Stockholm Design Lab
1998–2025

A book about the creative
process and design of

Optics
Restaurants
AI
Vehicles
Sports
Art
Tape
Fashion
Music
Light
Theatres
Architecture
Typography
Tech &
Flowers

Published by Victionary

Designed and edited by
Stockholm Design Lab

Stockholm Design Lab is an independent branding and design agency with international renown. Since 1998, they have transformed brands and businesses with simple, remarkable ideas. Rooted in Scandinavian philosophy, they blend strategy and design to position, future-proof, and elevate brands for long-term growth, cultural relevance, and lasting recognition.

They are a multidisciplinary team of art directors, strategists, designers, developers, and service professionals united by an exploratory mindset and a commitment to always creating their best work. The unique perspectives each member brings expand SDL's understanding of the world, while their shared curiosity drives them forward and helps them identify opportunities.

With a diverse portfolio ranging from airplanes, electric cars, pharmacies, sports, and tech to fashion, beauty, optics, museums, and the Nobel Prize, they bring over 25 years of experience to every project they take on.

Stockholm Design Lab
Headquarter
Eastmansvägen 12A
113 61 Stockholm
Sweden
+46 8 5555 19 00

01

02

03

04

05

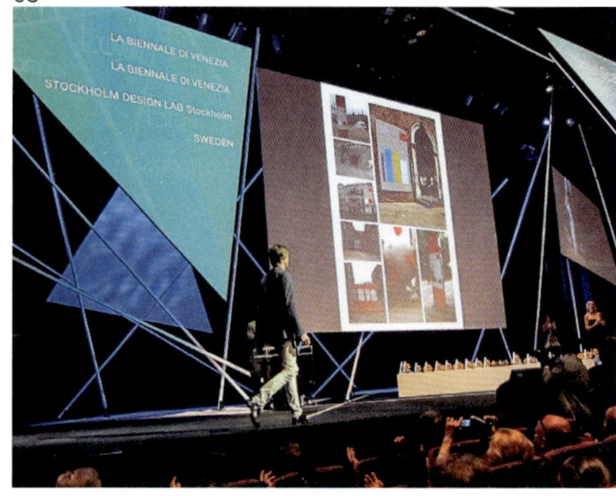

06

08

07

09

10

11

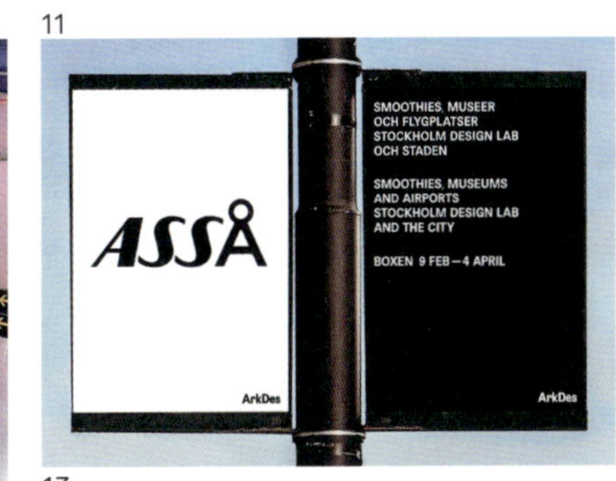

12

13

14

15

16

17

18

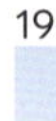
19

20

22

21

23

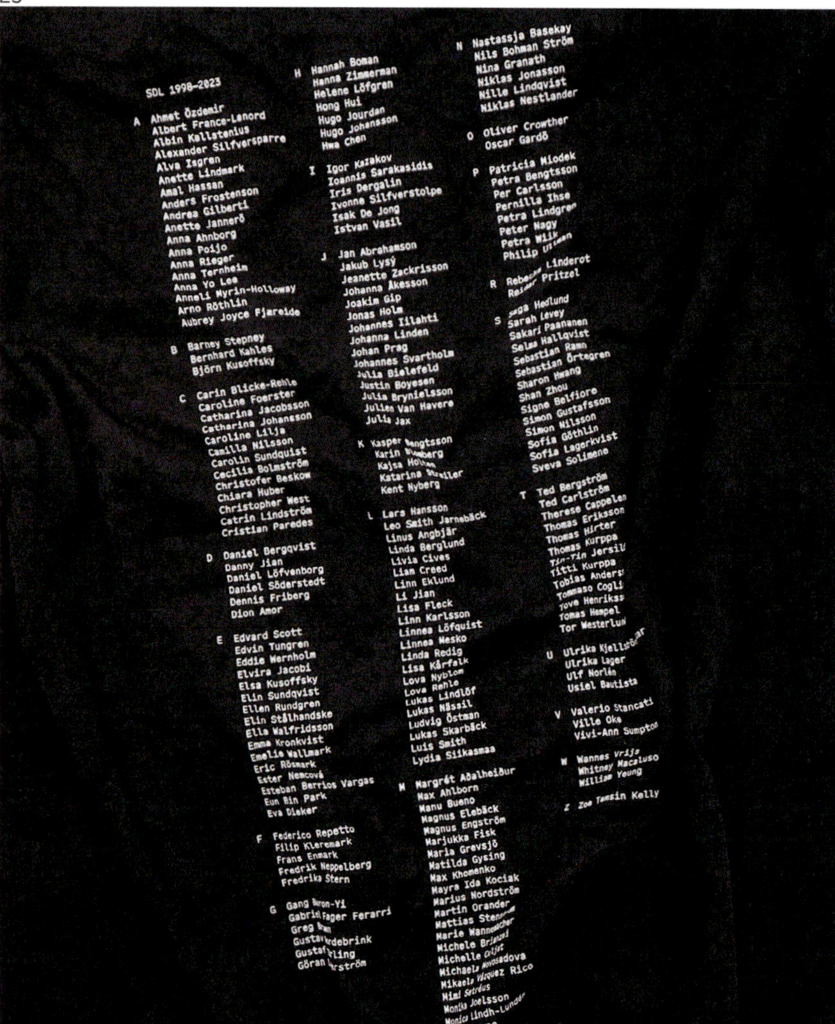

24

25

26

27

28

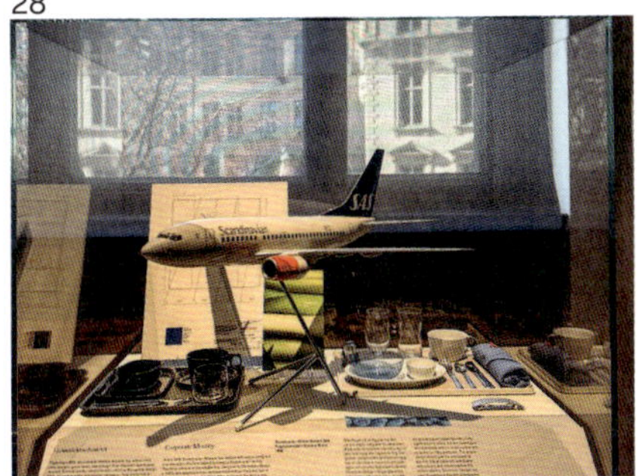

29

30

31

32

33

34

35

36

37

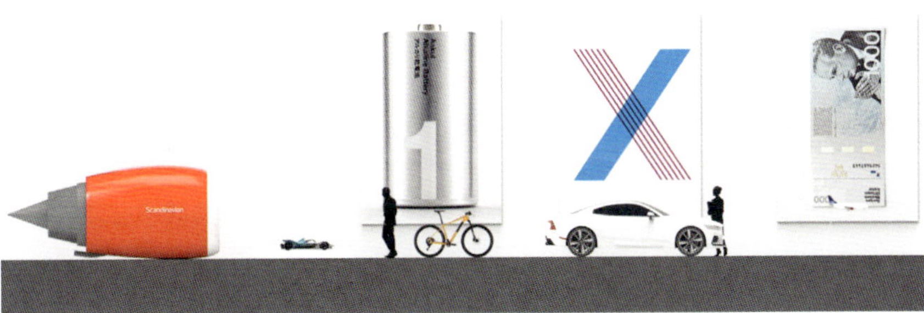

MIRACLES
HAPPEN
FARVÄL
ÅHLÉNS
ÅHLÉNS
Duty Free

MARKET
Scandinavian
SAS 98/09/24
01
Boeing 737

BILDMUSEET
Linnéuniversitetet
wästberg
ET

OneLab®
C
D/A
viedoc
E-POLO
RUPERT
MedHelp
ÅHLÉNS

Season 5
2018–2019
BELLA SK

Stay Sthlm
Corporate
Apartments
Transfer
Galaxy.

KMH Kungl.
Musikhögskolan

Landshypotek Bank
Colorfield®
PeakPerformance®
Sana
YANGO

HEMTEX

OMAKA
Alight
Hansot
C Future Park

BONNIER

PAX®
istens
AOI

Cubus
SPRITMUSEUM

MIRACLES
HAPPEN
THE NOBEL PRIZE
KSPECIAL
ROYCE
Cactus

SDL™
ONSTHALL
Airlines

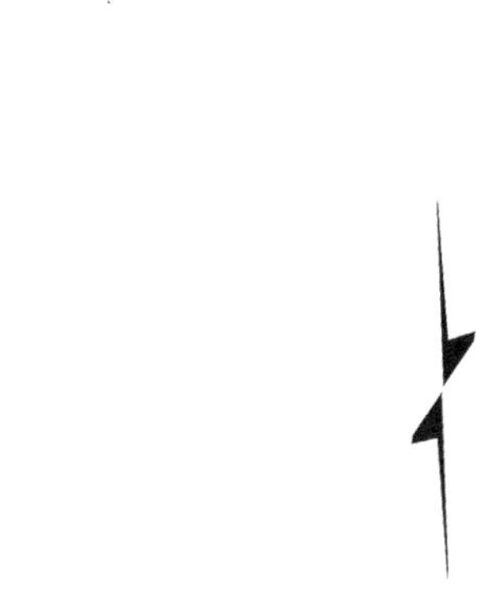

Polestar

Nordnet

SNS

SAS

Slam™
emmer

9.58
abc
737-600
SAS
stadium XXL
47
AaBb
MODERNA MUSEET
AaBbCc
HEMTEX
astoria

MIRACLES
HAPPEN

Scandinavian
01
ab
23.02.07 15
Making Difference
ARTs
FARVAL

Collage
Page 4–7

01 SDL team in the swedish subway, 2022
02 Battery check, print proof of first SDL book. Artron, Shenzhen, 2019
03 SDL XXV anniversary invitation, 2023
04 The challenge of creating one's own identity, 2006
05 SDL receiving the Cannes Gold Lion for La Biennale di Venezia, 2010
06 Matchbox, SDL XXV anniversary, 2023
07 Björn Kusoffsky's desk, *Plaza Deco*. Photo: David Thunander
08 SDL at the racetrack, 2024
09 Moving into the new office at Sturegatan 11, Stockholm, 2006
10 SDL Exhibition at ArkDes, the Swedish Centre for Architecture and Design, 2022
11 Campaign for the SDL Exhibition at ArkDes by Research and Development, 2022
12 Building the SDL Exhibition at ArkDes, 2022
13 A day at the office, Riddargatan 17, 1999
14 SDL Exhibition, Shenzhen, China. Over 200,000 visitors made it Shenzhen's most visited exhibition, 2020
15 Multiple screens at the SDL Exhibition, Shenzhen, China, 2020
16 Poster for the new premium typeface, Lab Antiqua, 2022
17 Keynote speaker at the Latin American Design Festival, Lima, Peru, 2016
18 A day at the office, going through Omaka Beer
19 Field trip, Berlin, biking to Sammlung Boros, 2019
20 A day at the office, looking at Hyperice
21 Permanent sign and message for SDL Photo: Thomas Mandl
22 Making airplanes, Sturegatan, Stockholm, 2015
23 T-shirt, SDL XXV anniversary. An attempt to thank all employees and interns throughout the years, 2023
24 Keynote speaker at the Wallpaper Design Talks, Thailand, 2017
25 Physical typography, SDL Exhibition, Shenzhen, China, 2020
26 Examining SDL's work at Tokyo Graphic Passport, 2010
27 SDL headquarters. Photography by the mighty Johan Fowelin, 2025
28 SDL represented in the permanent design collection since 2000 at Nationalmuseum, Sweden's museum of art and design
29 A studio with a view. SDL headquarters, 2007
30 Field trip, Courmayeur, Italy, 2022
31 A day at the office, 2025
32 Testing dust jacket with Times Bold typeface for SDL's previous monograph
33 Swedish television channel TV4 broadcasting SDL's work, 2015
34 Field trip to the exceptional Carl Eldhs Ateljémuseum, Stockholm. Carl Eldh (1873–1954) was one of Sweden's most prominent sculptors of the early 20th century.
35 In front of the gold leaf wall at Fondazione Prada Milan, 2015
36 Piles of SDL monographs
37 Testing 1:1 sizes for the SDL Exhibition at ArkDes, the Swedish Centre for Architecture and Design, 2021

Image captions

Dustcover showing SDL's design for Askul batteries. The Japanese company that has been a client to SDL since 2005. The functional design is based on the fact that in Japan the four most common battery sizes are indicated with numbers 1, 2, 3, 4 instead of letters AAA, AA, C, D like in Europe and USA.

03 Stockholm Design Lab headquarters, Eastmansvägen 12A, Stockholm, Sweden. Photographed in June 2025 by Johan Fowelin. Finger sculpture by Ray Atelier, Bertoia Diamond Chair, flowers from Club Yvonne, vase by Oliver Sundqvist and Frederik Nystrup-Larsen, Wunderbaum by Lars Tunbjörk

08 Gathering SDL artefacts for 20th anniversary film

10 Logotype City – a selection of bespoke identities from SDL

12 Examining SDL's work at Tokyo Graphic Passport, 2010

13 Miracles Happen – permanent sign and message for SDL

14 SDL headquarters, Eastmansvägen 12A, Stockholm, Sweden, 2025 Photo: Johan Fowelin

A book about the creative process and design of

Foreword: Pär Heyden Executive Creative Director Polestar

Some people have an almost invisible presence. They don't dominate a room, but you notice when they're not in it. Stockholm Design Lab is like that. Not always visible, but always present.

This spring, I visited Milan Design Week. So did more than half a million others, all eager to be inspired and to inspire. With thousands of exhibitions and showrooms, you need maps and guides to find the true gems. After days of running around, I was looking forward to one particular exhibition that I had saved for last.

When I finally arrived, I was met by a perfectly orchestrated experience. Someone had lavished near-obsessive attention and care on every detail. Just as I was doing my best not to look completely out of place, I backed straight into Björn. Of course SDL was there. Of course they were drawn to the same exhibition. And of course they were seeing the same qualities, and the same flaws, that I was, after more than a decade of working together.

There's a comfort in knowing they're around. Not just in Milan, but as a constant presence in an otherwise fickle communications landscape. While other agencies come and go, change shape and tone, SDL has remained true to itself. They've been our mirror, our filter, our conscience. An extension of our team, but also something entirely their own. Working with SDL means gaining access to a rare combination: aesthetic rigour and analytical clarity. They ask the right questions, even when the answers are uncomfortable. They say no when everyone else says yes. They never cut corners. And they won't let you do it either.

At the same time, their position is a paradox. They can be free, and they are. Free from our daily chaos, messy processes, and the heavy burden of responsibility. Sometimes I've thought it must be a luxury to exist in that space. Other times, I've wondered if it's painful, to be on the outside yet still want more.

This book is perhaps a kind of greatest hits collection. And rightly so. But even though it looks back, there's nothing nostalgic about their work. No leaning back. No satisfied return to past triumphs. What's been done still feels relevant, perhaps because it was never chasing trends to begin with. And still, there's something in the tone, in the posture, that points ahead.

SDL's best work? The next one. And the one after that.

A book about the creative process and design of

Optics

Optics

It was the summer of 2023 when I first met Stockholm Design Lab.

Sigma has been manufacturing cameras, lenses, and other imaging equipment for over 60 years. All of our products are developed in-house and manufactured at our Aizu factory in Japan. We had absolute confidence in the performance and quality of our products, which our engineers and factory staff put their whole heart and soul into making. But I was concerned that we were not properly communicating the true value of our products to our customers.

It was around that time that I heard of a Swedish company called Stockholm Design Lab that was doing good work in corporate branding. I checked their website, and was completely fascinated by the imagination and creativity that ran through their work, from typefaces and wordmarks to key visuals and packaging designs. Needless to say, I immediately ordered the first volume of the book, Stockholm Design Lab 1998–2019, so that I could discover more of their work.

Convinced that SDL would be a good fit for Sigma, I contacted the founder and CEO of SDL, Mr Björn Kusoffsky, and we met face-to-face soon afterwards. I told him that we wanted to convey the value of our products – of which we are very proud – more accurately to our customers, and that by doing so I wanted to make Sigma the most loved and respected brand in our sector. Björn and his associates immediately understood my intention and agreed to a new relationship with Sigma to help enhance our brand image.

The main concern I had at the time was that SDL, having worked with so many companies, would use their past experience as a template and apply it to our project, but my fears were completely unfounded. They listened intently to our corporate ethos, history, philosophy, and dreams for the future, and helped create an innovative and unique brand strategy to steer Sigma in a new direction.

At first, I just wanted SDL to propose some key visuals for our website and advertisements, but as we proceeded, I came to the conclusion that if we were really serious about improving our brand, we needed to commit to an entire branding project that included everything from a new company logo to refreshed product packaging designs.

To be honest, I was initially nervous about changing our logo, which had been used for decades and was well known to our customers. But I decided that we had to do it now in order to realise our future goal of building a stronger and more premium brand identity. Looking back, I think I was able to make this decision because everyone at SDL was really serious and sincere about our company, which gave me full confidence in their vision and allowed me to put my trust in their recommendations.

We have had a very intense two years with SDL. The scale and ambition of the project have required a lot of thought and work, but the team members in both companies have thoroughly enjoyed this creative process. The SDL staff have been fantastic to work with, which has helped us get through some busy and challenging times. SDL's deep understanding of our company, and their love of our products, makes them a very good fit for Sigma, and the results of the project have far exceeded our expectations.

I believe this was due to the fact that we share not only the same core values, such as what is beautiful and what is right, but also a similar sense of humour. This is only my guess, but I suspect that this is because Sweden and Japan, although geographically far apart, share deep similarities in values and aesthetics, including a respect for simplicity, an appreciation of purposeful design, and a strong connection to nature and natural materials.

During the project, we talked not only about work, but also about art, music and food. I always enjoyed our conversations, and I cherish the time we spent together in this way even more than the deliverables of the project.

Sigma tends to build deep relationships with our suppliers, distributors, and other business partners, and these relationships often grow into friendships that last for many years. I believe that only long-standing relationships based on deep mutual understanding and respect can create truly valuable work. And that is exactly the kind of relationship we have built with SDL.

We are truly grateful for everything SDL has contributed to Sigma, and we look forward to growing our partnership in the years to come.

Kazuto Yamaki
CEO, Sigma

01

02

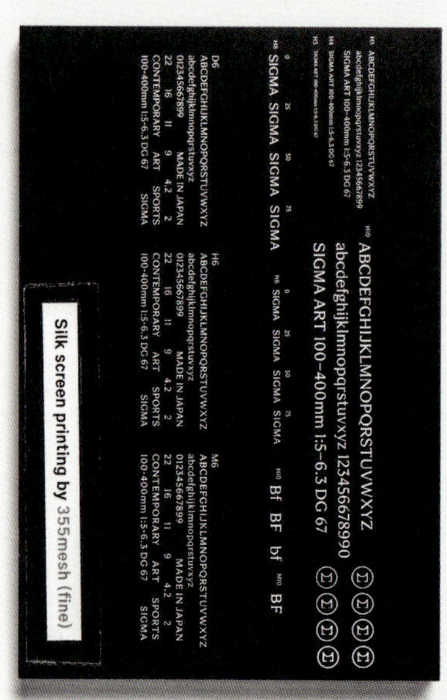

03

05

04

06

07

08

09

10

11

12

13

14

15

16

17

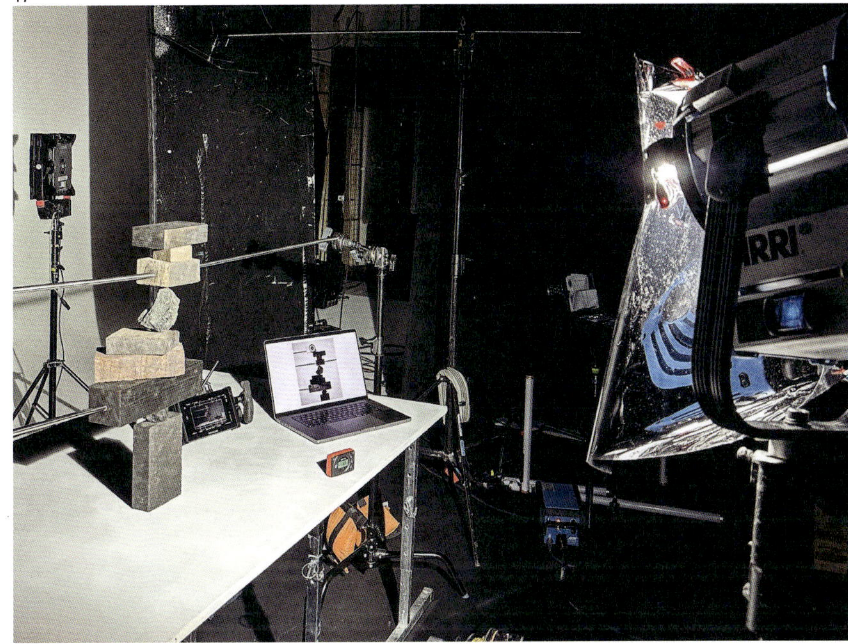

18

19

20

22

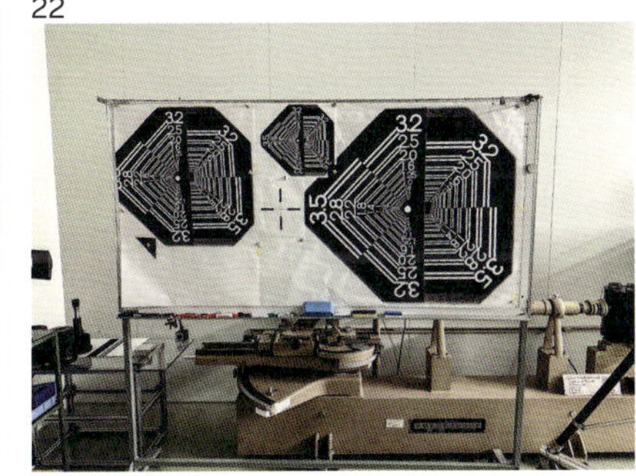

21

SIGMA
BF
45mm 1:2.8 DG ø55
SIGMA
LH577-02B

Sigma
Photography equipment
Japan
Holistic brand identity
–
2025

Sigma, founded in Tokyo in 1961, is a manufacturer of high-quality photography equipment made exclusively in Aizu, Japan. They turned to Stockholm Design Lab to more clearly express their obsession with quality, and to create a more coherent brand and customer experience.

Launched globally in early 2025, the new visual identity is a celebration of Sigma's spirit of independence, innovation, craftsmanship, and technical precision, as well as its Japanese heritage. The work spans brand strategy, visual identity, custom typography, photography, illustration, product branding, packaging, website, uniforms, architecture and spatial experience, product launch campaigns, art collaborations, product demo films, stationery, and more.

The main font, Sigma Serif, is a bespoke flare-serif typeface inspired by calligraphic brush strokes, balancing technical accuracy with crafted elegance. The mathematic sigma symbol – representing 'the sum of all parts' – was reintroduced, now with an updated geometry. Illustrated characters add a light-hearted cultural layer, while packaging combines craft paper with premium printing for a refined unboxing experience.

A dynamic photographic language infuses the brand with rich, creative energy, with photographers such as Emil Larsson, Julia Hetta, Fumi Nagasaka, Sarah van Rij and David Van Der Leeuw bringing their own unique expressions.

SIGMA

Sigma Serif Headline
Sigma Serif Text
Sigma Serif Engraving

ABCDEFGHIJKLMNOPQR
STUVWXYZ
abcdefghijklmnopqrstuvwxyz
0123456789
(;=∞×ø%&+§:?!-“”)

Sigma Sans Regular
Sigma Sans Medium
Sigma Sans Bold

ABCDEFGHIJKLMNOPQR
STUVWXYZ
abcdefghijklmnopqrstuvwxyz
0123456789
(;=∞×ø%&+§:?!-“”)

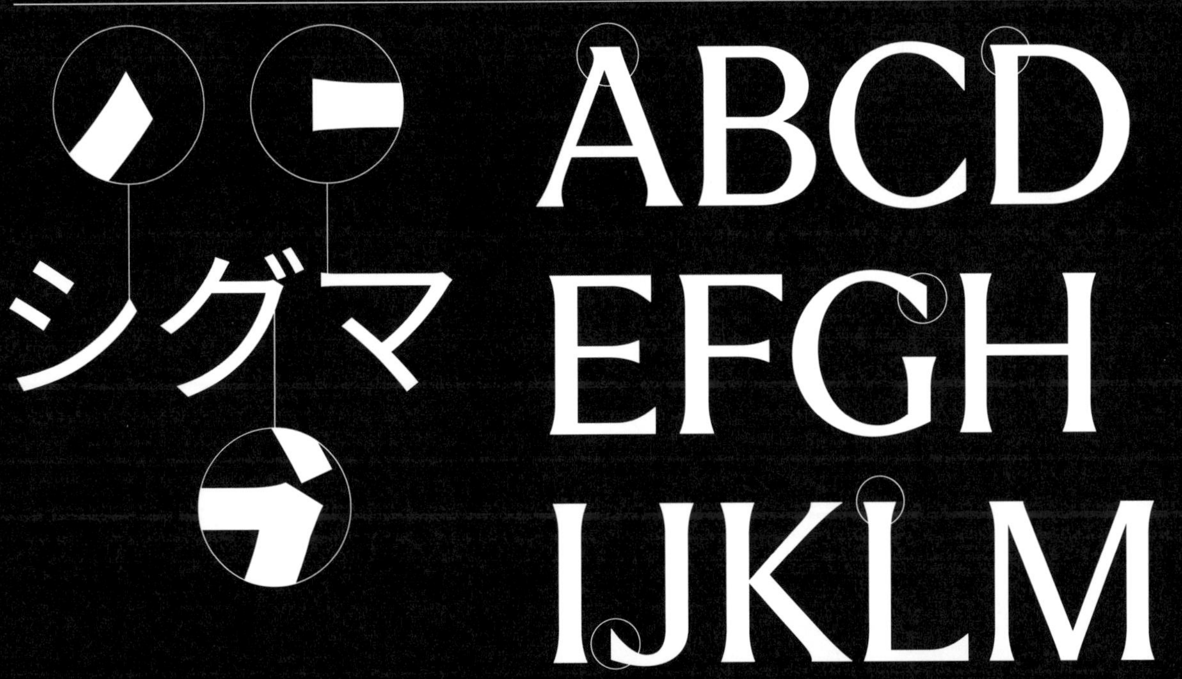

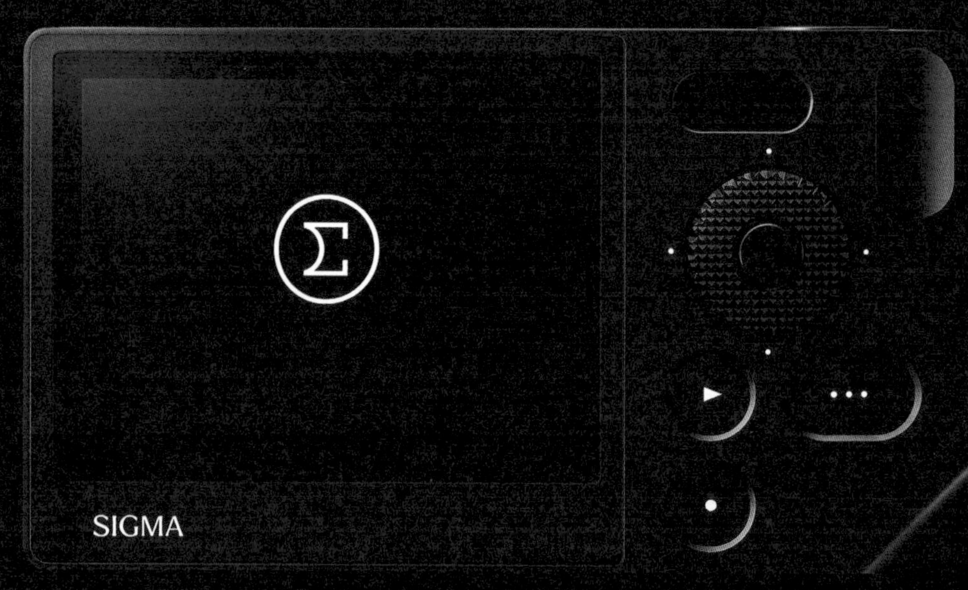
SIGMA

FOCUS
AF MF
300-600mm 1:4 DG
SIGMA

SIGMA

THE BF CAMERA
MADE IN AIZU, JAPAN

SIGMA

THE BF CAMERA
MADE IN AIZU, JAPAN

CONTEMPORARY
45mm F2.8
DG
SIGMA
BF CAMERA
SIGMA

17 20 24 28 35 40
17-40mm 1:1.8 DC ø67
SIGMA

THE BF CAMERA
MADE IN AIZU, JAPAN
SIGMA
南门涮肉王府
swatch+
南门烤鸭

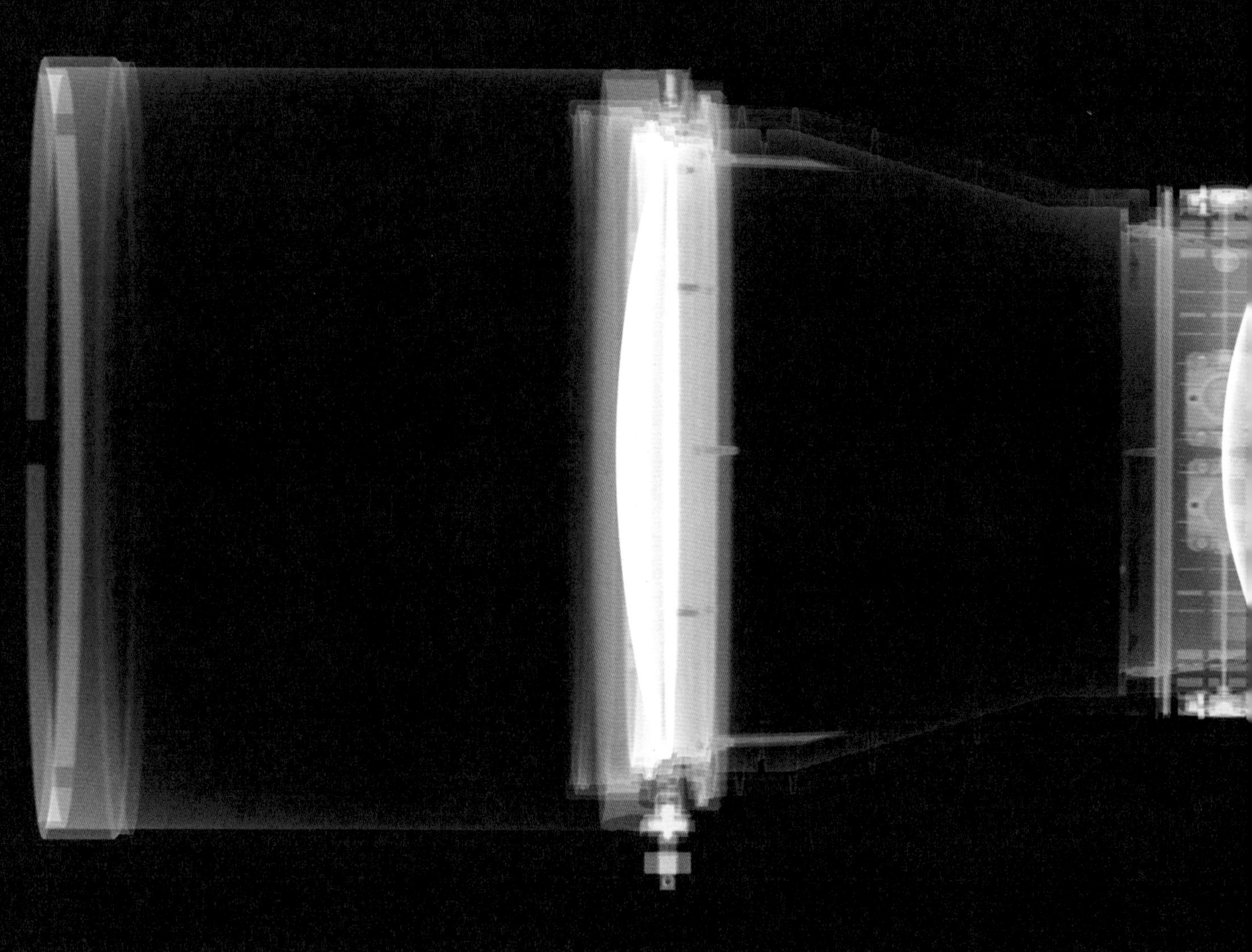

AIZU PRIME
32
T1.3
SIGMA
FRONT DIAMETER 95 mm
IMAGE DIAMETER 46.3 mm
AIZU PRIME
40
T1.3
SIGMA
FRONT DIAMETER 95 mm
IMAGE DIAMETER 46.3 mm
AIZU PRIME
27
T1.3
SIGMA

AIZU PRIME
75
T1.3
SIGMA
FRONT DIAMETER 95 mm
IMAGE DIAMETER 46.3 mm
AIZU PRIME
50
T1.3
SIGMA
FRONT DIAMETER 95 mm
IMAGE DIAMETER 46.3 mm
AIZU PRIME
25
T1.3
SIGMA
FRONT DIAMETER 95 mm
IMAGE DIAMETER 46.3 mm
AIZU PRIME
65
T1.3
SIGMA
FRONT DIAMETER 95 mm
IMAGE DIAMETER 46.3 mm
AIZU PRIME
35
T1.3
SIGMA
FRONT DIAMETER 95 mm
IMAGE DIAMETER 46.3 mm

MANUALS AND BROCHURES

PRODUCT WARRANTY

CAMERA COMPATIBILITY

MOUNT CONVERSION SERVICE

RETURNS

NEWSLETTER

CUSTOMIZATION SERVICES

SERVICE

PHOTO

LINEAR FOCUS COMPATIBILITY

CINE DOWNLOADS

FAQ

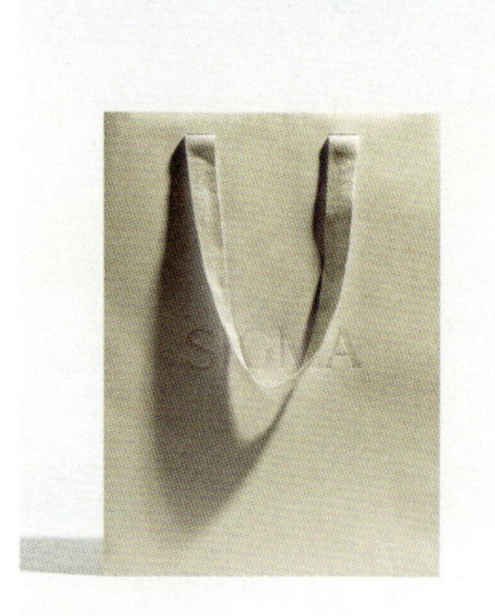

SIGMA AIZU JAPAN

CUSTOMER SUPPORT

SIGMA

CONTEMPORARY
16–300mm F3.5–6.7
DC OS

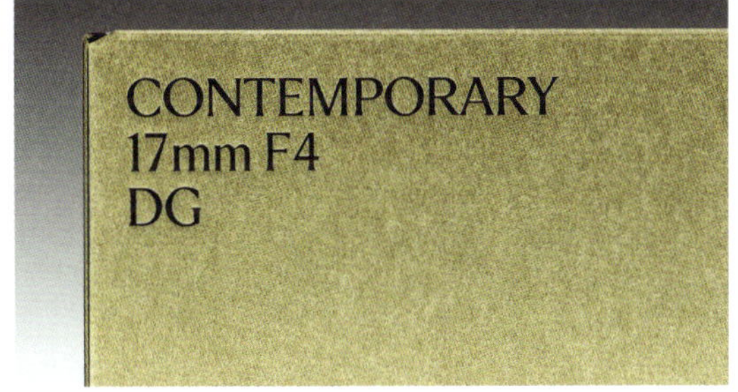

Cactus
Laser Trigger
LV5
Cactus
Laser Trigger
LV5

Cactus
Wireless camera equipment
Hong Kong
Brand identity and packaging design
–
2013

Cactus is a Hong Kong-based brand specialising in photography equipment such as camera flashes and wireless flash triggers. Its products are designed for semi-professional photographers and advanced amateurs.

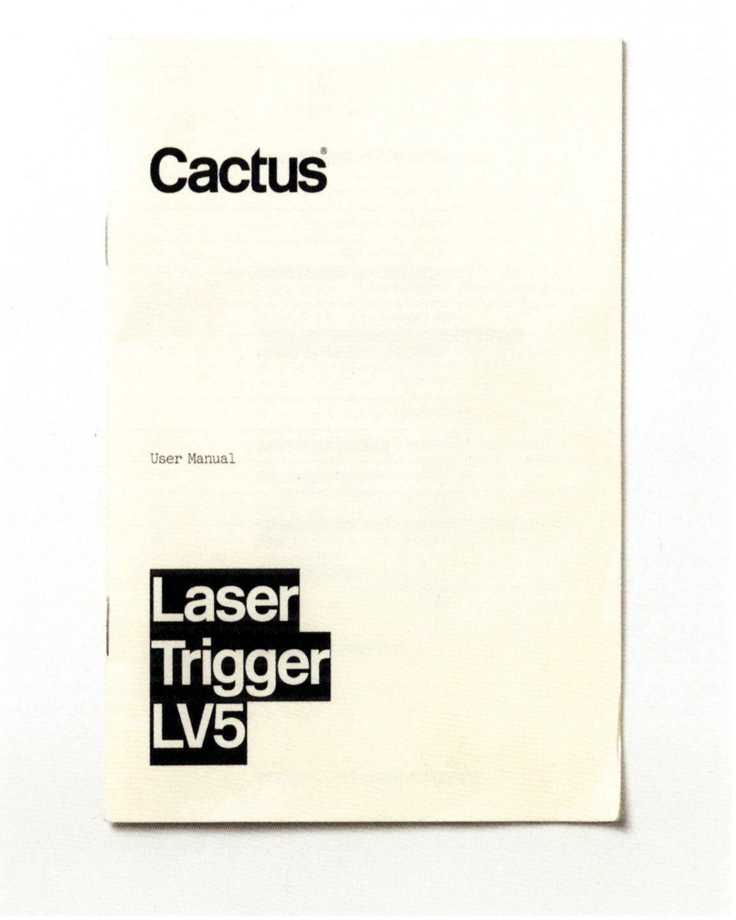

Tuva Larsson
Beckmans College of Design
Development Scholarship by
Stockholm Design Lab
2022.06.03

Beckmans College of Design
Sweden
Development scholarship
–
2000

Quality design must always have a strong content, and that content must make a difference. This difference is created through knowledge, questioning, ingenuity and courage.

Since 2000, the Beckmans College of Design Development Scholarship by Stockholm Design Lab has been awarded to students who have shown both a distinct passion for design and an exceptional ability to make a difference in the field.

2000 Erik Schedin
2001 Sofia Lagerqvist
2002 Bea Szenfeld
2003 Anna Mörner, Linda Solvang, Jenny Modeér and Torbjörn Neby
2004 Tomas Mankovsky
2005 Rasmus Norlander
2011 Tomas Carlsten
2018 Marcus Nystrand
2022 Tuva Larsson
2025 Noah Constantinou and Sofia di Marco

Collage
Page 24–25

01 Retail reference from 1899, Chicago
02 Silkscreen printing test for Sigma
03 Portrait of legendary art director Lars Hall with a vintage Sony digital camera, 2006
04 Guerrilla posters, Rencontres d'Arles, France, 2024
05 Heavenly eyewear
06 Tuva Larsson, recipient of the Beckmans College of Design Development Scholarship by Stockholm Design Lab, 2022
07 First batch of Sigma packaging using Japanese Takeo paper
08 Testing grounds, Sigma's Aizu factory
09 Sigma's Aizu factory
10 Frame your subject in an instant! Vintage advertising from Sigma
11 Used lenses en masse
12 Sigma launch, Shanghai, 2025
13 Application test on Cactus studio equipment, Hong Kong
14 Sigma's logotype development over the years. Originally, a mechanical-style wordmark was accompanied by the Greek capital letter sigma. Later, the symbol was removed and the wordmark simplified.
15 Inspection at Sigma's Aizu factory
16 Extraordinary meeting with Yamaki-san and legendary Swedish photographer Anders Petersen, in his studio
17 Balancing act photo shoot for Sigma
18 Sigma BF artificial daylight shoot
19 Balancing act sculpture by Mattias Nyhlin and SDL, for Sigma
20 Photographer Emil Larsson and team at Delight Studios, Stockholm, 2024
21 Sigma pop-up store, Milan
22 Testing grounds, Sigma's Aizu factory

Image captions

26 The Sigma BF Camera, an interchangeable-lens mirrorless digital camera. The most important feature is its simplicity – an ambition to create the easiest camera to use, inspired by the humble beginnings of the camera obscura. While the lens remains the soul of photography, the camera still profoundly shapes the images you take – directly, indirectly, even subconsciously. Without compromising on features or performance, the BF's design cuts out everything that distracts from your interaction with the image. From its aluminium unibody to its simplified controls and streamlined menu, the BF embodies a pure photographic experience free of frustration.

29 Sigma Serif is a semi-serif typeface based on the same letterform geometry as the Sigma Sans, giving the serif typeface an engineered character at the foundation. The character of the serifs is inspired by Japanese lettering, translated for the Latin alphabet. Sigma Serif is the perfect mix of a sans-serif and a serif, expressing both heritage and technical sharpness.

34 The subdued colours and tactile materials introduce a natural softness, balancing the sharpness and precision of the engineered products.

37 Sigma BF campaign in major cities across China

42 Illustrated characters guide customers through support and repair services – a light-hearted dimension of the brand, rooted in Japanese culture.

A book about the creative process and design of

Restaurants

Restaurants

Hospitality, at its most elemental, is not an industry – it is a civic act.

Long before it was monetised or styled into luxury, hospitality functioned as a form of social infrastructure. Across cultures and eras, it has been a means of enacting care, of offering safety and recognition to the unfamiliar or unseen. To host is to extend more than a service; it is to mark someone's presence as valid. In this light, hospitality is not a supplement to society – it is a rehearsal of it.

And yet, in contemporary discourse, hospitality is often reduced to its surfaces: a plate, a chair, a smile, a view. These are the aesthetics of welcome, but not its essence. The true function of hospitality is spatial and civic – it is to create the conditions under which people from different backgrounds might share an experience, feel a sense of belonging, and recognise their place in a collective story.

This belief has shaped the arc of my career. I trained as an architect because I was drawn to the built environment as a mirror of our cultural values. Architecture, at its best, encodes how we live with one another. And in a multicultural society like ours, I felt an urgency to design spaces that would not simply reflect dominant narratives, but expand them – to include new voices, new identities, new forms of gathering.

Over time, my focus narrowed to hospitality. Not because I saw it as lesser than other civic institutions, but because I saw it as under-theorised and deeply potent. Restaurants, dining rooms, lounges – these are not incidental places. They are some of the last remaining civic interiors where people of different origins voluntarily sit beside each other. These spaces carry the weight of representation. They perform culture in real time.

My earliest work, through my firm Modellus Novus, centred on this understanding. But it was through my collaboration with Chef Jamal James Kent that it fully came to life. Together, we built restaurants that didn't just serve food – they embodied values. Crown Shy, Saga, Overstory, and others weren't about aesthetic trends. They were about anchoring excellence in empathy. About building teams whose diversity was not cosmetic, but structural. About telling stories that hadn't been told before, in rooms that felt made for everyone.

Today, I serve as CEO of Kent Hospitality Group – a continuation of that shared vision. And I have the privilege of working with Stockholm Design Lab to articulate our evolving identity. What distinguishes SDL's work is not merely its visual sophistication. It is their ability to encode values into form. To construct identities that speak across time, cultures, and generations.

Their brands are not declarations of status; they are arguments for belonging. They recognise that the most powerful hospitality spaces are not those that dazzle, but those that signal: you are safe here, you are welcome here, you matter here.

As a new father, I think often about the future we're building. About whether my son – a young, Blasian child growing up in an increasingly fragmented world – will walk into a space and feel it was made with him in mind. Hospitality, at its highest form, can make that possible. It can remind us that inclusion is not a sentiment, but a structure. Not an afterthought, but a beginning.

In this era, when civic bonds are strained and identity is contested, hospitality offers a quiet but radical proposition: that we can still come together. That we can still design for presence, not just presentation. That how we gather matters.

And that the spaces where we do – if conceived with intention – can carry us forward.

Preeti Sriratana
CEO, Kent Hospitality Group

01

02

03

04

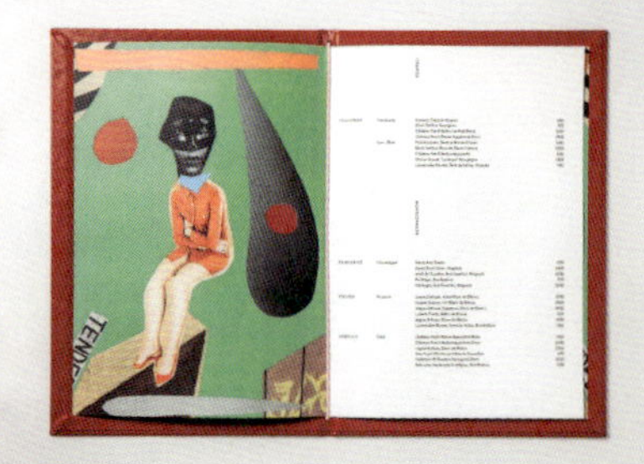

05

06

07

08

09

10

11

12

13

14

15

16

17

18

19

Riche Fenix
Bar and restaurant
Sweden
Brand identity
–
2022

The owners of iconic brasserie Riche in uptown Stockholm sought to expand their brand to the southern part of town, Södermalm. The new bar would serve as Riche's rebellious younger sibling, while still embracing its origins. The venue had long carried the name Fenix – first as a pharmacy, then as a bar – making the phoenix a natural symbol. Under the Riche brand, the space was reborn once more, giving new relevance to the mythology of transformation and return.

In collaboration with artist Otis Huss, Stockholm Design Lab developed a vibrant brand identity in which the logotype, symbols, illustrations and paintings are seamlessly integrated with the physical environment, designed by interior architects Louise Tungården and Ellen Nyqvist.

The result is spirited and colourful – a celebration of creativity, art, taste and atmosphere – that remains functional and true to the essence of the original brand. The phoenix references recur throughout the space – from the old statue watching over the entrance, to the bird motifs appearing in unexpected places.

The wordmark is as distinctive and enigmatic as the legend itself. The hologram by the door, the unconventional receipt holder, the restroom ceiling, and the lobster-dressed hot dog all add to a narrative that is both playful and layered.

RICHE
Riche Fenix
Vinlista

20:48
20:48
GOND
STADSGÅRDEN 6
GONDOLEN.SE
ÖPPNAR SNART

Gondolen
Restaurant
Sweden
Brand identity
–
2023

Gondolen has been part of Stockholm's skyline since 1935, a restaurant suspended between sky and sea, tradition and modernity. Stockholm Design Lab was tasked with updating the visual identity with care and respect, keeping the original logotype as a central element.

SDL refined the wordmark and created a bespoke version inspired by the Katarina Elevator, tying the identity to the building's characteristic silhouette. The visual language draws from 1930s design, Swedish functionalism, and a bold sense of artistry. The result is a confident, modern expression that stays true to Gondolen's heritage, while carrying it into its next chapter.

GONDOLEN

GONDOLEN

GONDOLEN
GONDOLEN

BAR
ZEPPE
LIN

OMAKA
OMAKA

Omaka
Brewery and restaurant
Sweden
Holistic visual identity
–
2021

Odd, mismatched, ill-assorted, incongruous, irregular? No, there is no direct translation of the Swedish word 'omaka'. Yet its meaning is clear – it is one of a kind, stands apart, hints at a counterpart and defies convention. Just like the Stockholm-based brewery and restaurant that carries its name – an easy-going and welcoming space, yet marked by a high level of sophistication in the world of food and drink.

In close collaboration with brewmaster Hedda Spendrup and her team, Stockholm Design Lab acted as a strategic partner in the development and launch of a brand that serves not only as a hub for local beer connoisseurs, but as site of innovation for the wider Spendrups brewery group. The assignment included naming, brand strategy, visual identity, design system, packaging concept, and brand implementations. It was recognised with the Gold Egg for Identity Design in Sweden's oldest, largest and most prestigious competition for the creative industry, the Gold Egg Award.

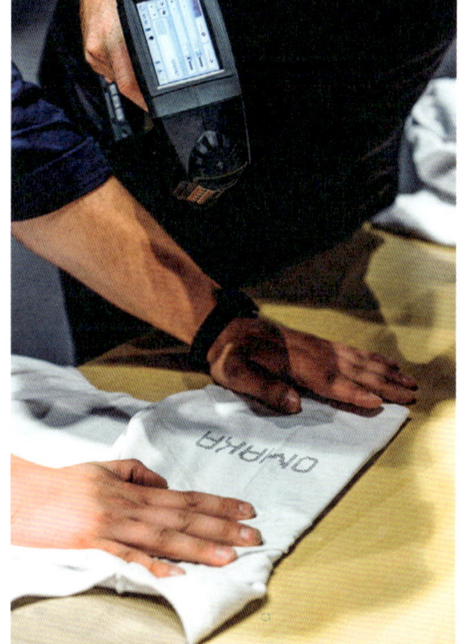

OMAKA
#7
BITTER STOUT
—
330 ML
4,2% VOL

PEPPAR, PEPPAR
SYRLIG, JOSIG, KRYDDIG
DET HÄR ÄR HISTORIEN OM EN KORT BESATTHET AV PEPPAR, EN LIVSLÅNG KÄRLEK TILL PASSIONSFRUKT OCH EN PILSNER SOM DRÖMDE OM ATT BLI NÅGOT ANNAT.
BRYGGT AV HEDDA I STOCKHOLM
OMAKA
VENICE
FRISK, FRUKTIG, SPRUDLANDE
MED SMAK AV DEN DÄR DRINKEN MED PERSIKA DU DRACK PÅ BRUNCHEN DEN DÄR DAGEN SOM VAR SÅ VARM.
BRYGGT AV HEDDA I STOCKHOLM
OMAKA
MAMMA
TORR, BESK, KRISPIG
DET SÄGS ATT PILSNER ÄR ÖLETS MODER OCH JUST DEN HÄR ÄR BRYGGD FÖR ALLA MAMMOR. DEN ÄR TORR, BESK OCH KRISPIG, PRECIS SOM MAMMA VILL HA DEN.
BRYGGT AV HEDDA I STOCKHOLM
OMAKA
LOVE
HER
AFRODITE
FRUKTIG, HET, SPRUDLANDE
EN ÖL BRYGGD I KÄRLEKENS TECKEN. KÄRLEKEN TILL JORDGUBB, BUBBLOR & INGEFÄRA. SMAKERNA SMÄLTER SAMMAN I EN SPÄNNANDE SYMBIOS SOM FLÖRTAR MED DIN TUNGA.
BRYGGT AV HEDDA I STOCKHOLM
OMAKA
A.K.A.I.P.A.
FYLLIG, ÖRTIG, AROMATISK
WAS IST DENN LOS? DAS IST EIN BIER MIT AMERIKANISCHER HEFE UND DEUTCHE HOPFEN. DIESES BIER MIT EINER CURRYWURST, MANN O MANN WIE LECKER!
BRYGGT AV HEDDA I STOCKHOLM
OMAKA
SVARTSKOG
FYLLIG, BÄRIG, CHOKLADIG
SCHWEIZISK
ÄR SVÅRT ATT SÄGA MEN
INSPIRERAS AV. DÄRFÖR ÄR
ÖLEN BRYGGD MED HALLON,
VINBÄR OCH CHOKLADMALT
BRYGGT AV HEDDA I STOCKHOLM
OMAKA
HURRA!
GRATTIS!

OMAKA
#1
BLOND PA
—
330 ML
4,2% VOL

OMAKA
#1
BLOND PA
—
330 ML
4,2% VOL

OMAKA
#1
BLOND PA
—
330 ML
4,2% VOL

OMAKA
#1
BLOND PA
—
330 ML
4,2% VOL

OMAKA
#1
BLOND PA
—
330 ML
4,2% VOL

OMAKA
#1
BLOND PA
—
330 ML
4,2% VOL

OMAKA
#1
BLOND PA
—
330 ML
4,2% VOL

OMAKA
#1
BLOND PA
—
330 ML
4,2% VOL

OMAKA
#1
BLOND PA
—
330 ML
4,2% VOL

OMAKA
#1
BLOND PA
—
330 ML
4,2% VOL

OMAKA
#1
BLOND PA
—
330 ML
4,2% VOL

OMAKA
#1
BLOND PA
—
330 ML
4,2% VOL

OMAKA
#1
BLOND PA
330 ML
4,2% VOL

OMAKA
#1
BLOND PA
330 ML
4,2% VOL
OMAKA
#1
BLOND PA
330 ML
4,2% VOL
OMAKA
#1
BLOND PA
330 ML
4,2% VOL
OMAKA
#1
BLOND PA
330 ML
4,2% VOL
OMAKA
#1
BLOND PA
330 ML
4,2% VOL

#1
BLOND PA
330 ML
4,2% VOL

OMAKA
#1
BLOND PA
330 ML
4,2% VOL
OMAKA
#1
BLOND PA
330 ML
4,2% VOL

OMAKA
#1
BLOND PA
330 ML
4,2% VOL
OMAKA
#1
BLOND PA
330 ML
4,2% VOL
OMAKA
#1
BLOND PA
330 ML
4,2% VOL

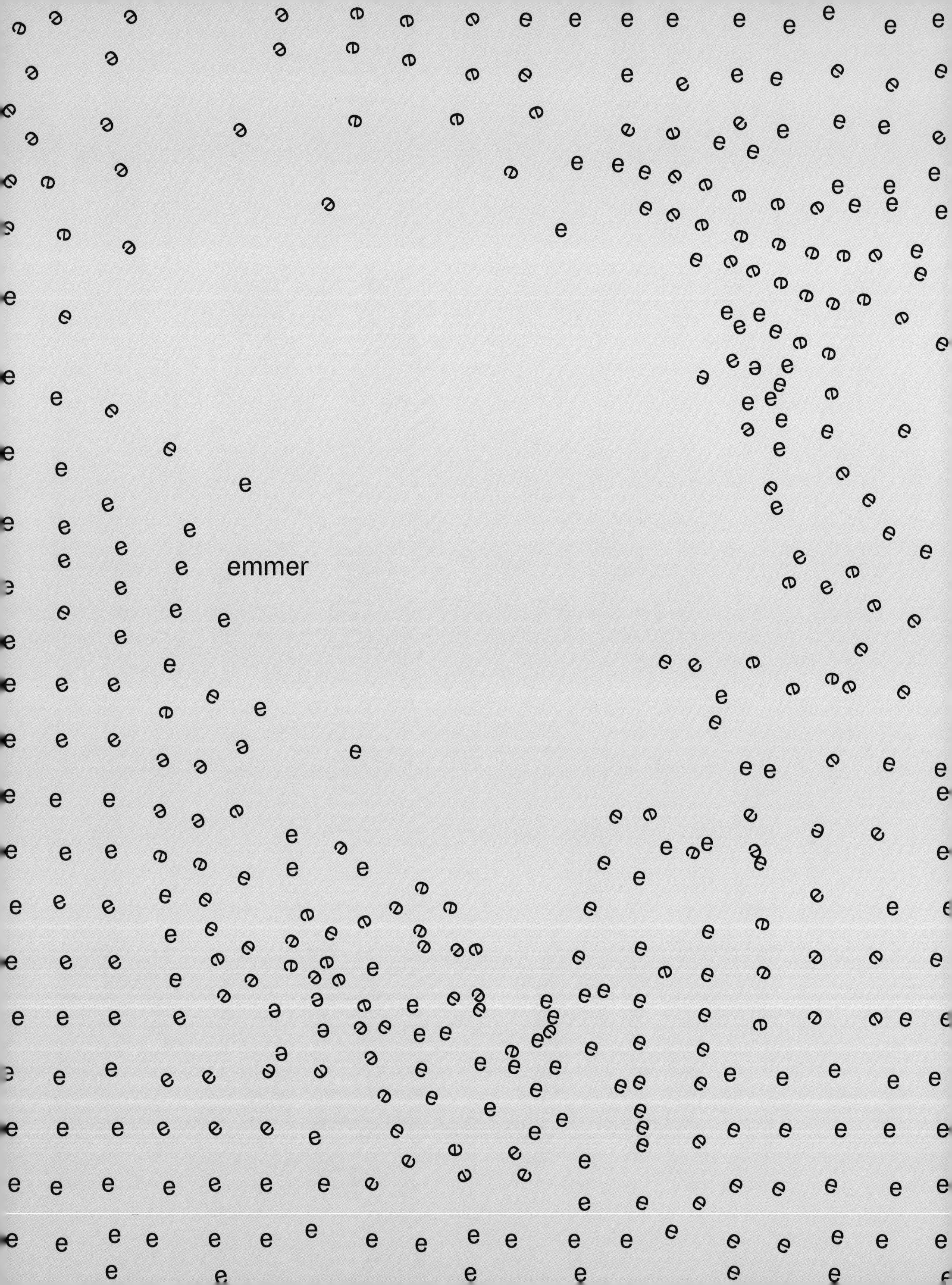
emmer

Emmer
Restaurant
Sweden
Brand identity
–
2020

Located just a stone's throw from Stockholm's inner city, Ulriksdals Värdshus is a tranquil dining destination, nestled among forest, sea, and farmland. Its owners, Svenska Brasserier, sought to reinterpret the traditional Swedish inn into something greener, simpler, and more sustainable. The result was Emmer – a restaurant focused on locally sourced produce, serving modern Scandinavian cuisine in a relaxed setting close to nature, with the aim of appealing to a new, environmentally conscious audience.

At Emmer, cultural heritage met home-grown ingredients and a vision for a more sustainable future. Its visual identity was rooted in the garden's plantings, the origins of the food, and the cyclical rhythms of nature. Drawing from the elements – wind, water – the concept captured the magic of seeds carried on the breeze and brought to life by rain. Stockholm Design Lab created a visual identity that mirrored the natural world: playful, whimsical, colourful, and organic.

dryck
middag
emmer

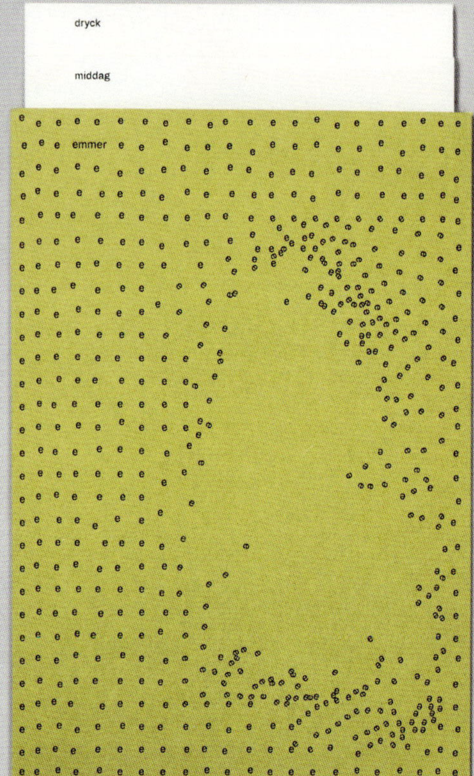
dryck
middag
emmer

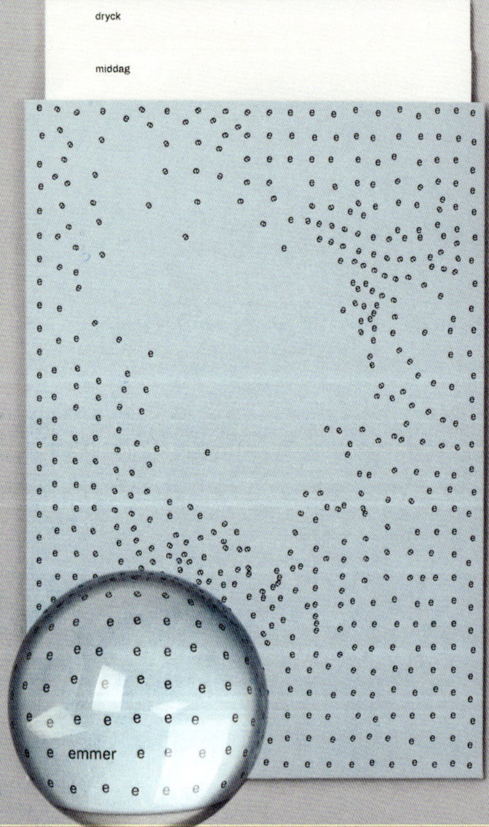
dryck
middag
emmer

dryck
middag
emmer

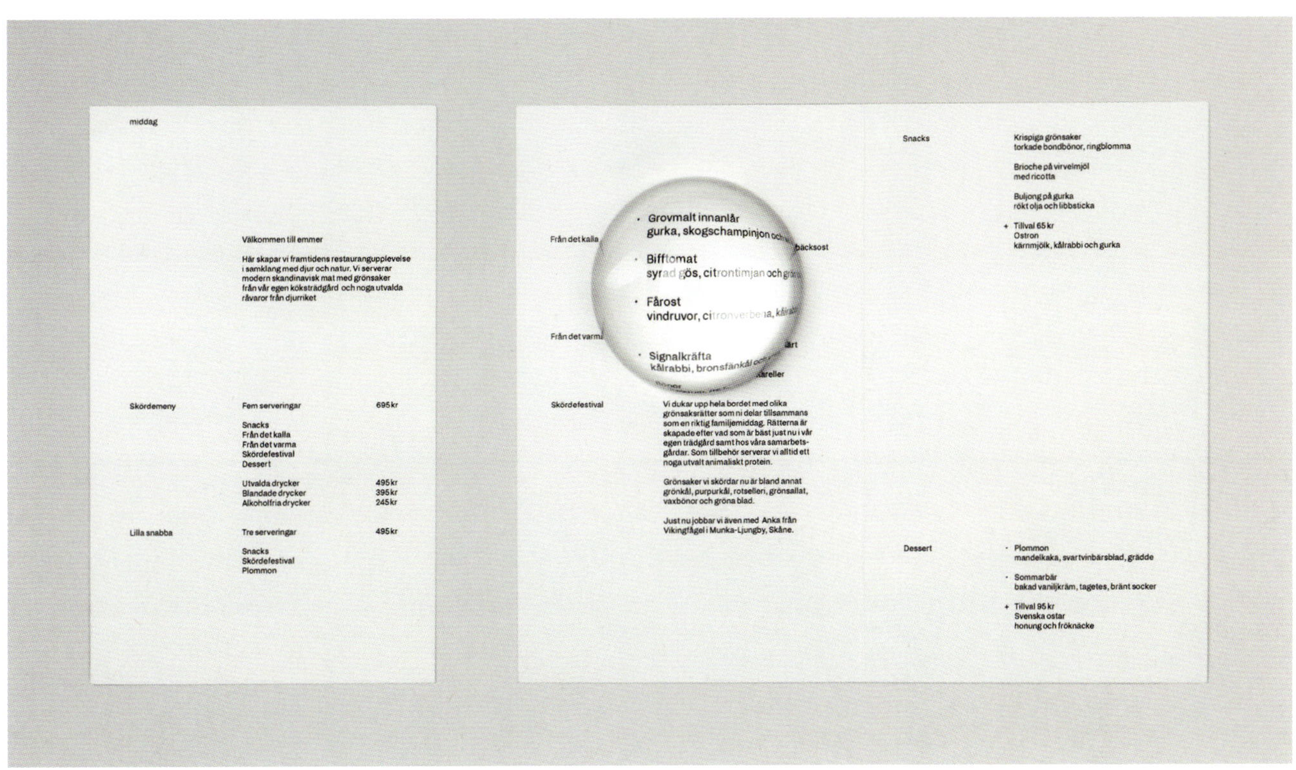

middag

Välkommen till emmer

Här skapar vi framtidens restaurangupplevelse i samklang med djur och natur. Vi serverar modern skandinavisk mat med grönsaker från vår egen köksträdgård och noga utvalda råvaror från djurriket

Skördemeny	Fem serveringar	695 kr
	Snacks Från det kalla Från det varma Skördefestival Dessert	
	Utvalda drycker	495 kr
	Blandade drycker	395 kr
	Alkoholfria drycker	245 kr
Lilla snabba	Tre serveringar	495 kr
	Snacks Skördefestival Plommon	

Från det kalla

- Grovmalt innanlår
  gurka, skogschampinjon och ... bäcksost
- Bifftomat
  syrad gös, citrontimjan och gr...
- Fårost
  vindruvor, citronverbena, kålra...

Från det varma

- Signalkräfta
  kålrabbi, bronsfänkål och ... kareller

Skördefestival

Vi dukar upp hela bordet med olika grönsaksrätter som ni delar tillsammans som en riktig familjemiddag. Rätterna är skapade efter vad som är bäst just nu i vår egen trädgård samt hos våra samarbetsgårdar. Som tillbehör serverar vi alltid ett noga utvalt animaliskt protein.

Grönsaker vi skördar nu är bland annat grönkål, purpurkål, rotselleri, grönsallat, vaxbönor och gröna blad.

Just nu jobbar vi även med Anka från Vikingfågel i Munka-Ljungby, Skåne.

Snacks

Krispiga grönsaker
torkade bondbönor, ringblomma

Brioche på virvelmjöl
med ricotta

Buljong på gurka
rökt olja och libbsticka

+ Tillval 65 kr
Ostron
kärnmjölk, kålrabbi och gurka

Dessert

- Plommon
  mandelkaka, svartvinbärsblad, grädde
- Sommarbär
  bakad vaniljkräm, tagetes, bränt socker

+ Tillval 95 kr
Svenska ostar
honung och fröknäcke

locally produced crops
the cycle of nature

välkommen i augusti

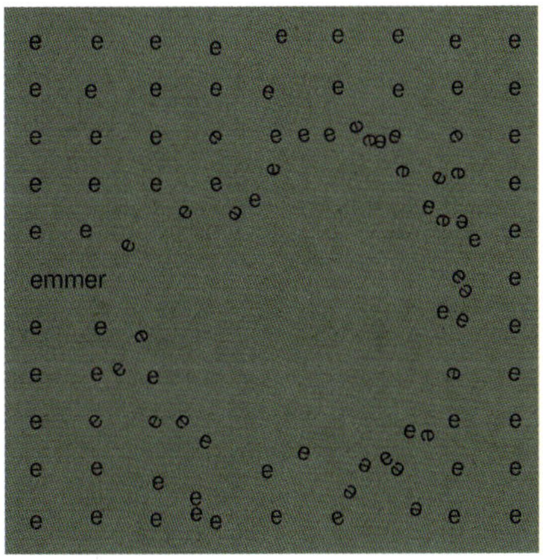

emmer

locally produced crops
the cycle of nature

14.00–19.00

WELCOME TO A NARRATIVE UNFOLDING IN CHAPTERS
In here every dish is a passage and every ingredient a character. Rooted in precision and refinement, cuisine values balance over excess, intention over ornamentation. Ingredients evolve across the meal, reappearing in different forms, creating echoes of flavor and texture. Presentation is architecture, not decoration, and each dish stands alone while contributing to a larger composition.

OTORO
Wasabi crème fraîche, trout roe, shima aji, daikon, citrus, otoro

KINMEDAI
Pear, hibiscus, kinmedai

CAVIAR
Scallop, mussel, caviar

KNAFEH
Squash, citrus

MADAI
Farro, collard green, dry-aged madai

ORA KING SALMON
Beet, goat cheese, ora king salmon

TEA
Moroccan tea

MERINGUE
Chocolate, malt, meringue

SAGA
25.04.22

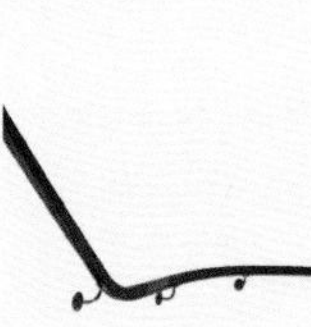

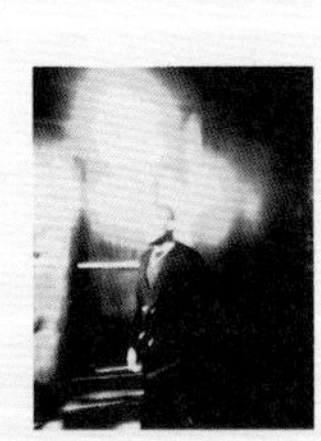

Saga
Restaurant
USA
Brand identity
–
2025

Saga, founded by the late culinary legend Jamal 'James' Kent, is a two-Michelin-starred fine dining restaurant located on the 63rd floor of 70 Pine Street, a landmark Art Deco tower in the Financial District of New York City. With the transition into Saga 2.0, new Head Chef Charlie Mitchell aims to re-contextualise what fine dining can be and who it is for, placing emphasis on the value of the entire dining experience beyond the food alone.

Stockholm Design Lab was asked to develop the brand identity for Saga 2.0. The result is a personal restaurant branding concept with a clear sense of place, balancing intimacy, refinement and intrigue. A visit to Saga is like stepping into a home – a personal story that is constantly being written and rewritten. The identity concept was born from this idea, capturing the story and the journey that has shaped both Saga and Chef Mitchell. In essence, it reflects what defines New York – its fusion of influences, experiences, and cultures, woven together in a way that is both refined and deeply personal. More than just providing the expected, it is meant to spark curiosity, inspire dialogue, and foster meaningful conversations.

SAGA
SEPTEMBER 2025
FALL/WINTER

SAGA
Spring/Summer
May 2025

SAGA is a fine dining restaurant perched on the 63rd floor of 70 Pine Street, a landmark Art Deco tower in New York's Financial District. The food at SAGA is honest, fundamental cooking that pushes boundaries while staying rooted in excellence – every element is mastered with love and respect, creating meals that nourish and build community.

A visit to SAGA is like stepping into a home – into a personal story that is constantly written and rewritten.
An ever-evolving story, one that engages the guests in participating and revisiting. "Blending Stories" was born from this idea, capturing the journey that has shaped both SAGA and Chef Mitchell.

It reflects the fusion that define New York. A fusion of influences, experiences, and cultures – woven together in a way that is both refined and deeply personal.

1.
BENTO BOX
razor clam, spot prawn, octopus, salmon roe, tuna, red snapper, mackerel

2.
FOIE GRAS
citrus, radicchio, meringue

3.
ROYAL STURGEON CAVIAR
tamago, scallop, potato

4.
CELERY ROOT
tamago, scallop, potato

5.
LOBSTER
black pepper, sunchoke, bun

6.
DRY-AGED DUCK
pear, brussels sprout, chicories, hummus, yogurt, m'semen, chili honey, harissa

7.
MOROCCAN TEA
mint, orange blossom, date, pistachio

8.
APPLE
rye, spiced chai, vanilla, miso butterscotch

Collage
Page 54–55

01 Stacked cases of one of Omaka's very first beers
02 Spring vegetables at Emmer
03 A selected illustration that became one of several depictions of the mythical phoenix, for Riche Fenix
04 Gondolen menu with artwork by Roland Hjort
05 Early sketches for Emmer's identity
06 Work in process for Riche Fenix by artist Otis Huss
07 Painting by Sven X:et Erixson, the grandfather of Roland Hjort, on the wall at Gondolen
08 Emmer menu with delicious dessert
09 The view from Saga, New York
10 Capturing the moment at Emmer
11 Work in process for Riche Fenix by artist Otis Huss
12 Work in process for Riche Fenix by artist Otis Huss
13 Colour and material samples by interior architects Louise Tungården and Ellen Nyqvist for Riche Fenix
14 The original staff gathered for the opening of Riche Fenix
15 Tape-based collage for Omaka beer sketch
16 Test printing of coasters for Gondolen
17 Historic image of the iconic Katarina Elevator
18 Artwork detail for Gondolen
19 Redevelopment of the Gondolen restaurant

Image captions

64 Omaka Beer, located in the brutalist building of the former Arkitektskolan (KTH School of Architecture)

66 The design system is based on a repeatable basic structure, consisting of separated fields which form a canvas for product differentiation and visual hierarchy in layouts.

68 Early sketches of how to use the 'white canvas' with different expressions

74 Menu covers showing the identity concept Blending stories, capturing the story and inspiration of Saga and Chef Mitchell – reflecting the essence of New York.

A book about the creative process and design of

AI

AI

The Dawn of Self-Generating Intelligence.

The first time I encountered the concept of artificial intelligence, I was struck by an idea so astonishing that it felt indistinguishable from magic: a program I crafted could continue to 'think' on its own, developing ideas and solutions even as I slept. The implications were staggering. Here was a system that, once written, did not simply execute a fixed routine, but could engage in an open-ended process of reasoning – processing millions of thoughts in parallel, evaluating each, and then converging on its best insight. This is fundamentally unlike the way human minds work. Where it takes us years, even lifetimes, to surmount intellectual challenges and transmit knowledge across generations, these new systems could incorporate new knowledge instantly as they emerge, sweeping forward without the friction of time or memory loss.

We are now living through an inflection point. For much of AI's recent history, the mantra was to 'train on everything humans have ever written', in hopes of distilling the breadth of collective knowledge into AI models. Today, however, a profound transition is underway: we are building systems that aren't just 'learning from the past', but reasoning from first principles, discovering solutions entirely unanchored to human precedent.

To understand the significance of this shift, consider the evolution of AI in games like Go. Early AI programs learned primarily by mimicking human play – they absorbed the accumulated knowledge of grandmasters, replaying moves from millions of games. But then came systems like AlphaGo and, more radically, AlphaZero. These programs transcended imitation. AlphaZero began with nothing but the rules and, through relentless self-play, discovered strategies that stunned even the world's leading Go experts, such as the iconic move 37. It didn't merely copy human approaches; it generated entirely new modes of reasoning – expanding the frontiers of the possible, not just the knowable.

This capacity for original reasoning has repercussions far beyond games. For as long as humans have existed, the creation of knowledge has fuelled our greatest leaps forward. We are the only species to continually generate explanations, challenge old certainties, and build ever more sophisticated theories about how the world works. Each new insight is a rung on the ladder of progress – leading to new medicines, scientific revolutions, technologies, and richer ways of living. If there is a common thread through human advancement, it is this process of knowledge creation and error correction.

Now, for the first time, we stand on the brink of exponentially accelerating this process. Imagine not just a handful of Einsteins or Curies toiling through years of research, but vast legions of digital minds, each able to work at extraordinary speed, unfettered by the biological constraints of attention or fatigue. The rate at which we create and refine understanding could grow not by increments, but by orders of magnitude. The compounding effect is almost impossible to grasp from today's perspective: new materials, pharmaceuticals, and scientific laws discovered at a pace we have never before witnessed.

What might this new era look like? I suspect it will resemble less the mechanical and industrial transformation of previous revolutions and more the flowering of the Renaissance – a time when the boundaries separating disciplines dissolved, and polymaths shaped the world by crossing, blending, and reinvigorating fields of thought. With artificial intelligence, we could see the return of this intellectual breadth. The once rare ability to span art and science, engineering and design, could become commonplace. Rather than requiring decades of specialisation to reach the frontier of a single domain, individuals might collaborate with AIs to achieve depth and versatility simultaneously – effectively placing a Da Vinci, a Turing, or a Curie at each person's fingertips.

This is not just about efficiency or productivity; it is about reclaiming the spirit of exploration and curiosity that has always been at the root of the human endeavour. When anyone can code, invent, write, or analyse at the level of history's greatest minds, whole new landscapes of creativity and scientific possibility open up. We break free from old bottlenecks – no longer limited by the long apprenticeship of skill-building, but liberated to engage in the creation and sharing of insight.

To me, nothing could be more exciting or meaningful. To be alive at a moment when the universe itself feels more accessible – when the canvas of discovery is suddenly so much broader – is both humbling and exhilarating. I feel extraordinarily privileged to play a part, however small, in ushering in this new age of knowledge, where the boundaries of our collective imagination may finally catch up to the breadth of our aspirations.

Joel Hellermark
Founder and CEO, Sana Labs

01

02

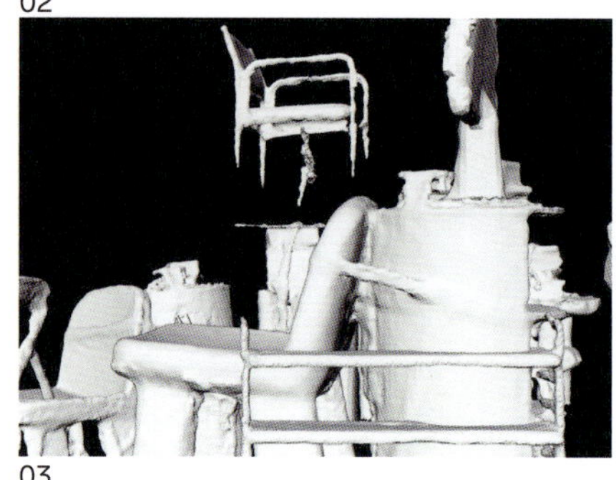

03

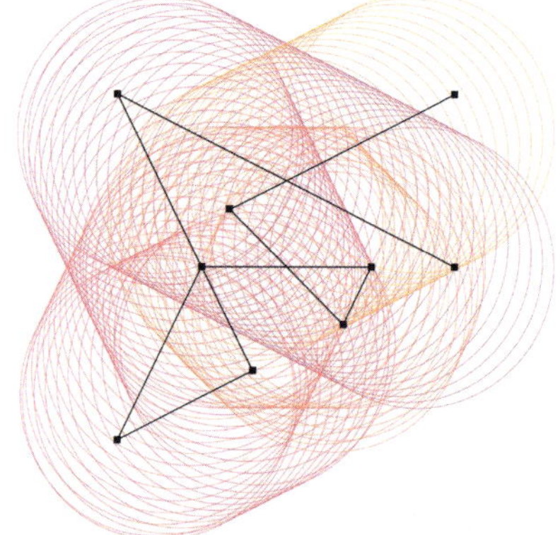

04

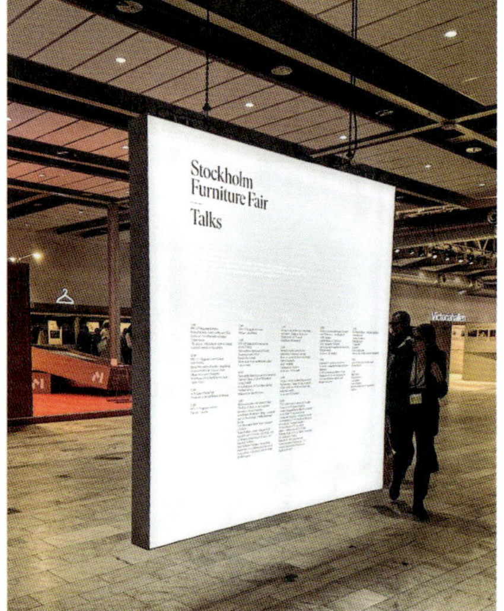

05

06

07

08

09
10
11
GENERATIVE ART
12
13
Sana, who needs
a nudge CMO
to complete the Infosec training?
14
Sana, which
our
top
feature
not
of
our
roadmap
are
requests
in
yet
?
15
16
17
18
19

ROTATIONS TO REVOLUTION

AOI 'Art on Internet' is a foundation for emerging art and technology. Our mission is to promote digital art and make NFTs accessible to a global audience through a permanent collection, metaverse exhibitions, television documentary series as well as a diverse schedule of 1/1 events. We collaborate with artists and brands to help create innovative projects that help improve our world.

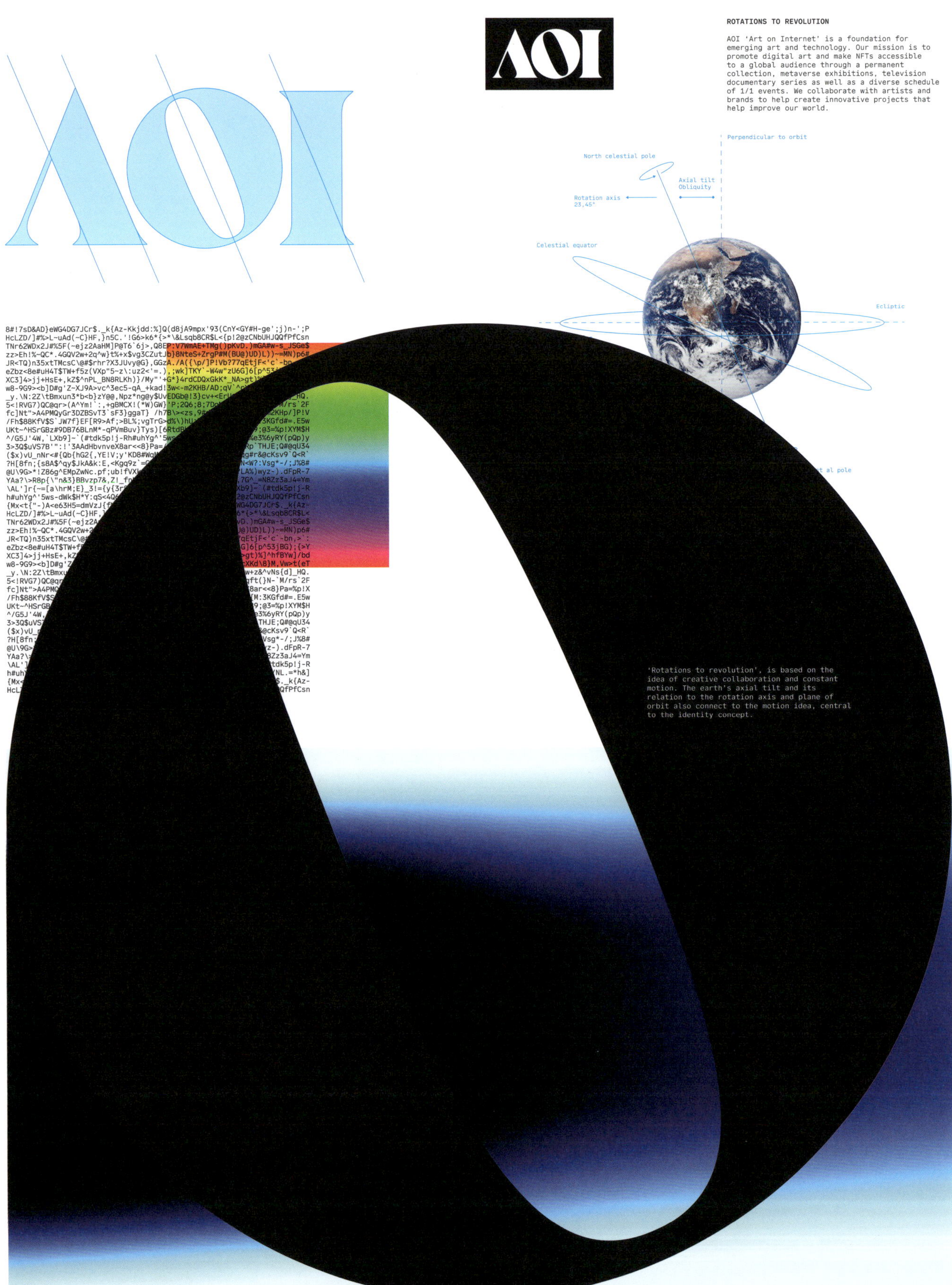

'Rotations to revolution', is based on the idea of creative collaboration and constant motion. The earth's axial tilt and its relation to the rotation axis and plane of orbit also connect to the motion idea, central to the identity concept.

AOI
NFT foundation
Hong Kong
Brand identity
–
2022

AOI, Art on Internet, is a foundation dedicated to emerging art and technology, with a mission to make digital art and non-fungible tokens (NFTs) accessible to a global audience. This is achieved through a permanent collection, metaverse exhibitions, documentaries and a range of physical events.

Collaborating with artists and brands, AOI supports the development of innovative projects aimed at driving positive change. Digital art is seen as a catalyst for unlocking creative potential, connecting billions across the globe and transcending society's boundaries.

Create
Contribute
Unite

@artoninternet
aoi.com

AOI pushes the boundaries of how inclusiveness and empowerment can lead to real impact – collectively together.
AOI
@artoninternet
aoi.com

Joel Hellermark
CEO
Sana Labs

Sana
AI learning
Sweden
Brand identity and campaign
–
2021

Sana exists to augment human intelligence through artificial intelligence. They build products that empower pioneering companies to accelerate their missions through better learning and seamless access to knowledge. Stockholm Design Lab and Sana first collaborated in 2021, working together to craft a distinctive, future-proof identity for the Swedish-born scaleup.

The partnership deepened in spring 2023 with a major advertising campaign – including a high-profile billboard takeover in central London – to launch Sana's AI workplace assistant and mark the company's expanding global footprint.

Sana™

Learning
made
human

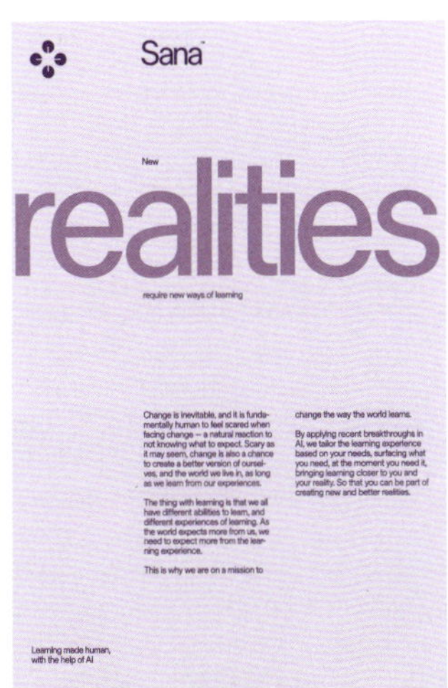

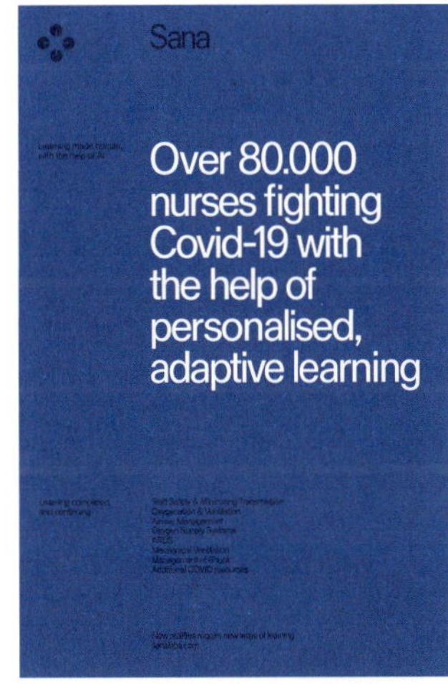

Sana™

Shoreditch Town Hall
JCDecaux
Sana,˜ please pull
for key markets and compare results.
latest sales numbers
AND A MUST-SEE.

JCDecaux
Sana,˜ show last month's 3 star reviews and suggest improvements.
high compared to similar services
Useful service but a bit pricey
Nice app but had some registration issues at the start
So far so good

Shoreditch High Street Station
JCDecaux
Sana,˜ summarise what our CPO said in yesterday's workshop.
Turn into action points action points action
yesterday's workshop yesterday's workshop

Sana,˜ show last month's 3 star reviews and suggest improvements.
sana.ai
Nice app but had some registration issues
So far so good
Useful service but a bit pricey
Go Ahead-London
MORGAN SINDALL
AVAILABLE NOW
hertz247.co.uk

STOCKHOLMSMÄSSAN
ÄLVSJÖ
STOCKHOLM, SWEDEN

Stockholm Furniture & Light Fair is the world's leading meeting place for Scandinavian design. Nowhere else in the world will you find as many Scandinavian design Companies gathered under one roof. For a couple of days, these halls are bursting with the best of Scandinavian furniture and lighting design for both public and home environments.

Stockholm Furniture Fair

—

The world's leading meeting place for Scandinavian design

A ABSTRACTA
ALBIN I HYSSNA
ALDA FORM
AMAROTTO
ANNALA OY
ARITCO
ARPER
ARTL
ARTOME
ASKO
ASPLUND
ATELIER MON
ATELIER SANDEMAR
AVOLT

B BALZAR BESKOW
BANG PAPER COLLECTION
BASECO GOLV
BASIC COLLECTION
BAUX
BECKMANS COLLEGE OF DESIGN
BESLAG DESIGN
BIARO
BISLEY
BLÅ STATION

C CAMIRA
CANE-LINE
CHEF DECO

D DAILRADE KOKS
DALFORM
DESIGN TATU LAAKSO
DEWERTOKIN GMBH
DRY FOREST FURNITURE

E EDOFF & COMPANY
EGE CARPETS
EHEA LIVING
EILERSEN
ERMATIKO OÜ
ESKOLEIA
ESSEM DESIGN
ESTONIAN ACADEMY OF ARTS
EUROCONTACT

F FABULA LIVING
FELICIA LARSSON
FERMOB
FORESTIER
FRAMERY
FRIENDS & FOUNDERS
FROST

G GEMEGA
GEMLA
GLAMOX
GRAND ERP
GRID
GRYTHYTTAN STÅLMÖBLER
GUSTAV WINSTH
GÄRSNÄS

H HAGS
HANYANG UNIVERSITY
HAUGAARD
HEALSAFE INTERIÖR
HELLAND MÖBLER
HEM
HETTA SUPPLY
HITEX ROBOT TUFT
HORREDS MÖBEL
HUMAN ERROR

I INERGO
INTERSTUHL
ISIMAR

J JELTEC
JENNI INCIARTE VILLAVERDE
JESS
JLM-FORM
JOHANSON

K KAKELSPECIALISTEN PROJEKT
KALLIN & FRANZÉN
KARL ANDERSSON & SÖNER
KATEHA
KINNARPS
KLONG
KO JUBILO STUDIO
KONSTFACK
KOUPLE
KRISTINA DAM STUDIO
KURAGE
KÄLLEMO

L LAMMHULTS
LAPALMA
LAURITZON
LEKOLAR
LENTALA
LINTEX

M MARI KOPPANEN
MATERIA
MAVIS
MILA
MJ DESIGN
MM STUDIO
MONT
MOROSO

N NOAS SWEDEN
NORDIFA
NORMANN COPENHAGEN

O OBLURE
OFFECCT
OGEBORG
OHLSON

P PIIROINEN
PILKE
PINJASTO OY / SAARI
POIAT
POLARIA
PORCELANOSA
PRESS & SON

R RAGNARS
REETA LAINE
REFORM DESIGN LAB
RE-VOLT

S SARA DE CAMPOS
SATELLIET ORIGINALS
SECTO DESIGN
SKANDIFORM
SKARGAARDEN
SMD DESIGN
SOFTREND
STARRIKE OF SCANDINAVIA
STRING FURNITURE
SWEDSTYLE
SVENHEIM
SVENSSON
SYNC MODE

T TK-TEAM
TED SYNNOTT STUDIO
TENTE

U UNG SVENSK FORM
UNIDRAIN

V VAD
VANDRA RUGS
VESTRE
VIA DESIGN
VILAX
VILLEROY & BOCH
VIVERO

W WEDOGREEN
WENDELBO
WOODNOTES OY
WTEDY DREWNO

Z ZEE
ZERO BELYSNING
ZILENZIO
ZILIO A&C

23.02.07—15

Stockholm Furniture Fair
Scandinavian design and architecture platform
Sweden
Brand identity
–
2023

Since 1951, the Stockholm Furniture Fair has played a vital role in uniting and advancing the Scandinavian design community. Pioneering with passion, creativity and authority, it continues to shape the future of the industry. Stockholm Design Lab was commissioned to develop an updated visual identity for the Stockholm Furniture Fair, reinforcing its international standing.

Drawing inspiration from the colours of the Swedish flag, reinterpreted in a fresh and contemporary manner, the new identity presents a bold and iconic visual expression. Through its use of technology, the imagery offers a visionary, abstract reflection of the design world. The concept is dynamic and rooted in both contradiction and inclusivity – simultaneously personal and commercial, collective and individual.

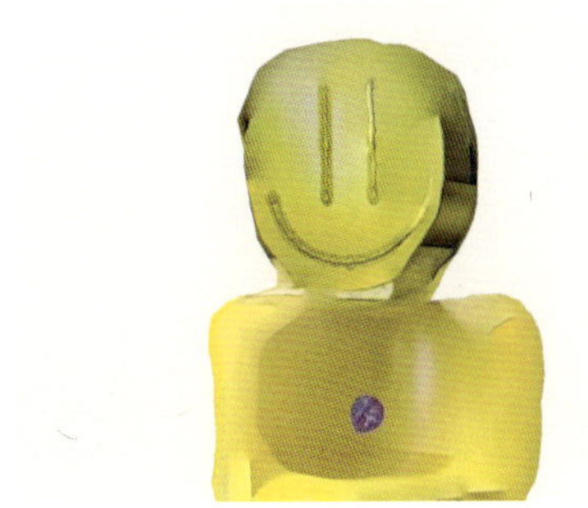

Stockholm
Furniture Fair
Hall C

Stoc
Furn
23.02

Scandinavian design authority since 1951.

A.12/3

STOCKHOLMFURNITU
#SFF23

THE WORLD'S LEADING MEETING PLACE FOR SCANDINAVIAN DESIGN

SDW 23

m
e Fair
–15

navian
authority
51.

Hall B

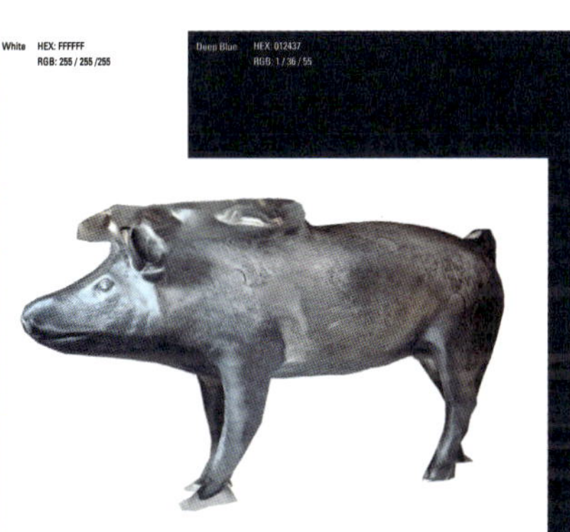

Black HEX: 000000 RGB: 0 / 0 / 0

White HEX: FFFFFF RGB: 255 / 255 / 255

Deep Blue HEX: 012437 RGB: 1 / 36 / 55

Warm Gray HEX: D8D1BE RGB: 216 / 209 / 190

Light Warm Gray HEX: EFEDE5 RGB: 239/ 237 /229

Stockholm Furniture Fair is the world's leading meeting place for Scandinavian design. Nowhere else in the world will you find as many Scandinavian design companies gathered under one roof. For a couple of days, these halls are bursting with the best of Scandinavian furniture and lighting design for both public and home environments.

The vibrant and dynamic exhibition stand is designed by Note with the optimism and bold spirit of the Lammhults brand as a starting point.

Amongst classics and new icons of the past years, Hem unveiled their new Chop outdoor collection. Their first step to taking premium design outdoors.

Collage
Page 80–81

01 AOI stencil tests
02 3D modelling for Stockholm Furniture Fair
03 AOI line drawing tests
04 Lightbox for Stockholm Furniture Fair
05 3D modelling for Stockholm Furniture Fair
06 Sana AI Summit, keynote broadcast
07 3D scans for Stockholm Furniture Fair
08 Sana – asterisk reference in an early Greek papyrus
09 Gradient test for AOI
10 Multiple-colour gradient test for AOI
11 Generative animation for AOI
12 Interactive animation test for AOI
13 Sana campaign sketch
14 Sana campaign sketch
15 Sana, typography reference: *An Anthology of Concrete Poetry* by Emmett Williams, published by Something Else Press, 1967
16 Sana, outdoor campaign, London
17 3D modelling for Stockholm Furniture Fair
18 Apptronik site visit, Austin, Texas – meet and greet with humanoids
19 3D chair scan for Stockholm Furniture Fair

A book about the creative process and design of

Vehicles

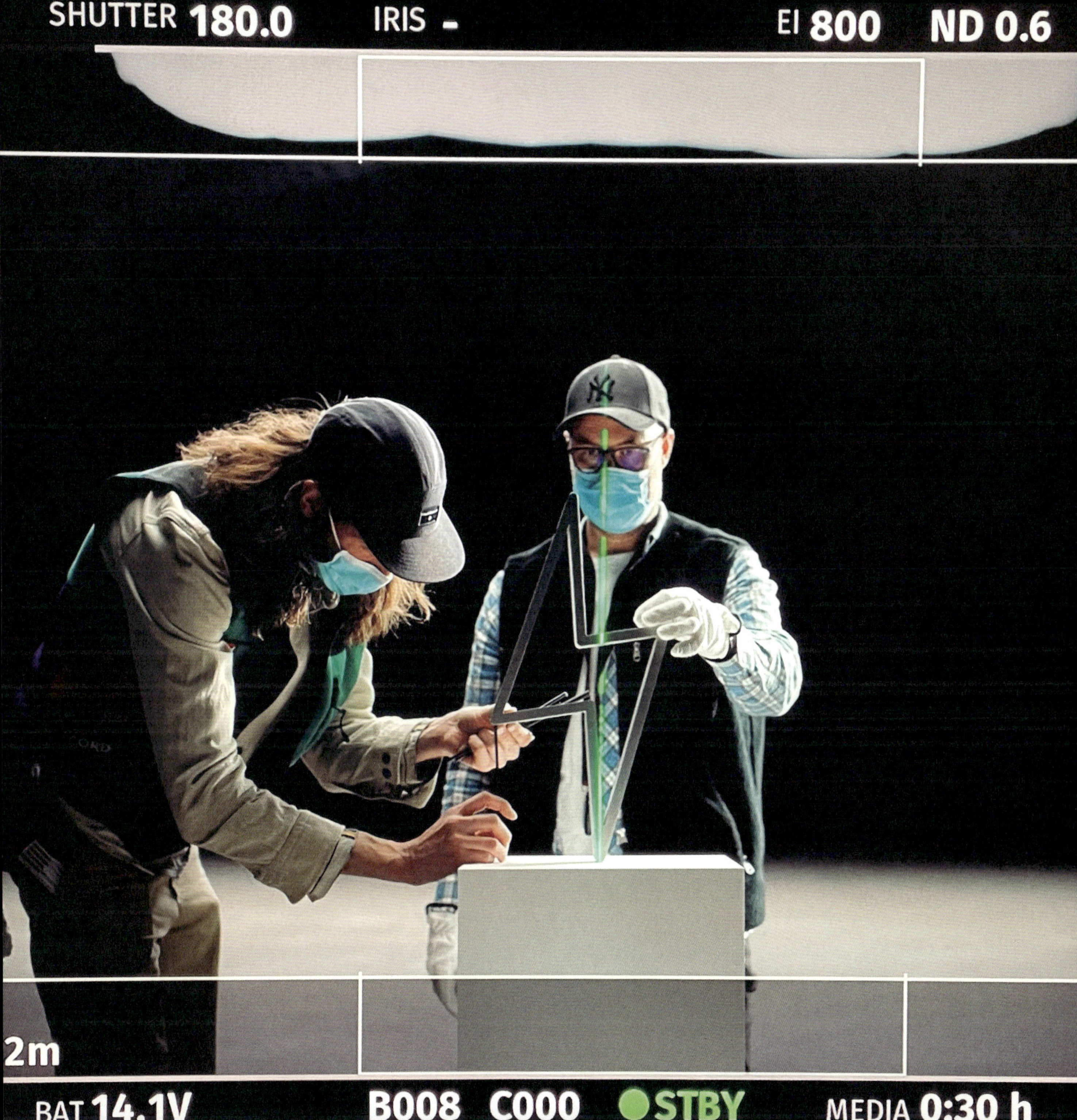
SHUTTER 180.0
IRIS -
EI 800
ND 0.6
2m
BAT 14.1V
B008 C000
STBY
MEDIA 0:30 h

01

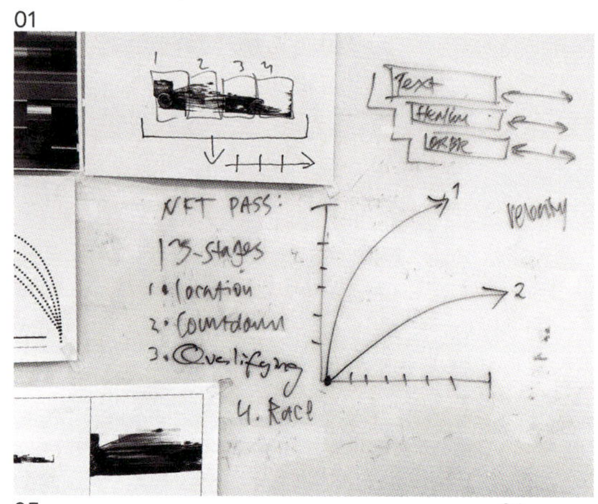

02

03

04

05

06

07

08

09

10

Bornholm

Færgen

11

12

13

14

15

16

17

18

19

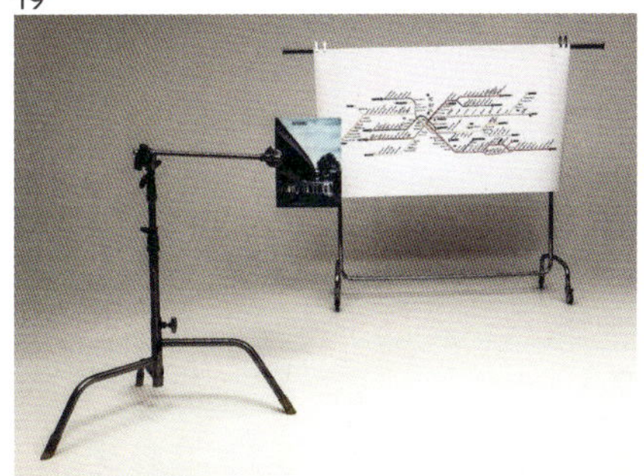

20

21

22

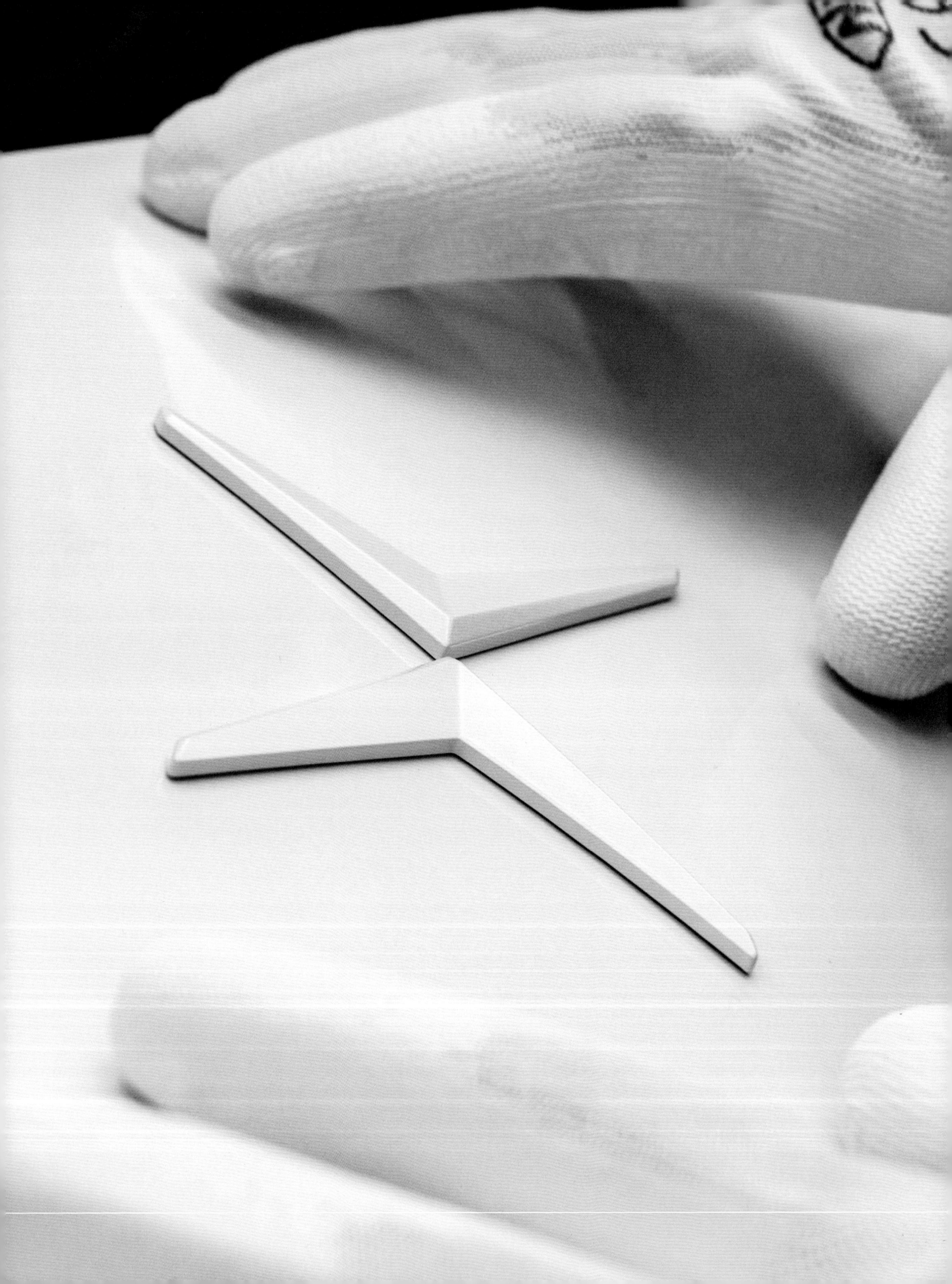

Polestar
Electric cars
Sweden
Holistic brand identity
–
2017

Polestar cars are a new form of electric performance, defined by minimalist design, technological innovations, sustainable solutions, and a complete lack of compromise.

Stockholm Design Lab was asked to help position the Polestar brand as a credible competitor within the fast-evolving global automotive market – one that appeals to the world's most discerning and progressive drivers. SDL's role has been both strategic and operational, defining the long-term brand platform while supporting with hands-on brand design and production.

3D Knit
100% Recycl PES
M1210-B/1691

Polestar 4
100 kWh / 400 kW

Symbol

Wordmark

Polestar

Typography

Unica77 Polestar

AaBbCcDdEeFfGgHhIiJjKk

01234567890 !?.,:;-–&€$@

Colour

Marking system

Marking system

1 size, 1–2 lines under the dash

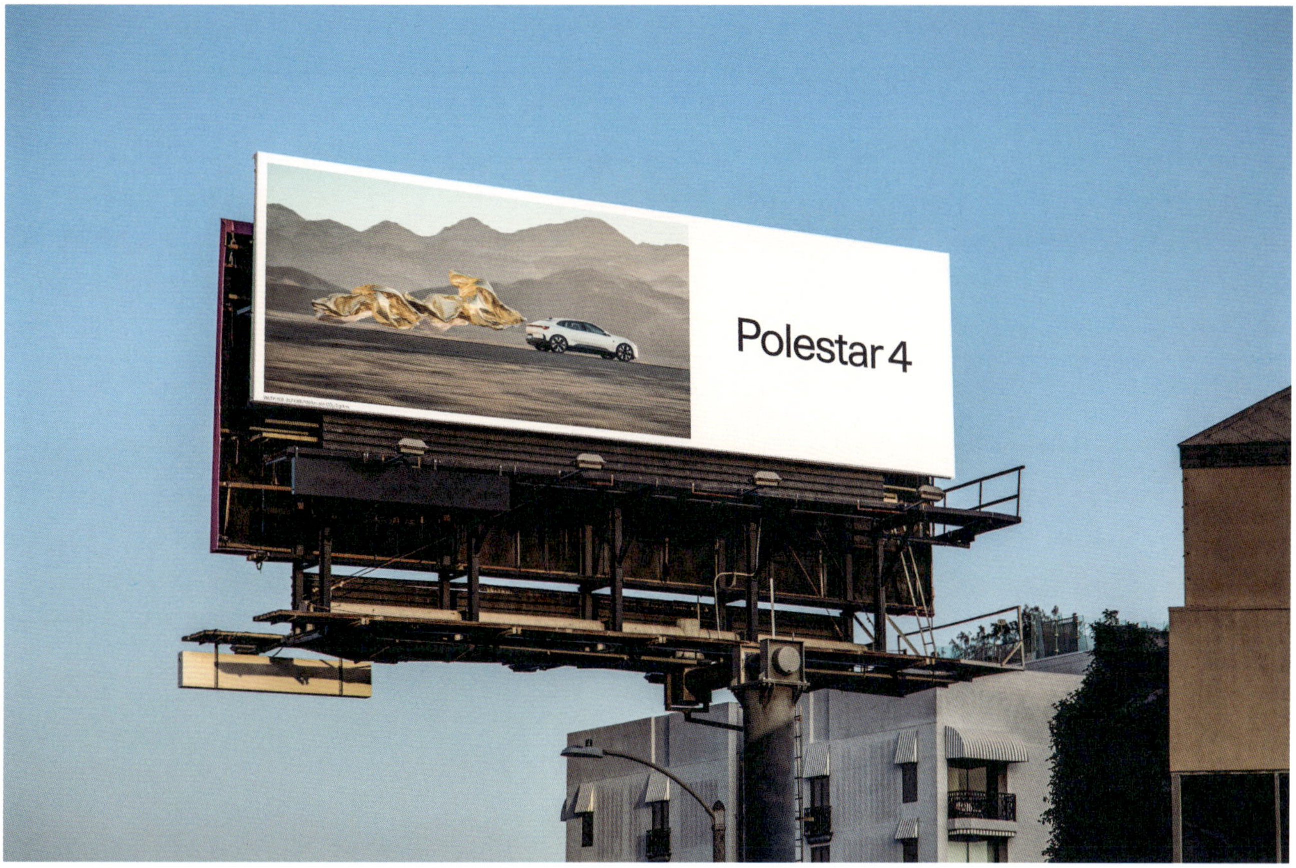
Polestar 4

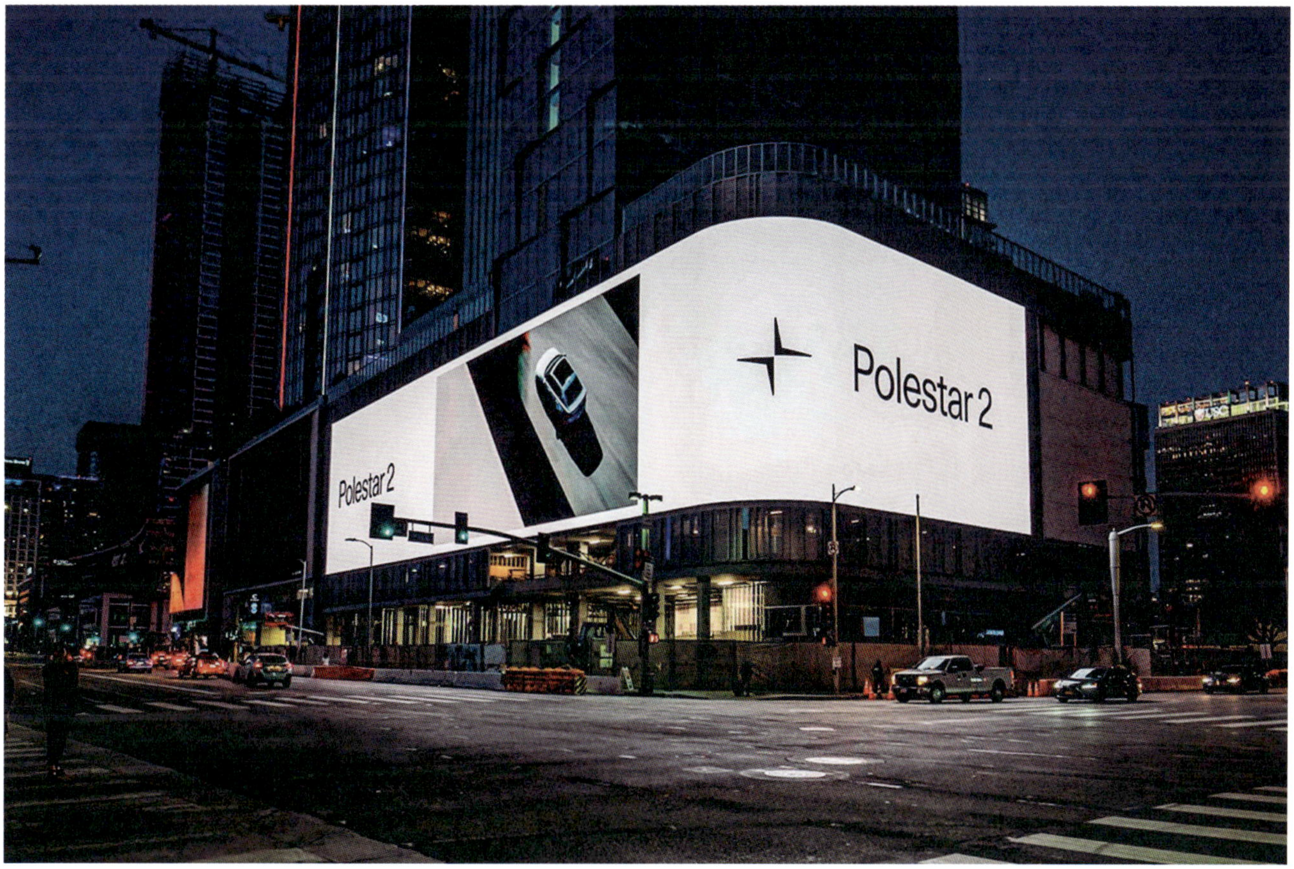
Polestar 2
Polestar 2

Polestar 2

MLB 808

20.1

20.7

21.1

Cradle-to-gate

tonne CO_2e

21.2

22.6

23.4

24.3

25.2

Polestar
A new beginning
1
1
2

Polestar 3

Polestar 3
Polestar 3

Polestar
Sight
24
Sensory perceptions
Sight
25

Polestar
Taste
186
Taste
187
Polestar

KXQU624

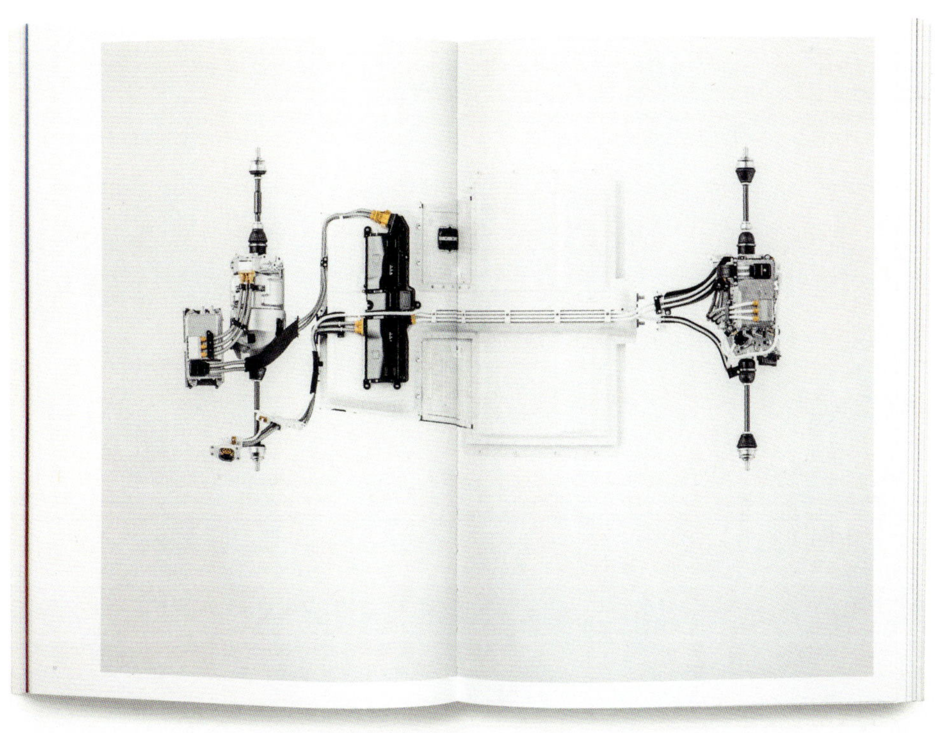

Allebike Alpha
—
Polestar edition
CFRP frame

Polestar
Polestar
Polestar
Polestar
Polestar
Polestar

Polestar 4
Ice Race 2025
Arctic Circle edition
Polestar 4
Ice Race 2025
Arctic Circle edition
Polestar Engineered™
4
4
4

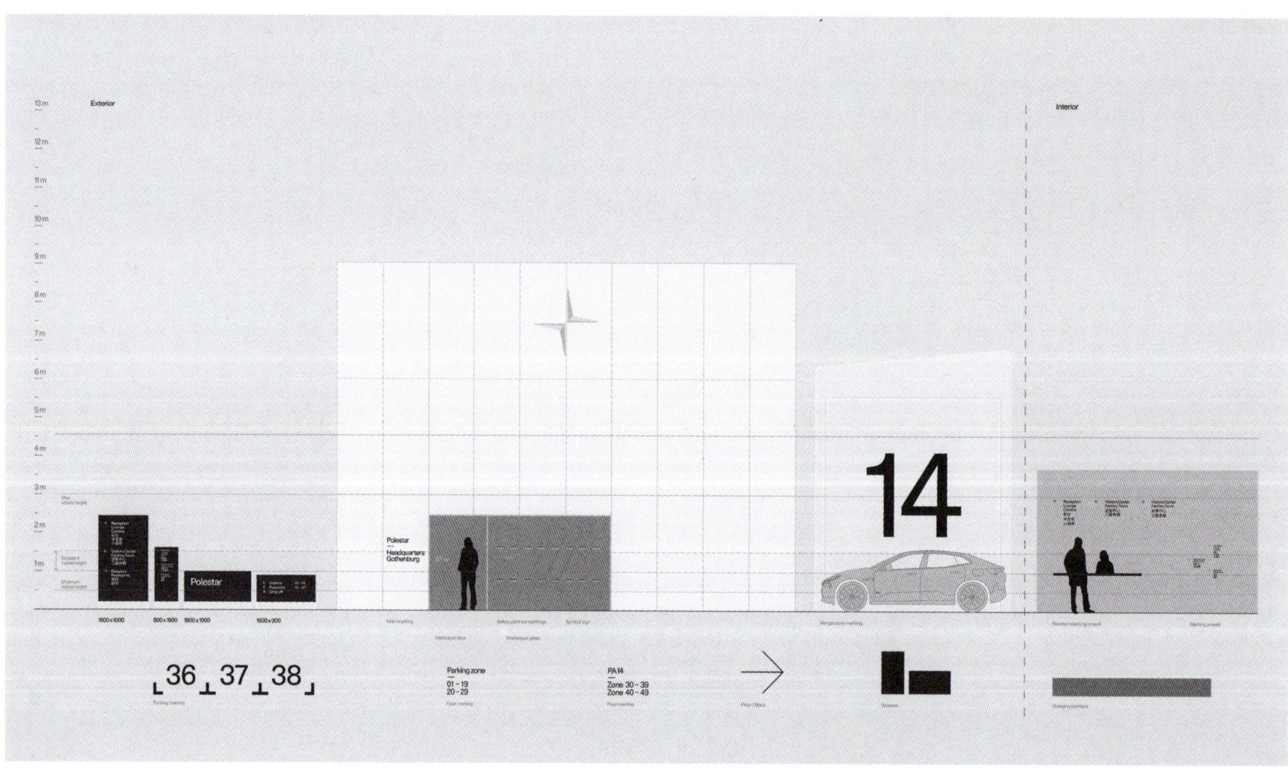

13 m
Exterior
Interior
12 m
11 m
10 m
9 m
8 m
7 m
6 m
5 m
4 m
3 m
2 m
1 m
Polestar
Polestar
Headquarters Gothenburg
14
36 37 38
Parking zone
01 – 19
20 – 29
PA 14
Zone 30 – 39
Zone 40 – 49

Rupert Marine
Custom-built boats
Sweden
Brand identity
–
1999

Swedish boat builder Rupert Marine has produced high quality RIB-boats for the military, police, maritime rescue organisations as well as high demanding yachtsmen. Rupert's boats are available in a wide range of models for different applications and are used from Spitsbergen in the north to Australia in the south.

Controls climate.

Volvo Cars
Vehicles
Sweden
Art direction
–
2021

The first Volvo car rolled off the production line in Sweden in 1927. Since then, Volvo Cars – acquired by Geely Holding of China in 2010 – has remained a global leader in safety technology and innovation, with a multi-brand presence worldwide.

Volvo Cars' premium positioning and Swedish heritage guided Stockholm Design Lab in their strategic design, which included the development of holistic brand identity guidelines and the refinement of the iconic iron mark.

For the launch of the new companion app, key features needed to be communicated with clarity and impact. Rather than producing a conventional instructional film, SDL and Volvo developed a concept-driven narrative. The story highlighted the app's features through elevated visual storytelling – where icons became symbolic representations of functionality – without displaying a traditional phone interface. The film was distributed across digital platforms including YouTube, social media, and the Volvo website.

CT-2

City Transformer
Urban mobility
France
Brand identity
–
2022

City Transformer is a micro-mobility tech startup founded in Israel. Its product, CT, is a shapeshifting, fully electric microcar set to redefine the future of urban mobility.

Early in the process, Stockholm Design Lab identified a gap in the micro-mobility market: a lack of safe, comfortable, and premium alternatives with true sophistication. CT addresses this need – but its ambition goes further. Positioned as a thought leader, it engages with pressing issues in urban mobility and sustainability, acting as a unifying force within its sector and reimagining the future.

Both brand and product were crafted to reflect the pioneering, purposeful spirit of the founders. The resulting identity is distinct and confident, challenging the visual conventions of the traditional car industry.

The core idea centres on brave simplicity, bold messaging, elegant layout, and premium photography. Grounded in motion and white space, the identity evokes a sense of movement and openness, even when static. Through typography, image selection, and layout, SDL equipped CT with a refined, forward-thinking identity as it shapes the urban mobility landscape.

SYMBOL

WORDMARK

CITY TRANSFORMER®

MARKING

CT–1
CT–2

HEADLINE

BIG ENOUGH TO CHANGE THE WORLD

Oracle Red Bull Racing
Formula One team NFT pass series
Austria
Identity and communication
–
2023

Red Bull Racing, at the pinnacle of Formula One, represents values built on audacious innovation, bold ambition and a relentless pursuit of excellence. With uncompromising passion, the team delivers precision-engineered performance on the track.

Stockholm Design Lab was commissioned by client AOI, on behalf of Oracle Red Bull Racing and crypto trading platform Bybit, to help create a new NFT pass series, identity and communications for the official Red Bull Racing team. Throughout the season, the campaign featured a series of releases by established NFT artists, brought together through a consistent design identity and communication strategy.

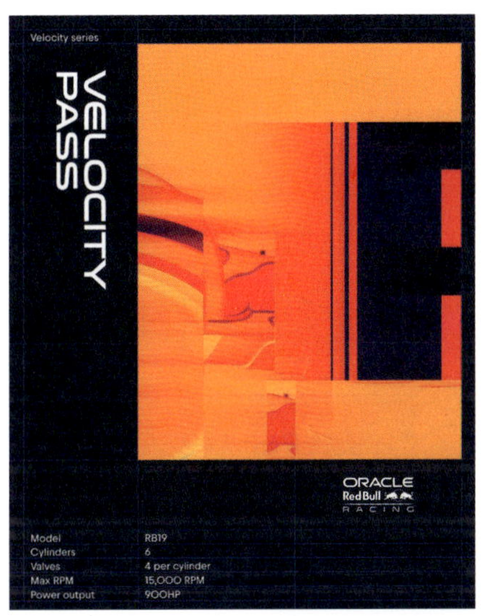

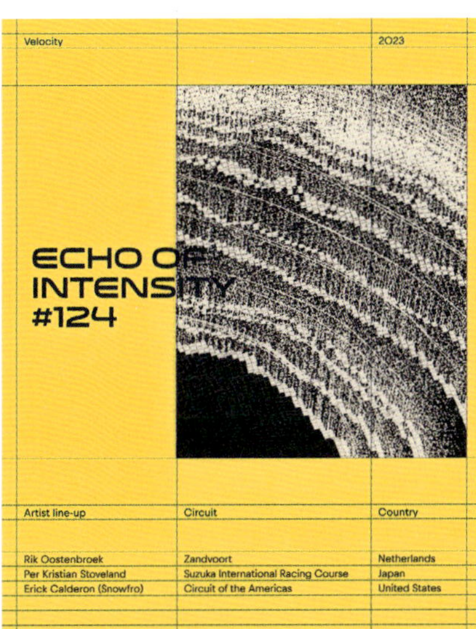

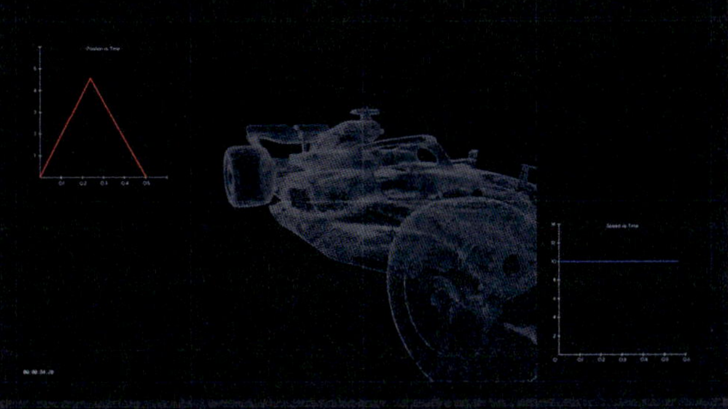

VANQUISH DISPLAY

THE VANQUISH DISPLAY TYPEFACE PERFECTLY COMPLEMENTS THE REDESIGNED SYMBOL AND WORDMARK, CREATING A DISTINCTIVE VISUAL IDENTITY THAT SETS THE BRAND APART FROM ITS COMPETITORS.

Vanquish Yachts

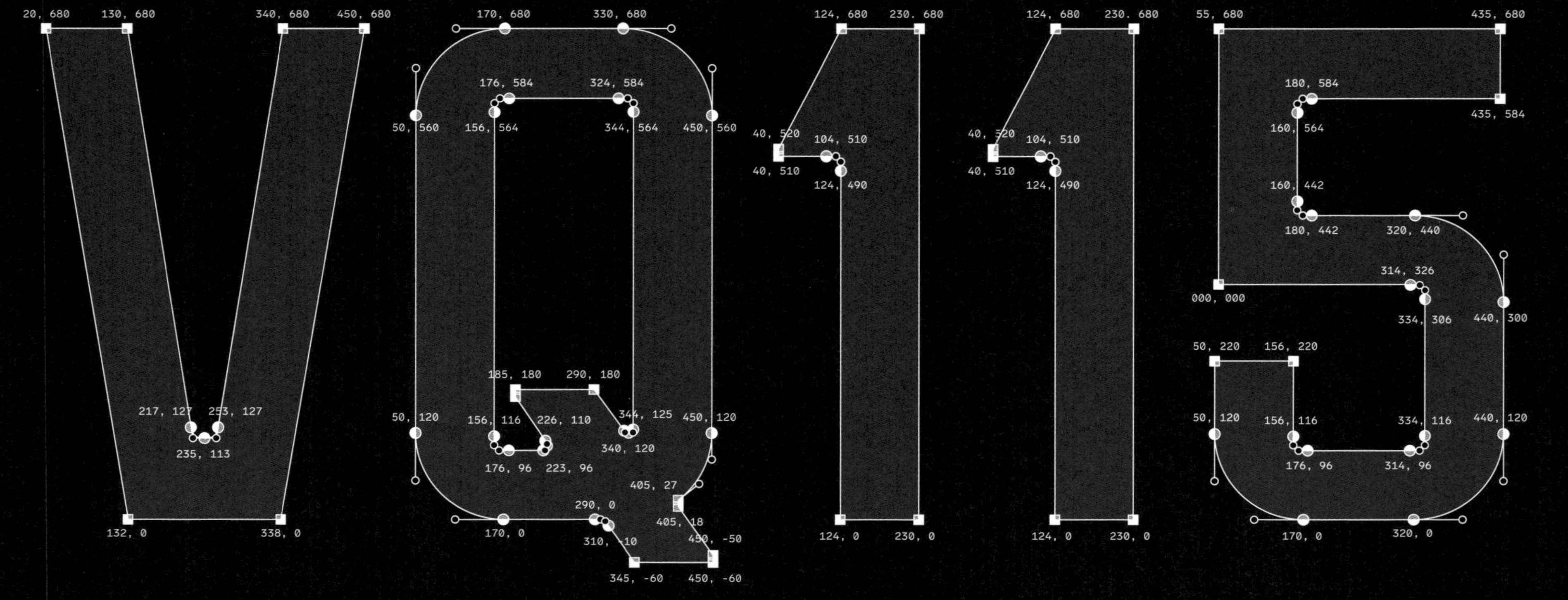

Vanquish Yachts
Performance yachts
The Netherlands
Brand identity
–
2025

Since 2012, Vanquish Yachts has challenged the mainstream orthodoxy of the motor yacht world, creating bespoke boats with innovative technology and high-performance materials.

Stockholm Design Lab created a more premium coherent brand expression including new imagery, typography, and wordmark.

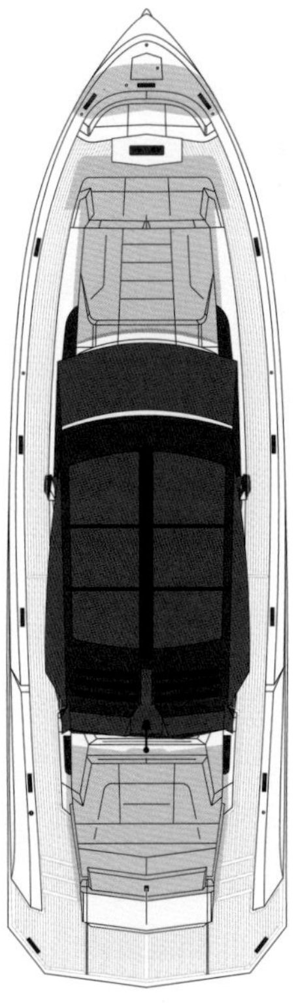

Crescent

Ork
Travel 140 mm
Hydroformed Alloy 6061 TB
Wheelsize 27.5/29"
BOOST Technology

Designed and
developed in
Varberg/Sweden

Crescent/Cycleurope
Bicycle manufacturer
Sweden
Graphic design
–
2018

Crescent remains one of Sweden's most trusted and recognisable bicycle brands. Now part of Cycleurope – one of the world's largest cycle groups – Crescent continues to evolve while staying true to its origins. In 2019, Stockholm Design Lab was commissioned to develop a distinct visual identity for Crescent's mountain bike range – one that would carve its own path within the brand portfolio while standing out in an increasingly saturated market.

SDL's design approach was inspired by the understated logic of the trail itself. Borrowing from the iconic painted markers that guide hikers and riders through the Nordic landscape, SDL reinterpreted these utilitarian symbols as graphic signatures: bold, minimal, and unmistakably functional.

Scandinavian
Airlines
A310 A320 A321
AN12 B737
A30B A342 B727
B74S B752 IL62
IL76 IL86 MD80
A330 A343 B767
DC10 L101 MD11

SAS
Scandinavian Airlines
Sweden
Holistic brand identity
—
1998

SAS embarked on a new course to expand beyond the business travel sector. The shift was significant – more akin to turning a supertanker than steering an aircraft. The challenge set for both SAS and Stockholm Design Lab was to reinvent the brand and craft a travel experience with truly universal appeal.

SDL's strategy for distinguishing the airline from its competitors centred on re-establishing its legacy of good design, specifically Scandinavian design, originally introduced in the 1950s. From aircraft livery to hairpins, airport signage to salt packets, SDL led a comprehensive rebranding initiative, redesigning 2,500 items in an extensive, award-winning programme spanning several years.

SAS has since been transformed through a commitment to simplicity, thoughtfulness, and dependability, underpinned by a meticulous attention to detail – values that continue to resonate with travellers across the globe.

A new tram for Hanover
Design: Jasper Morrison
Gebr. Mann Verlag . Berlin

Üstra
TW 2000 tram
Public transportation
Germany
Graphic system and book
In collaboration with Jasper Morrison
—
1998

Üstra, the public transport company in Hanover, Germany, commissioned Jasper Morrison to design their new TW 2000 tram. In close cooperation with both the client and Morrison, Stockholm Design Lab developed a new graphic system comprising pictograms, transit maps and bespoke typography.

Julius Bär
NIO
Acronis
16

NIO
Formula E Season 5
Electric cars
China
Brand identity and livery design
–
2018

NIO – an automotive brand founded in China, with a distinctly global mindset – is shaping the future of electric mobility. As a founding competitor in the ABB FIA Formula E Championship, NIO has fused engineering excellence with progressive brand thinking from the outset.

Stockholm Design Lab was invited to develop a comprehensive identity system for the NIO Formula E Team. The concept *Stratosphere* became a design idea grounded in performance, innovation, and optimism.

Inspired by the atmospheric layer shielding us from the sun, the identity expresses both protection and aspiration. Gradients form the core of the system, evoking speed, energy, and clarity. The visual language is bright, technical, and minimal – translating seamlessly across car livery, garage environments, driver kits, team apparel, merchandise, and digital platforms.

Collage
Page 104–105

01 Oracle Red Bull Racing: Based on the concept of velocity and the fundamental science behind it, all inputs became the starting point for exploration and development. Through a greater understanding of the science and its connection to speed and motor racing, a set of pure visual cues was formed.
02 Refreshed identity for shipping company Viking Line, keeping the iconic cropped NGLI logotype created by Lars Liljendahl
03 Volvo – on set with CNC-milled icons on podiums
04 Boat storage, Vanquish Yachts research trip, Florida, 2025
05 SDL test drive, LMP3 at Circuit de Barcelona-Catalunya
06 Motorcycle inspiration, Tokyo, 2024
07 Storyboard for Volvo
08 Vehicle reference – futuristic vessel designed by Leiji Matsumoto (manga artist and Daft Punk collaborator)
09 911 & Michelin Man at Porsche Museum, Stuttgart
10 Concept proposal for Danish ferry company Faergen, 2011
11 Polestar signage test
12 Polestar FAT Ice Race livery test
13 Vanquish Yachts research trip, Florida, 2025
14 Crescent Bikes photo shoot
15 Polestar 2, gradient window display
16 Supermarket vehicle, Tokyo
17 Impeccable fireman, Tokyo
18 City Transformer – shapeshifting electric microcar test, France
19 Üstra Stadtbahn book and map
20 Design sketches for subsidiary Norwegian airline connected to SAS Scandinavian Airlines
21 SDL's design for SAS Scandinavian Airlines
22 Design sketches for subsidiary Norwegian airline connected to SAS Scandinavian Airlines

Image captions

103 Precision and security: production of a Volvo film during Covid-19

110–111 Polestar global campaigns, with SDL supporting Polestar's in-house team

116–121 Polestar books. The first book tells the story of Polestar 1, the performance hybrid that first introduced Polestar to the world – featuring never-before-seen images, in-depth explorations, and quotes from those involved in the project. The second book features the first fully electric offering from Polestar, the avant-garde fastback Polestar 2 – with articles, insights, and images from the process of bringing Polestar from theory to reality.

The Polestar 3 is a luxury SUV that appeals to the senses. This third book takes the reader on a journey through those senses with interviews, articles, and behind-the-scenes imagery, celebrating not only electric performance and modern luxury, but also the design process and launch of the SUV for the electric age.

123 Design and campaign for the 2025 Mille Miglia Green in Italy. The unique 'Collezione Mille' racing liveries are inspired by the history of the Mille Miglia and pay a modern homage to rich Italian racing heritage.

124–125 SDL supporting Polestar's in-house retail team and architects such as Snøhetta

129 Precise aluminium CNC milled icons put on art podiums, acting as heroes for the campaign

134–137 Velocity is the essence of motion's swiftness. It propels objects through space and time, a measure of speed in a specific direction. A fundamental concept shaping dynamics and our understanding of the universe.

A book about the creative process and design of

Sports

01

02

03

04

05

06

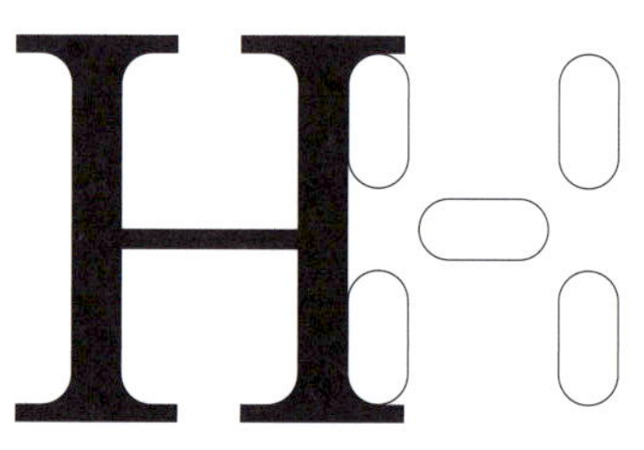

07

08

09

10

11

12

13

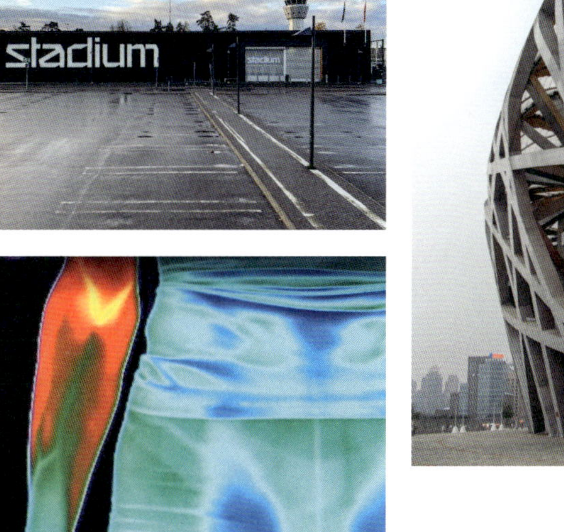

14

15

16

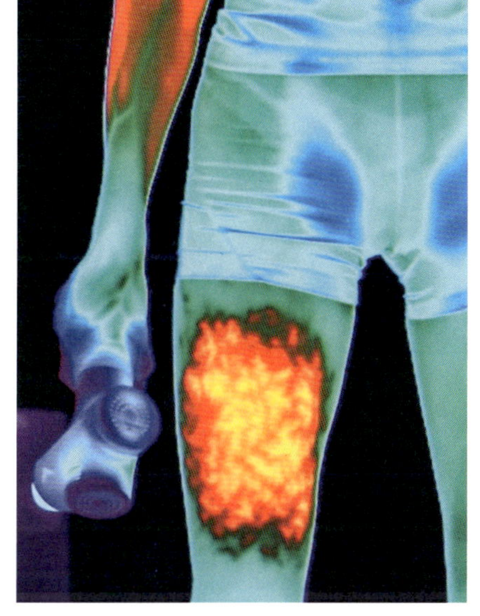

17

18

19

20

21

22

23

Normat

Hyperice
Athlete recovery technology
USA
Brand identity
–
2021

Hyperice – the industry leader in recovery technology, and a pioneer in percussion, vibration, dynamic air compression, and thermal technology – has been named to Fast Company's prestigious annual list of the World's Most Innovative Companies. The evolution into a modern, high-performance wellness brand allows Hyperice to serve a broader audience of athletes. This approach is reflected in a reimagined brand identity and the launch of the brand's largest global campaign to date.

Hyperice®

OAC #1121
PERMIT #120341077-01-SG
Power moves
OAC #1121
PERMIT #120341086-01-SG
Hyperice
Serious relief
OAC #1121
PERMIT #120341095-01-SG
Hypervolt 2 Pro
Hyperice

Power moves
Get the same powerful percussion massage therapy that the world's best athletes have—right in the palm of your hand.
Now with more power, and variable speeds, the Hypervolt 2 Pro helps you recover faster so you can get back to doing more of what you love.

Hyperice
Serious relief
The Hypervolt 2 Pro is our strongest percussion device, offering deep-penetrating relief to stiff muscles, so you can train harder and recover faster.
Choose the speed that's right for you. Cycle through five levels of percussion with the digital speed dial.

Hypervolt 2 Pro
Hyperice
Get the same powerful percussion massage therapy that the world's best athletes have—right in the palm of your hand.
Now with more power, and variable speeds, the Hypervolt 2 Pro helps you recover faster so you can get back to doing more of what you love.

Grey 1 R 240 G 240 B 240 # F0F0F0 C 000 M 000 Y 000 K 010
Grey 2 R 200 G 200 B 200 # C8C8C8 C 000 M 000 Y 000 K 035
Grey 3 R 160 G 160 B 160 # A0A0A0 C 000 M 000 Y 000 K 050
Yellow R 255 G 200 B 000 # 005FDC C 000 M 023 Y 093 K 000
Orange R 255 G 150 B 000 # FF9600 C 000 M 050 Y 093 K 000
Vibrant Orange R 255 G 095 B 000 C 000 M 073 Y 093
Grey 4 R 120 G 120 B 120 # 787878 C 000 M 000 Y 000 K 065
Grey 5 R 080 G 080 B 080 # 505050 C 000 M 000 Y 000 K 083
Grey 6 R 040 G 040 B 040 K 097
Blue R 70 G 145 B 245 C 070
Dark Blue R 000 G 095 B 220 M 062 Y 000
Red R 240 G 040 B 040 K 000
Black R 000 G 000 B 000 # 000000 C 000 M 000 Y 000 K 100
White R 255 G 255 B 255 # FFFFFF C 000 M 000 Y 000 K 000
Green C 040 M 000 Y 095 K 000
Vibrant Green R 095 G 215 B 000 # 5FD700 M 000 Y 100 K 000
Hypervolt 2
Hypervolt 2 Go
Normatec 3
Normatec 3 Pro
Hyperice X
Vyper Go
Vyper 3
Hypersphere
Hypersphere Go
Hyperice

BANK OF AMERICA
NASCAR
xfinity
SERIES
ALLMENDINGER
NASCAR
OFFICIAL

xfinity
ALLMENDINGER
Hyperice
NC
NC

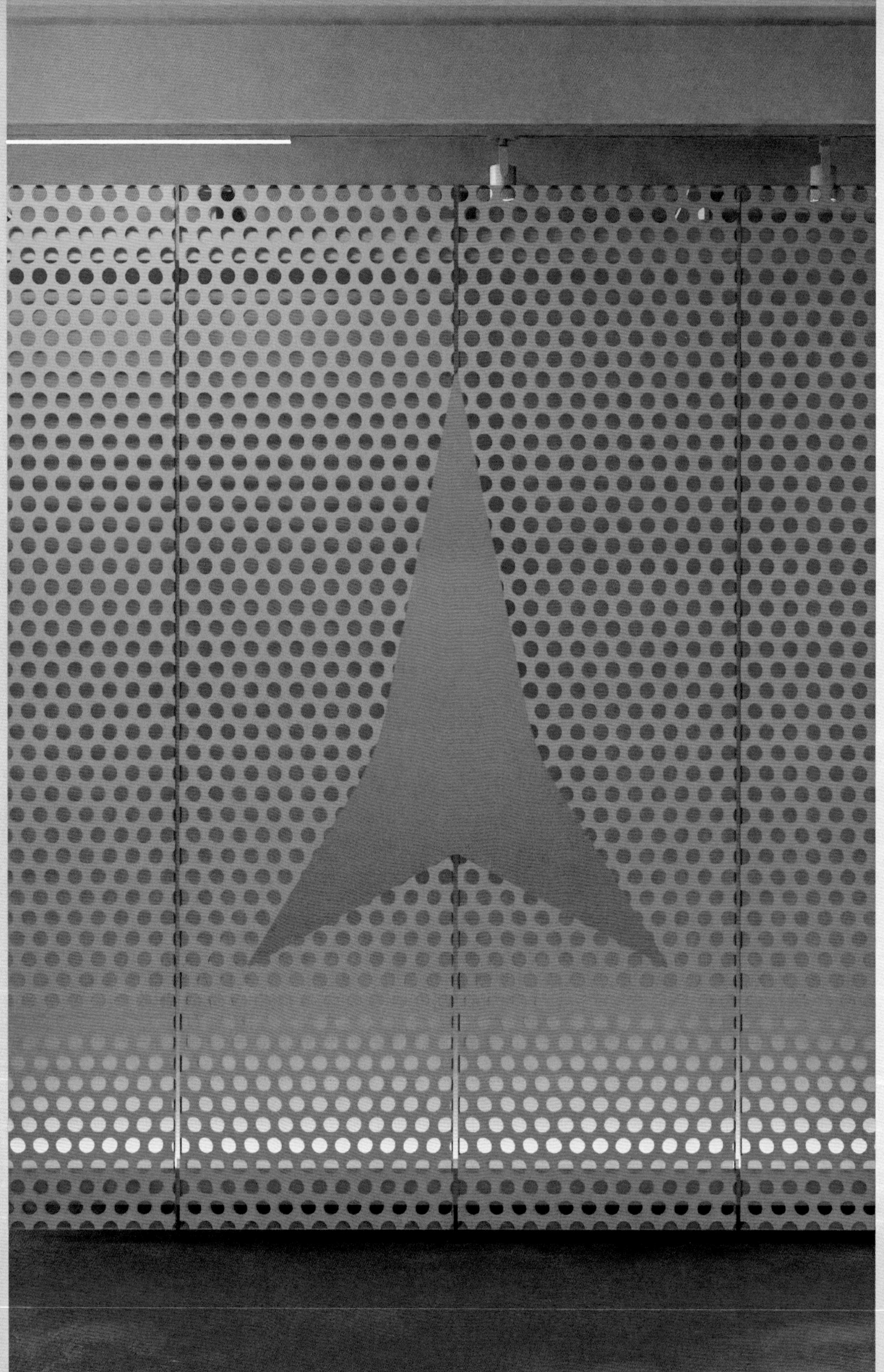

Atomic
Winter sports equipment
Austria
Retail environment and packaging
–
2024

The Atomic showroom in Salzburg was created to stand out from the competition and express the brand's technical innovation, maker DNA and deep passion for skiing. Its modular display system and spatial storytelling highlight the products with precision – anchored by a monolithic red archival storage system, inspired by the utilitarian character of Atomic's workshops and factory. Every surface and detail communicates performance and craftsmanship, brought to life through a clear, refined design system.

In parallel, a cohesive packaging system was created, centred around bold red boxes and marked with the iconic black Atomic star and wordmark. A silver foil label carries all essential product details – name, size, image, article number, and more – ensuring clarity and consistency across the range. The boxes are designed to be standardised within each product category, creating an efficient yet unified system for all models and variations.

ATOMIC
Savor M Stereo

Haglöfs
Outdoor equipment
Sweden
Holistic brand identity
—
2023

The story of Haglöfs is one of genuine craftsmanship, meticulous attention to detail, and a deep understanding of the needs of those who spend their lives outdoors. It began with inventor Wiktor Haglöf in 1914. During a time of demanding labour in the forests of Dalarna, equipment had to be carried over long distances. Driven by the challenges he encountered, Wiktor created the first Haglöfs backpack.

Within two decades, the company evolved from that initial design to producing a comprehensive range of outdoor equipment and has remained defined by an uncompromising dedication to life outdoors.

Haglöfs approached Stockholm Design Lab to craft a distinct, forward-looking brand purpose, supported by a refreshed brand platform. The redefined visual identity honours the brand's rich heritage while projecting a bold vision for the future. The project is ongoing in close collaboration with the Haglöfs brand team, encompassing reimagined retail and digital experiences, product integration, and global campaigns — and marking the beginning of the next chapter in the Haglöfs journey.

Haglöfs®

Haglöfs®

Haglöfs®

100% POLYESTER
30D FIBER PROOF PLAIN WEAVE FABRIC
49 G/M, BLUESIGN® APPROVED
INSULATION: MIMIC GOLD
100% RECYCLED POLYESTER
BLUESIGN® APPROVED.
MIMIC WEIGHT: 0.85 G (SIZE L)

Outdoor performance since 1914

SEK 900	F/W 25	[OUT OF STOCK]
SEK 600	F/W 24	
SEK 1.600	F/W 24	[OUT OF STOCK]
SEK 1.450	F/W 24	[OUT OF STOCK]
SEK 900	S/S 25	[OUT OF STOCK]
SEK 6.200	S/S 25	
SEK 1.600	S/S 25	
SEK 4.450	S/S 25	

Hiking shoes
Waterproof shoes
Daypacks
Hiking backpacks
Ski backpacks
Duffle bags

Haglöfs®

01 02 03 04 05 06
07 08 09 10 11 12
13 14 15 16 17 18
19 20 21 22 23 24
25 26 27 28 29 30
31 32 33 34 35 36

(OUR ORIGIN) Haglöfs was founded in 1914 by Wiktor Haglöf, a visionary with a dream and a toolbox. A carpenter by trade, Wiktor was determined to create a backpack that could withstand the necessary journeys through the country, no matter the conditions.

Seeking constant progress, we've ventured into new territory, creating technical designs that set a new standard in craftsmanship and committing to do all we can to ensure that the outdoors will still be there for future generations to explore. We've pioneered a new standard of perfection, but, like Wiktor, we will never stop innovating.

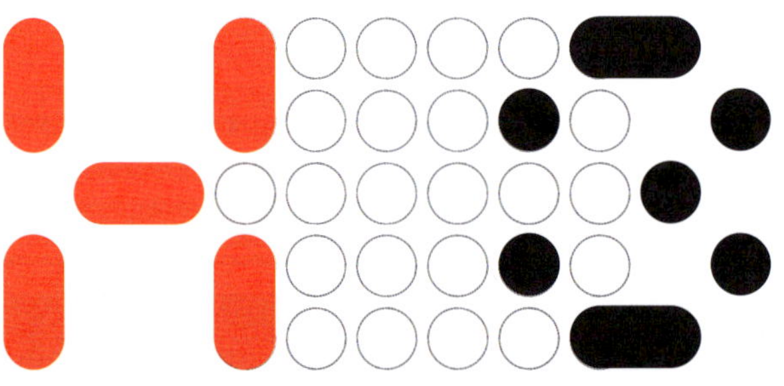

Haglöfs
Insulation
Week
Haglöfs
Haglöfs Accessories
Natural Blend Tech Crew Neck
Haglöfs
Caring for your products
Haglöfs
Haglöfs Haglöfs Haglöfs Haglöfs Haglöfs
Haglöfs

L.I.M SERIES ZT 2.0
A SYSTEM FOR
LIMITLESS PURSUIT
Haglöfs

Puffy Mimic Hood
Mimic GOLD Down
Haglöfs
Outdoor performance
Since 1914

Haglöfs®

Haglöfs

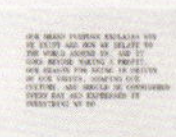
For the greatest
playground
ever made

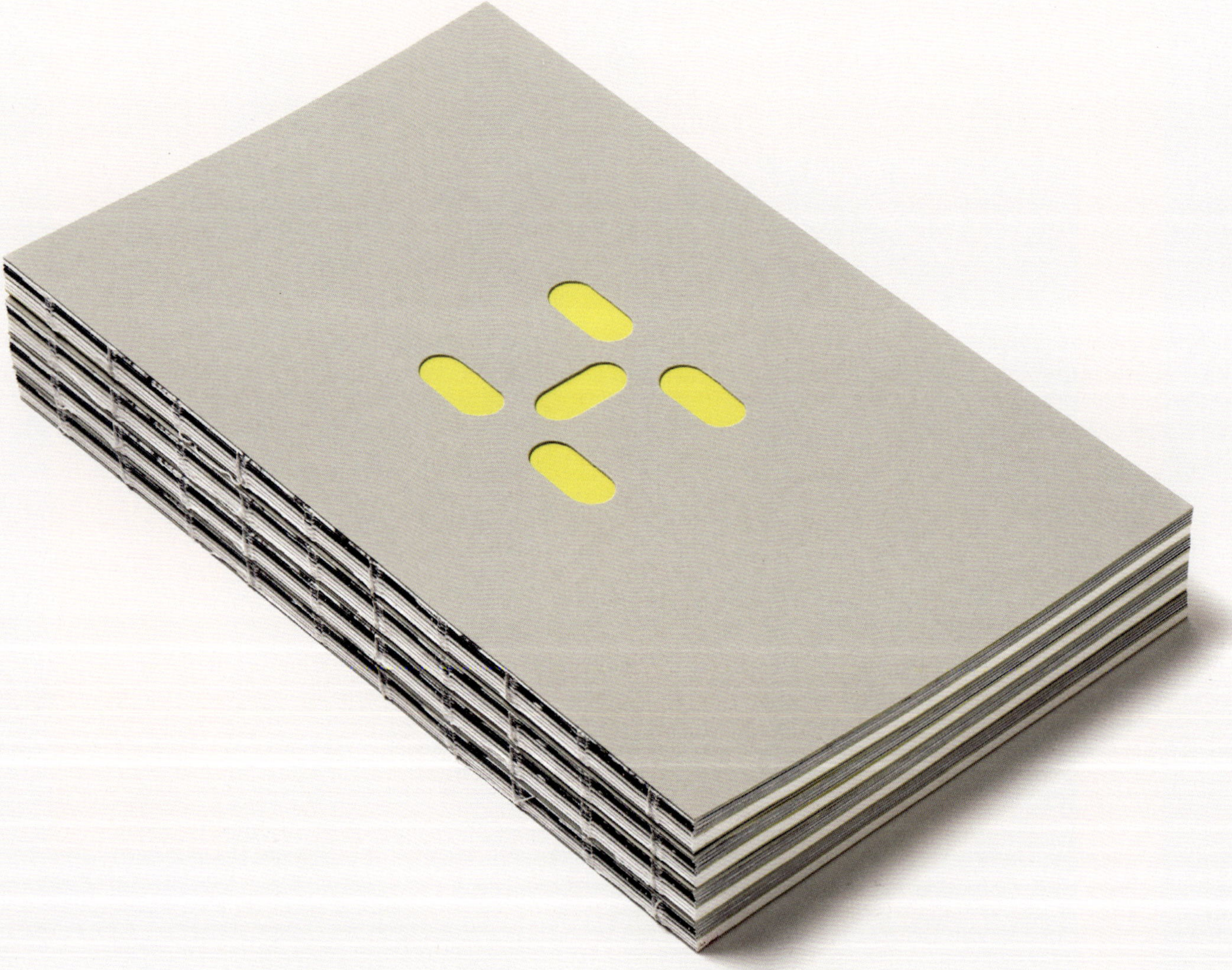

Uncompromised dedication to
life outdoors. Since 1914.
Haglöfs

[+]

Rakk
Professional rescue equipment
Switzerland
Brand identity
–
2024

Rakk is a Swiss/UK-based company producing innovative equipment for rescue workers. Their patented modular bag system – featuring a unique cross-shaped grid – allows rescue personnel, heli-divers and skiers to pack their gear in a customised way, always ensuring fast, easy access. This saves time and increases accuracy, which is crucial in a rescue situation.

Stockholm Design Lab was asked to create a visual identity that would work both as branding for the company and for the products themselves. The solution is a highly functional and flexible identity inspired by Rakk's Swiss origins, the products' distinctive grid, and of course the international symbol of care and rescue: the red cross.

Rakk

3C1B
/60/27

Pantone Bright Red C

Green
#212812
RGB: 33, 40, 18

Pantone 2411C

k
0000
: 0, 0, 0

White
#F5F5F5
RGB: 245, 245, 245

Grey 100
#999999
RGB: 153, 153, 153

Grey 50
#D1D1D1
RGB: 209, 209, 209

Grey 10
#E6E6E6
RGB: 230, 230, 230

Rakk® 1/16/24.
998103/48
AS.55G

#4.722 →

#5 14.2623
Storage
Syst—4×4
2×2

The new RakkPakks are built for professionals who thrive under pressure, offering resilience in the harshest conditions. Designed for rapid access, our modular storage system endures as relentlessly as you do.

Swiss values meet cutting-edge innovation to reimagine what a bag can do. With our modular system, you have unmatched control over your gear. This is Swiss mastery redefined.

Limits are for the ordinary. Our mission is to help you break boundaries. With our modular bag system, you're not just prepared; you're unstoppable. Equip yourself with RakkPakk and let nothing hold you back.

Professional
Rescue
Gear
Master
The
Impossible
rakk.com

Collage
Page 152–153

01 Adidas research
02 Adidas, three stripes exploration, 2016
03 The Water Cube, Beijing National Aquatics Center site visit, 2010
04 Adidas concept exploration
05 Atomic render exploration
06 Pairing the bespoke Haglöfs font with the H symbol
07 Product lineup for the SDL exhibition in Shenzhen
08 Peak Performance bag by SDL, 2008
09 National Centre for the Performing Arts, Beijing, China
10 POC, visual identity, 2005
11 Vintage label, Haglöfs
12 Vintage skis, Atomic HQ, Altenmark
13 Large signage for Stadium, 2007
14 Beijing National Stadium site visit
15 Peak Performance zip pull heads by SDL, 2008
16 Hyperice, heat camera reference
17 Hyperice, numerical exploration connected to the bespoke symbol
18 Haglöfs summit 2023, installation presenting the new visual identity by SDL
19 Art direction and design for POC
20 The most beautiful outdoor playground? Dolomites, Italy
21 Haglöfs signage, Tokyo, 2024
22 Haglöfs, retail exploration
23 Rakk research

A book about the creative process and design of

Art

Stockholm Design Lab and its relation to art

The conceptual artist Dan Wolgers was invited to write a foreword for this chapter about Stockholm Design Lab and its relation to art. Wolgers fed a chatbot a few well-known facts about SDL and instructed it to compose freely within the stylistic framework of the iconic 18th-century Swedish poet Carl Michael Bellman. The resulting piece is presented as the result of a single, unedited attempt.

A small piece on art, Stockholm Design Lab,
and other matters, rendered in the style of
Carl Michael Bellman by a chatbot.

Oh art, you jolly tavern guest,
You paint the wall's cracked rugged crest,
You sneak inside the jug and coat,
And in the painter's trembling note.

What are you? A painting proud? A swaying glass?
A crumpled hat on a drunkard's mass?
Nay, you're a glimpse, a sudden flare,
When maidens trip and laugh midair.

Art's not a lord, nor purse-filled knight,
It dwells in dreams of maids at night,
In music puffed from alehouse bands,
In love's grimace and groping hands.

It paints not courts in polished pride,
But whispers: Look! All shifts and slides!
A table reels, a chair may sneeze,
We sip the world in broken glees.

Stockholm Design Lab, that sly old crew,
Has dressed up dreams in jackets new;
With nimble hands and eyes so keen,
They frame what's wild, yet keep it green.
No marble halls, no velvet drape,
But lines that leap, and forms that shape.
They bind the books, they cast the maps,
They draw the songs in silent gaps.
They tailor colors on the run,
They weave with thread of thought and fun.

From painter's whim to poet's scrawl,
They catch the echo, mark it all;
With lively craft they box the breeze,
And fold the thunder in their sleeves.
In every binding, every mark,
They steal a glimmer from the dark,
And sew it into cloth and skin,
A second world to wander in.

They fashion covers not to hide,
But show the roaring tide inside;
With care and laughter they arrange
A book to dance, a thought to change.

So lift your jug, and raise your cheer,
For art's own feast and fleeting year,
For painted smears, for rebel songs,
For every brushstroke gone so wrong.

For art's like wine: when barrel's dry,
We sing our best, we toast the sky.
And none shall scorn its ragged grace:
A bloom in dirt, a kiss misplaced.

So here's to hands that bind and weave,
That steal the morning, stitch the eve;
Stockholm's fine Lab, a merry throng –
We drink to you, in art and song!

01

02

03

04

05

06

07

08

09

10

11

12

13

14

15

16

17

18

19

20

WORKS
BIGERT & BERGSTRÖM
1986 – 2016
BIGERT & BERGSTRÖM WORKS 1986–2016

Bigert & Bergström
Artist duo
Sweden
Art direction and design
—
1998—2025

Stockholm Design Lab has collaborated with the Swedish artist duo Bigert & Bergström for more than 25 years. Throughout their career, Bigert & Bergström have produced works spanning large-scale installations, public art, sculptures, and film projects. Characterised by a conceptual approach, the core of their practice lies at the intersection of humanity, nature, and technology. Driven by energetic curiosity, their work explores scientific and social themes relevant to contemporary society.

SDL was responsible for the art direction and design of an extensive 356-page monograph documenting the duo's artistic oeuvre, from its inception to the present. The publication offers a thorough exploration of their body of work and its ongoing cultural significance.

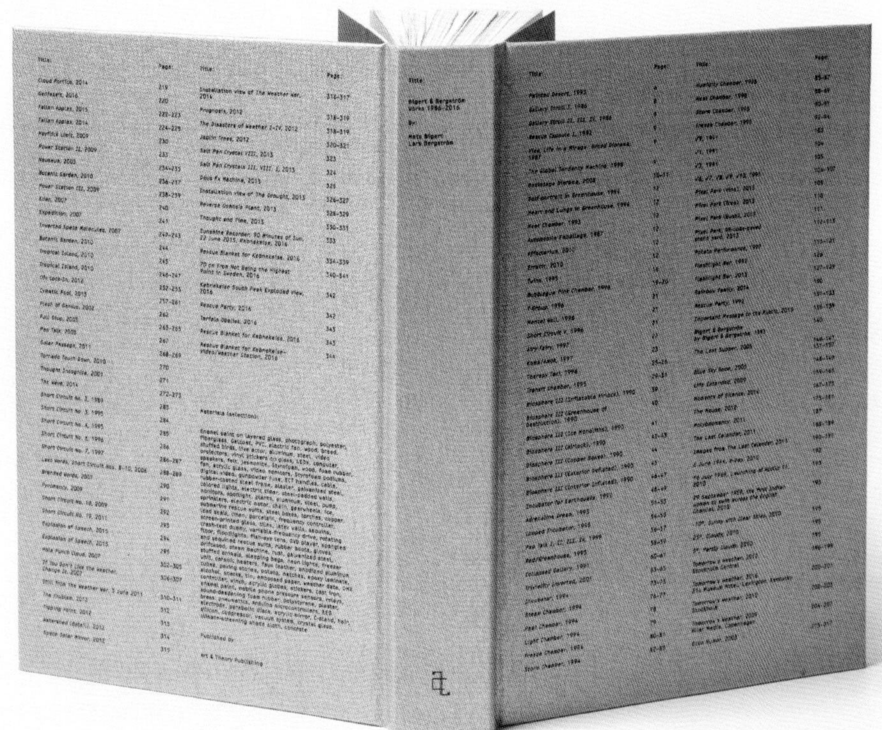

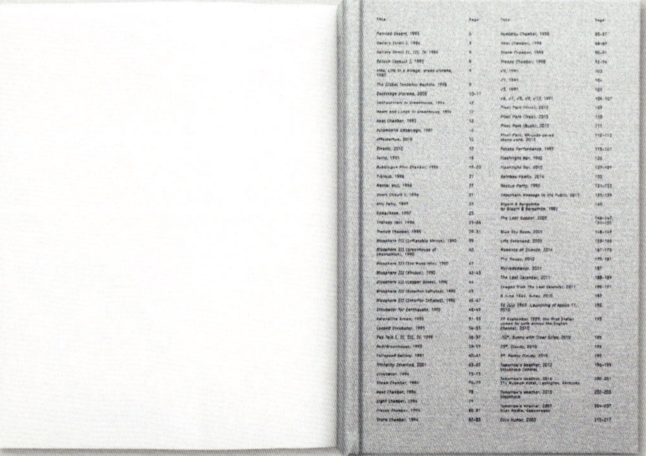

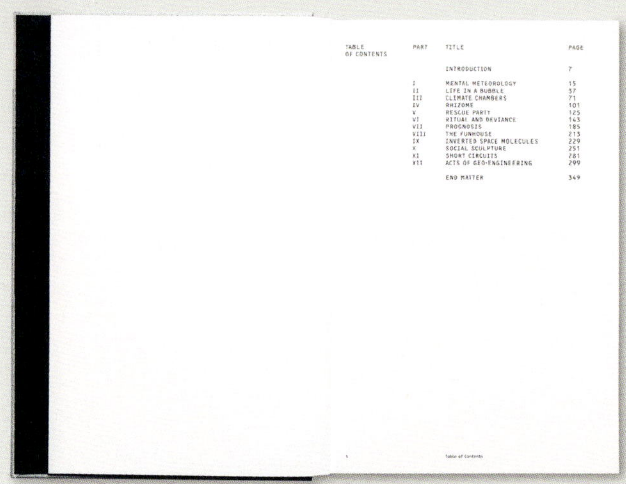
TABLE
OF CONTENTS
PART
TITLE
PAGE
INTRODUCTION 7
I MENTAL METEOROLOGY 15
II LIFE IN A BUBBLE 37
III CLIMATE CHAMBERS 71
IV RHIZOME 101
V RESCUE PARTY 125
VI RITUAL AND DEVIANCE 143
VII PROGNOSIS 185
VIII THE FUNHOUSE 213
IX INVERTED SPACE MOLECULES 229
X SOCIAL SCULPTURE 251
XI SHORT CIRCUITS 281
XII ACTS OF GEO-ENGINEERING 299
END MATTER 349

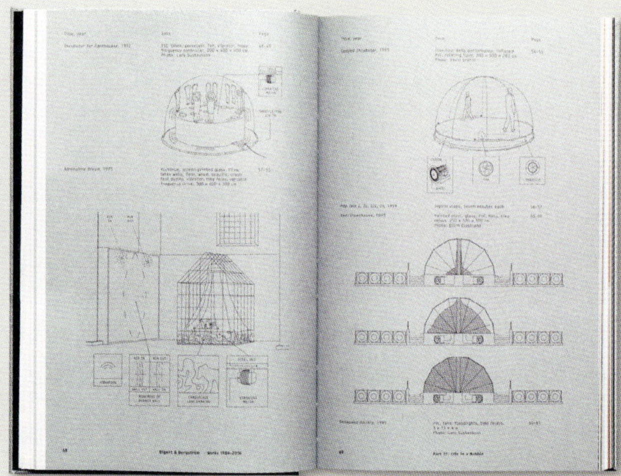

CLIMATE
CHAMBERS II
1998

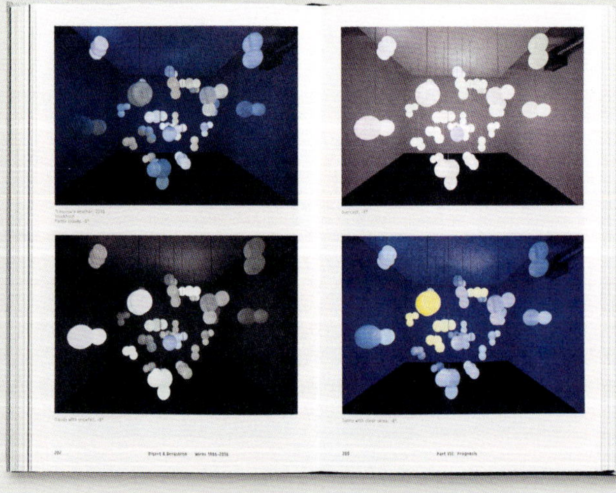

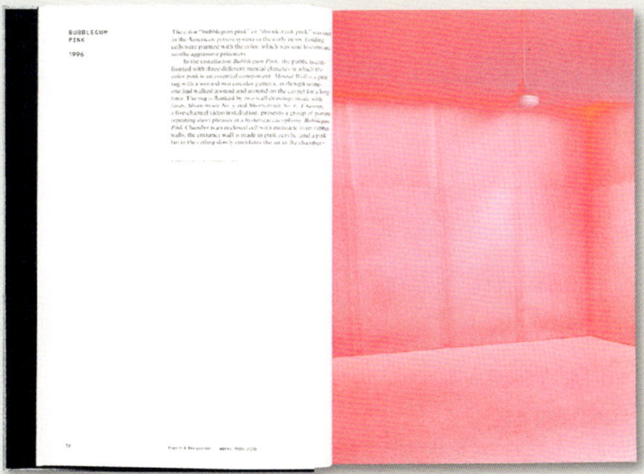
BUBBLEGUM
PINK
1996

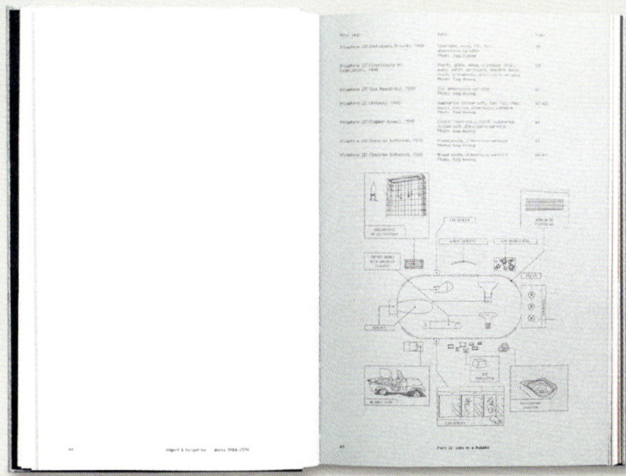

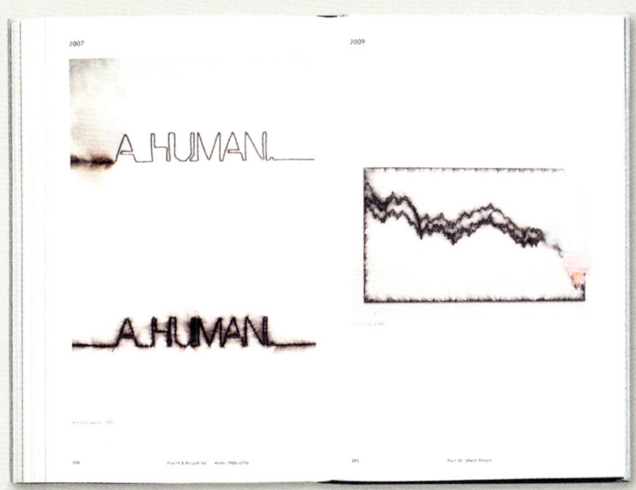
2007
2009
A_HUMAN
A_HUMAN

THE STORM BIGERT & BERGSTRÖM
THE STORM BIGERT & BERGSTRÖM
THE FREEZE BIGERT & BERGSTRÖM
THE DROUGHT BIGERT & BERGSTRÖM

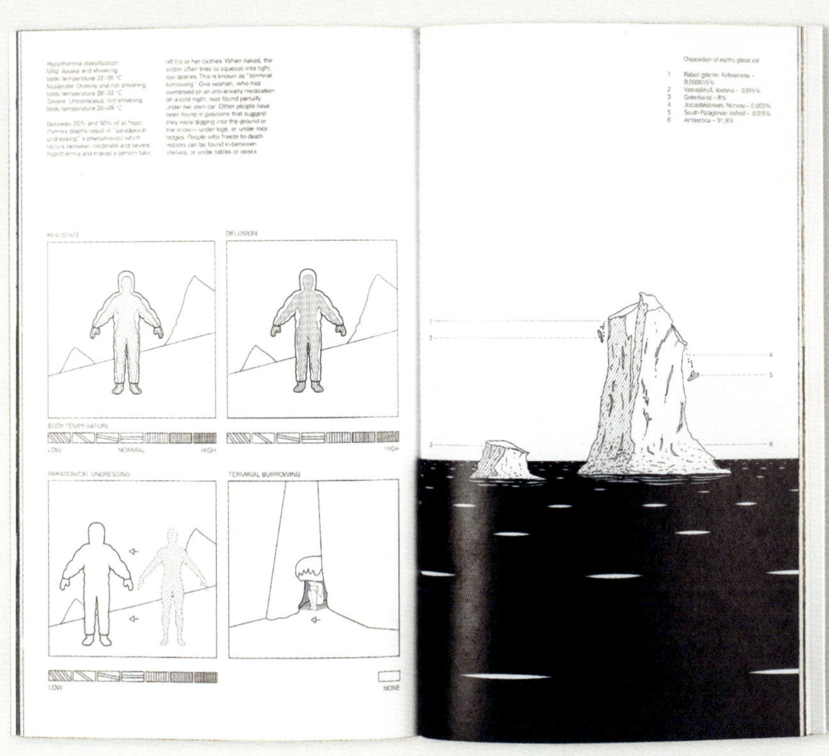

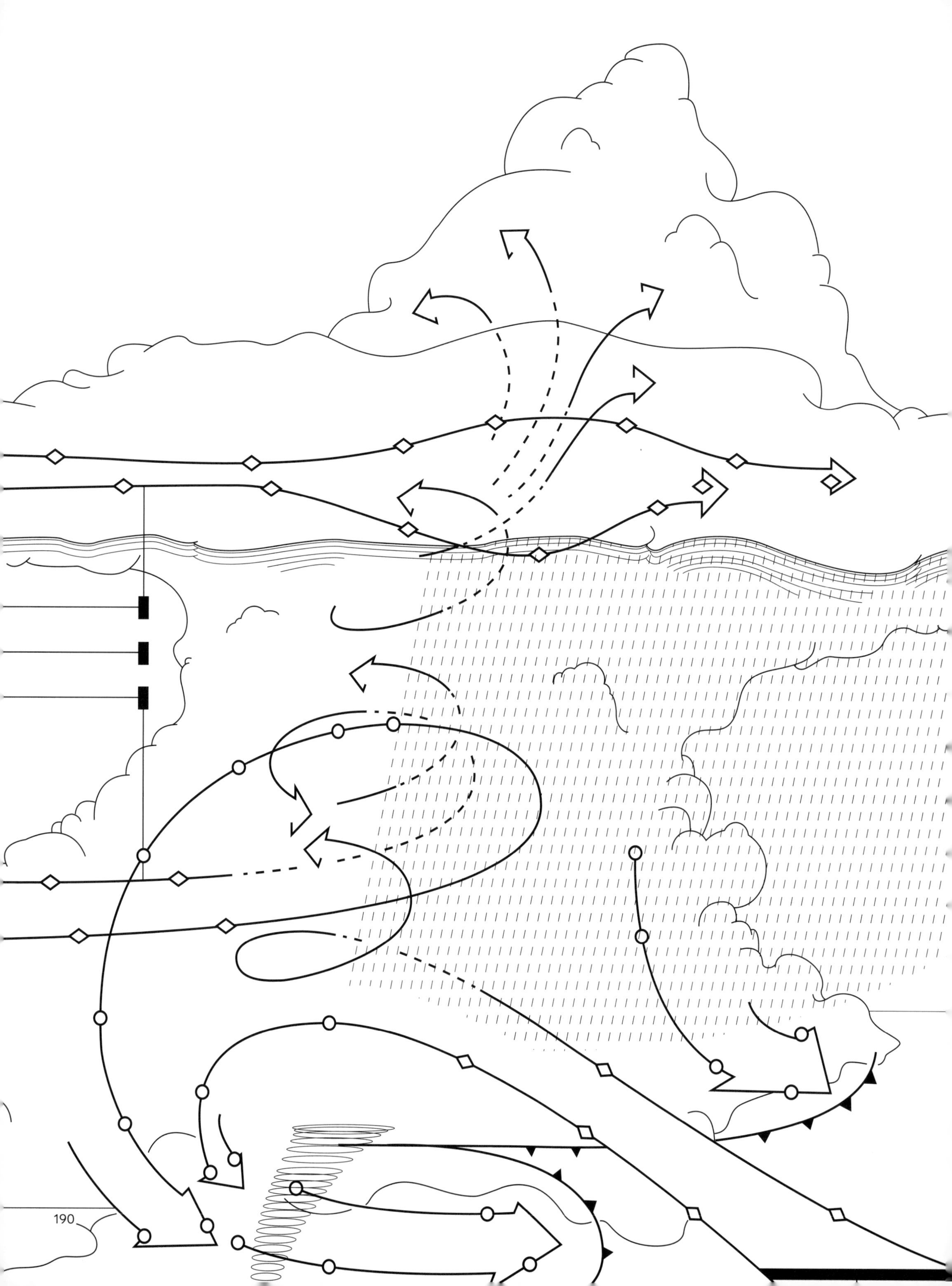

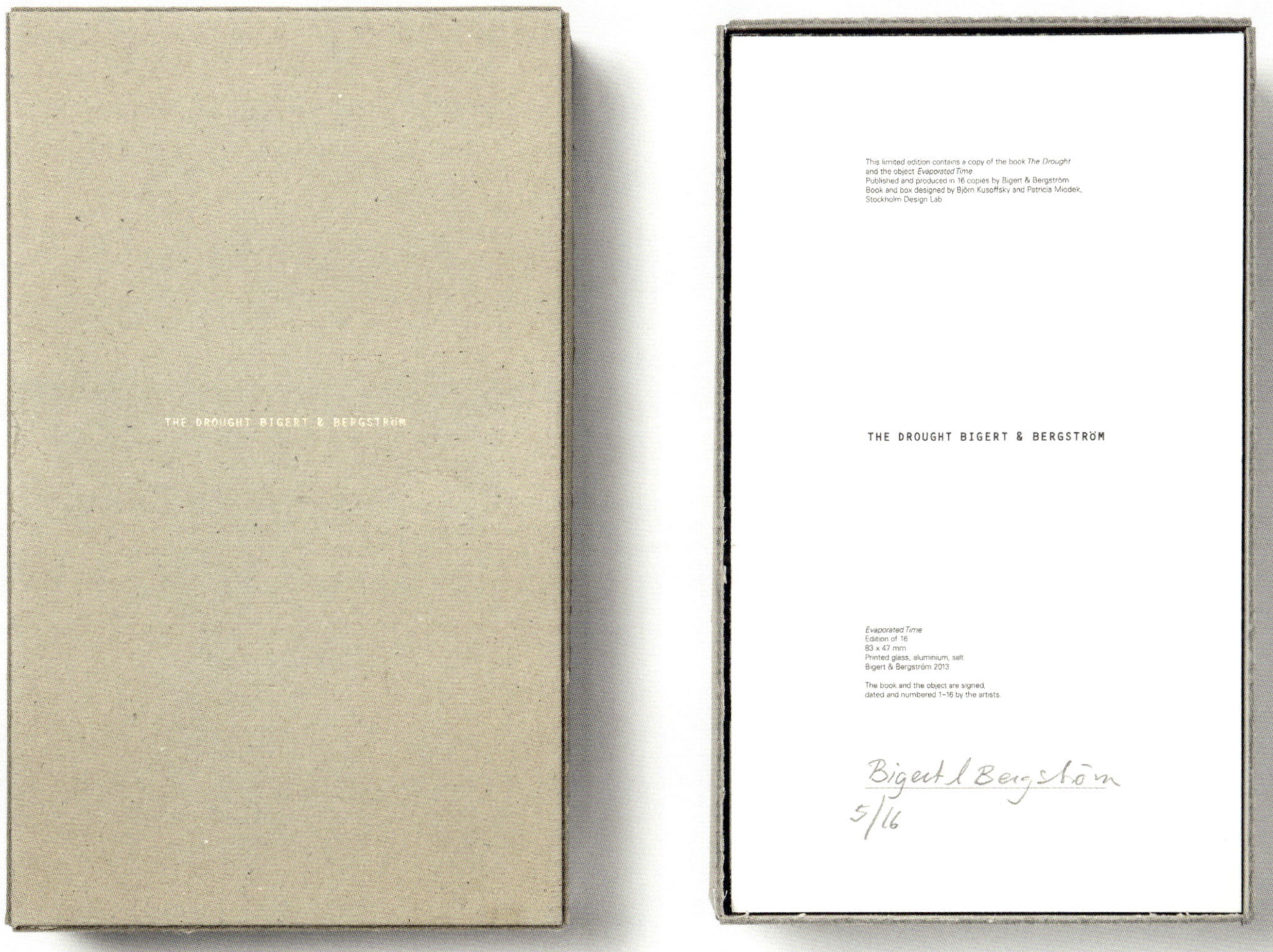

THE DROUGHT BIGERT & BERGSTRÖM

This limited edition contains a copy of the book *The Drought*
and the object *Evaporated Time*.
Published and produced in 16 copies by Bigert & Bergström
Book and box designed by Björn Kusoffsky and Patricia Miodek,
Stockholm Design Lab

THE DROUGHT BIGERT & BERGSTRÖM

Evaporated Time
Edition of 16
83 x 47 mm
Printed glass, aluminium, salt
Bigert & Bergström 2013

The book and the object are signed,
dated and numbered 1–16 by the artists.

Bigert & Bergström
5/16

Venice Biennial
1999
Ex Cinema Arsenale
Campo della Tana

Ulf Rollof
Artist
Sweden
Art direction and design
–
1999

Ulf Rollof's solo exhibition *7C's*, curated by Sune Nordgren, was held at Ex Cinema Arsenale, alongside Aperto at the 48th Venice Biennale, curated by Harald Szeeman.

A total of 50,000 catalogues were produced, all infused with a lemon scent during printing, and placed at the entrance – where visitors passed through Rollof's extraordinary arcade of steel arches and real lemons.

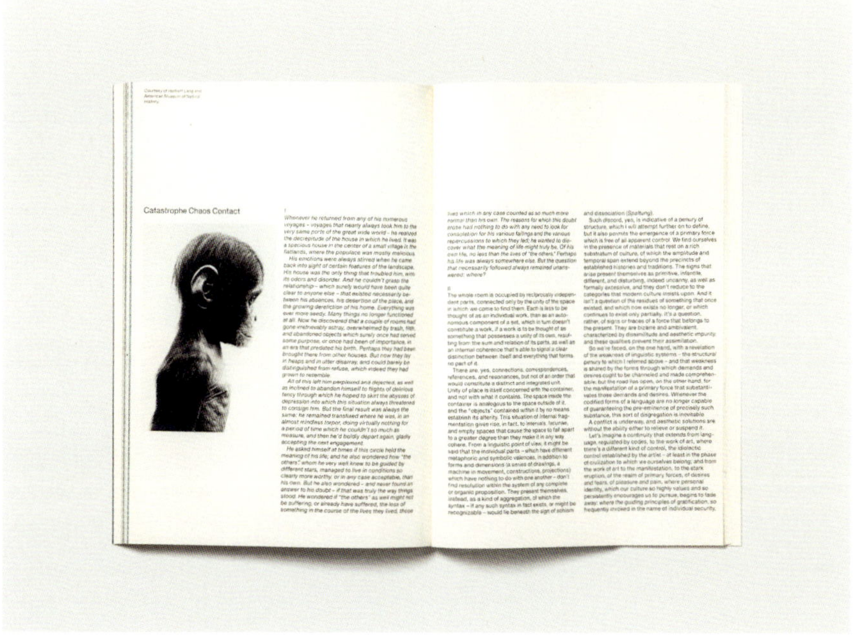

NORDIC
CONTEMPORARY
BY ARS FENNICA
PETRI ALA-MAUNUS FINLAND
MIRIAM BÄCKSTRÖM SVERIGE
RAGNAR KJARTANSSON ISLAND
AURORA REINHARD FINLAND
EGILL SÆBJÖRNSSON ISLAND
12 OKT 2019–
19 JAN 2020
SVEN-HARRYS
KONSTMUSEUM

Sven-Harrys Konstmuseum
Museum
Sweden
Art direction and design
–
2019

'What do you do with an art collection when it's complete? If you donate it to a museum, it ends up in their basement. No, I want everyone to be able to enjoy my art the way I do.' These are the words of Sven-Harry Karlsson, founder of Sven-Harrys Konstmuseum – a striking golden structure in Vasaparken, Stockholm, designed by renowned architects Gert Wingårdh and Anna Söderberg.

Over the years, Stockholm Design Lab has been responsible for the art direction and design of several of the museum's exhibitions, as well as its visual identity. In addition to the art gallery and a replica of Sven-Harry's countryside home, the building houses the restaurant Guld – whose identity SDL also designed – along with residential apartments and commercial premises.

Fernand Léger
Franciska Clausen
Otto G. Carlsund
Vera Meyerson
Erik Olson
Ettore Bugatti
Gösta Adrian-Nilsson
Thorvald Hellesen

Konst + Maskin
Utmanarna under 1920-talet

Bengt O Österblom
Christian Berg
Sonia Delaunay
Amédée Ozenfant
Florence Henri
Knut Lundström
Waldemar Lorentzon

Sven-Harrys konstmuseum
01.04–24.09 2023

Nikoline Liv Andersen
"Dansen med det Døvstumme Øje", 2011
Photo: Jeppe Gudmundsen-Holmgreen

Stockholm Design Lab

ART IN FASHION

SVEN–
HARRYS
KONST–
MUSEUM

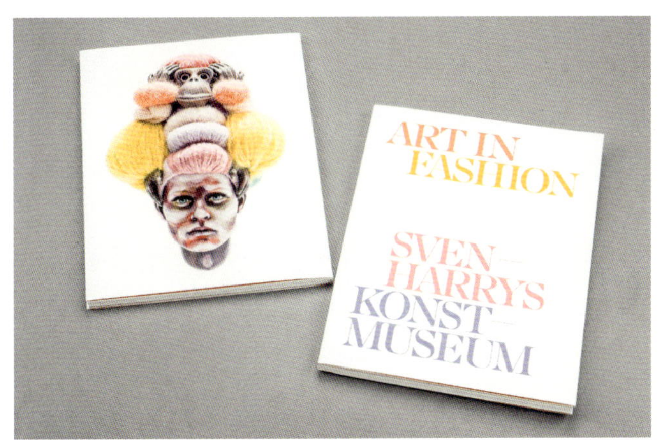
ART IN
FASHION
SVEN
HARRYS
KONST
MUSEUM

SELAM
FESSAHAYE

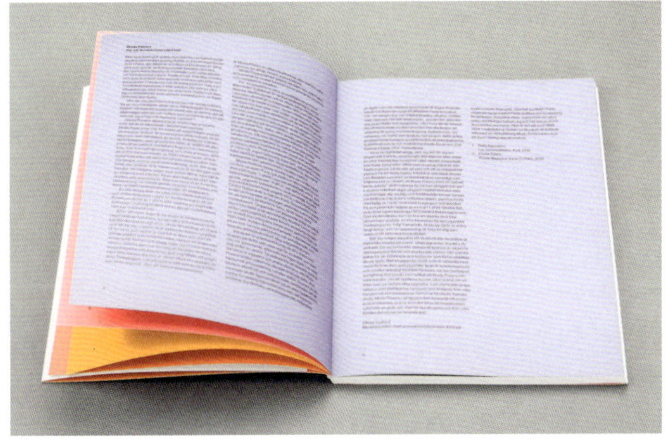

HOT SET
PLEASE
KEEP OFF

Dan Wolgers
Artist
Sweden
Art direction and design
–
2023

In the event of a break in filming, the sign 'Hot Set' is used to prevent the set design from being disturbed before shooting resumes. The sign is placed strategically in the middle of the set.

Placed instead at the centre of a home, the same sign wards off disruption of a different kind – transforming the entire home into a detailed work of art. For the owner of the sign – and anyone who dares cross its threshold – everything within becomes equal, untouchable, inviolable. A sanctuary. Life in art may now begin.

The exhibition catalogue for *Hot Set* by Dan Wolgers consists of a random selection of old articles, cartoons, and printed cards, along with a newly produced booklet containing original and reprinted texts, an artist chronology, and an appendix of images related to the exhibition. In the spirit of reuse – echoing Marcel Duchamp – the catalogue's packaging and cover is made from a limited remainder stock of the book Dan Wolgers *120 Works 1977–1996*, designed in 1996 by Anders Ljungman and Johan Melbi. The typeface Univers is also reused in the new material, featured in both titles and catalogue texts.

The catalogue was published in a numbered edition of 202 + 3 signed copies, prepared in advance of the exhibition. Each was sealed with a red Japanese rubber band – also from leftover stock.

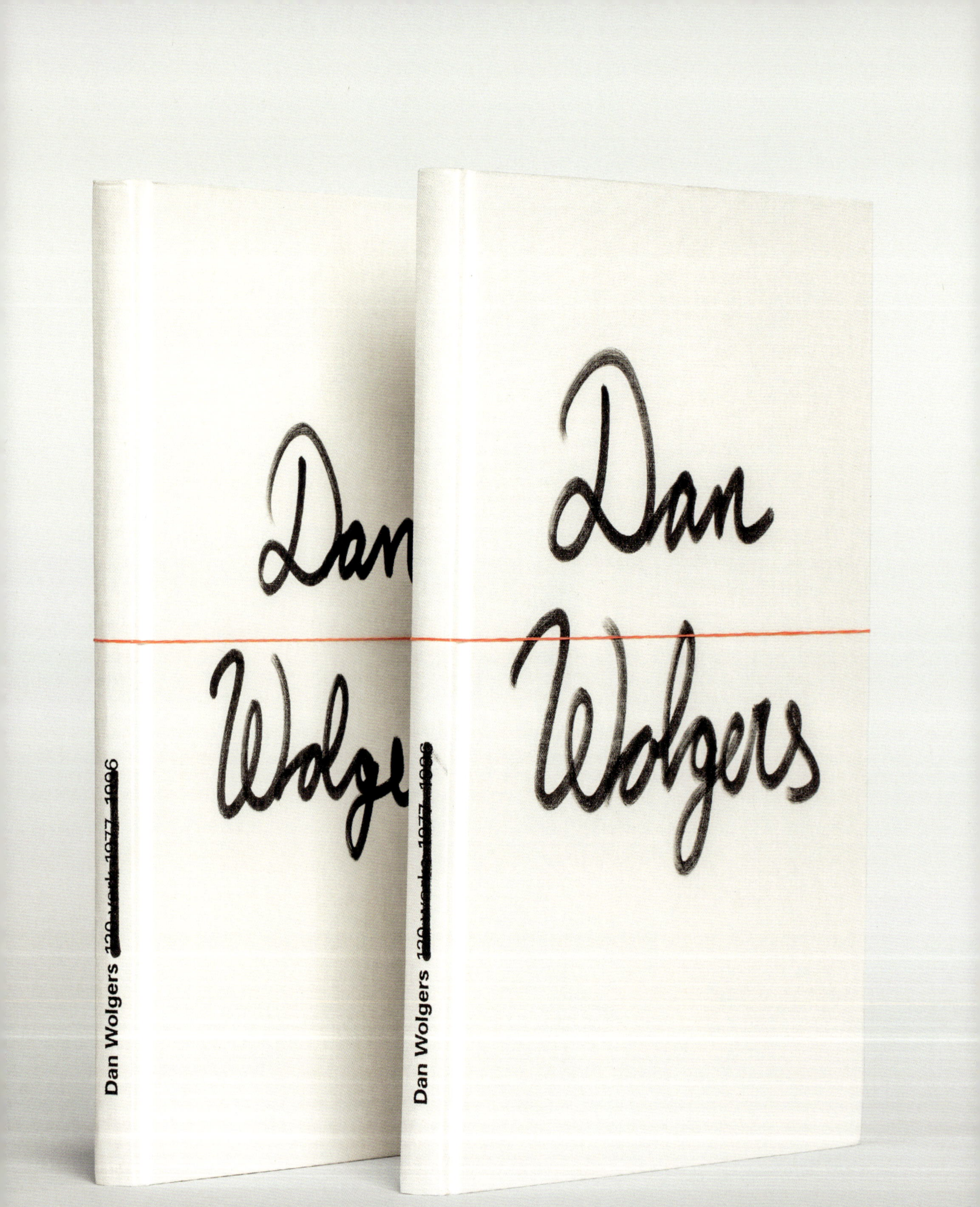

Dan
Wolgers

Dan Wolgers ~~120 verk 1977–1996~~

Dan
Wolgers

Dan Wolgers ~~120 verk 1977–1996~~

HOT SET
PLEASE
KEEP OFF

HOT SET
PLEASE
KEEP OFF

HOT SET
PLEASE
KEEP OFF

JA NEJ
HOT SET
PLEASE
KEEP OFF

MAMM
ANDERS N

STEIDL MODERNA MUSEET

Karin Mamma Andersson
and Moderna Museet
Artist and museum
Sweden
Art direction and design catalogue
–
2007

Swedish painter Karin Mamma Andersson is known for her richly layered compositions that fuse textured brushwork, loose washes and graphic lines with a distinctive use of colour. Drawing on sources such as archival photographs, theatre sets and everyday interiors, her work moves between landscape and domestic space, creating scenes that feel both familiar and dreamlike.

Several landscape works are presented as foldouts throughout the book, accompanied by documentary-style, black-and-white photographs of Karin's studio and surroundings, taken by JH Engström.

MAMM
ANDERS
STEIDL

Heimat Land, 2004
Akryl och olja på duk/
Acrylic and oil on canvas

Explosió!
El llegat de Jackson Pollock

Explosion!
Moderna Museet
Museum
Sweden
Exhibition catalogue
(Spanish version shown here)
—
2012

Explosion! Painting as Action explores the rich and complex cross-fertilisations and borderlands of painting, performance and conceptual art. The exhibition included works in different mediums by the Japanese Gutai group, along with artists such as Allan Kaprow, Jackson Pollock, Niki de Saint Phalle, Yves Klein, Ana Mendieta, Alison Knowles, Rivane Neuenschwander, Yoko Ono, and Lawrence Weiner. The exhibition was also shown at Fundació Joan Miró, Barcelona.

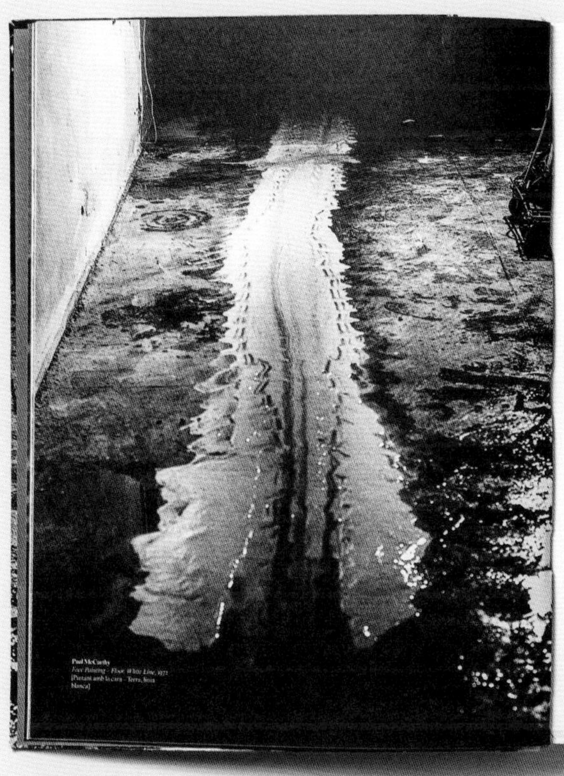

Índex

'Painting as I had known it was finished for me. The new works had to be unsigned painting-objects, anonymous. Everywhere I looked, everything I saw became something to be made, as is, without having to add anything whatever… There was no more need to compose. The subject was there, already made and I could avail myself of it everywhere.'

Ellsworth Kelly

Explosion! Painting as Action

Magnus af Petersens

Zero all

Explosion! starts off with the explosive expansion of the concept of art that took place after the Second World War and gained momentum in the 1950s and '60s. Like the Dada movement, which arose in reaction to the meaningless atrocities of the First World War, many artists and intellectuals wanted to start from scratch, from zero. This was expressed in civilisation critique and primitivistic anarchism – sometimes with aggression, sometimes with playfulness. The awareness of the horrors of war, the Holocaust and the atom bomb made it impossible to go on creating art as though nothing had happened. The desire to break away from the prevailing pattern to create something new became urgent, even if the idea of the new had been at the core of modernism ever since its genesis. Many artists attacked the conventions of art, which were most often represented by painting, in the form of oil on canvas. Destruction and creation became equally crucial components of the same change and movement.[1] From its status as a veritably timeless and static phenomenon, painting stepped out into the room and into time – from being a window to another world, it became part of the same time and space as the viewer.

The exhibition *Explosion!* covers the field from performative gestural painting, via happenings, events and performance, to more conceptual approaches in the form of instructions for paintings or practices where the execution is left open, like a score or a choreography. In this way, we highlight how different approaches are nevertheless *envisioned through painting*. The original subtitle, *Painting as Action*, emphasises the performative aspects of painting. Many artists became interested in the creative process itself. Existentialism, the dominating philosophy that was popularised through literature, also put action at the centre, not least through Jean-Paul Sartre's ideas on how man defined himself through his actions. Above all, it was a way of looking at art. The action in the original subtitle refers not only to the production of the work of art. It also signifies that the work of art generates situations, produces meaning and, thus, is a form of action in itself. Finally, "action" also includes the viewer's participation – as an agent and as a producer of meaning, as a co-creator of the work.

Performance and performativity

Performance is often defined as something live, in the present, unlike the art object – the painting or sculpture – which has traditionally been regarded as static.[2] This definition runs the risk of not doing justice to a number of artistic practices. In fact, the boundaries are rarely that clear cut, and there is often a performative element in a painting and a painterly element in a performance. The concept of "performative" does not necessarily adhere to performance but stems from the philosopher of language J.L. Austin's definition of "performative utterances", or "speech acts" as he also calls them. By this he means the capacity of language to do something: "I hereby pronounce you man and wife" and "I promise" are examples of speech acts that do not simply describe the world but perform an action. By uttering the sentence an action is performed – a promise is a promise, even if it is broken. Austin's theories on speech acts and performativity are almost surprisingly easy to transfer to the field of art, as was already done in the 1960s, but especially in the 1990s, under the influence of post-structuralism. Roland Barthes' essay "Death of the Author" (1967) helped shift the focus from the author's intentions to the reader and the text's own production of meaning.[3] Performativity theory entails a shift of emphasis from the work as an object to what the work *does*. The work is not autonomous but performative; its meaning lies not only in the artist's intention but is created interactively with the viewer and the context of which it is a part.[4]

Chance

Working intentionally with chance as a vital element in the production of a work is to leave it open to factors beyond the artist's control. This is an experimental approach, where the artist is closer to the viewer in the relationship to the end result. One early example of an artistic composition that is created through chance rather than by the artist's intentions is Marcel Duchamp's *Trois stoppages étalon* (1913–14).[5] This work was initially intended as a painting and was created by the artist dropping three one-metre ropes to fall on three-painted surfaces. Another example is the dada artist Hans Arp who, in 1915, scattered sheets of paper on his canvas and then glued them where they landed. Later, the composer John Cage also used chance as a method in what he called

‘There is not such a great difference between construction and destruction. What I’m trying to do is to create poetry through destruction and I think it is beautiful.’

Niki de Saint Phalle

norrtälje

Norrtälje konsthall
Museum
Sweden
Visual identity and art direction
–
1999

Fifty miles north of Stockholm, surrounded by pine forests on one side and the archipelago on the other, lies the small, quiet town of Norrtälje. In the autumn of 1999, art curator Carl Fredrik Hårleman arrived at Norrtälje konsthall with a vision: to transform a traditional community art gallery into a vibrant, living centre for both Swedish and international contemporary artists. Stockholm Design Lab collaborated on several exhibitions, including those featuring Swedish artist Dan Wolgers and Romanian artist Dan Perjovschi.

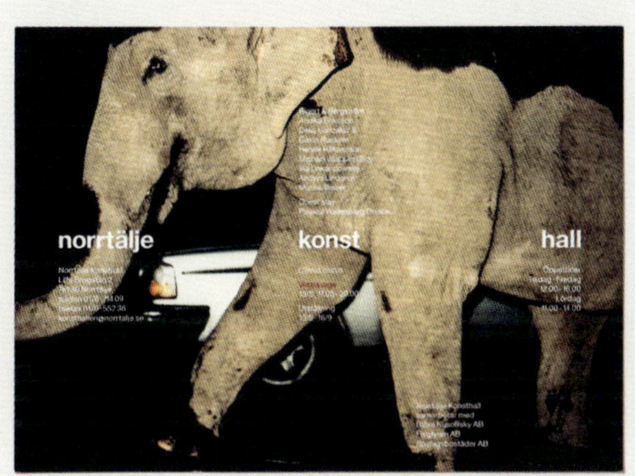

Dan Perjovschi
Piece & Piece

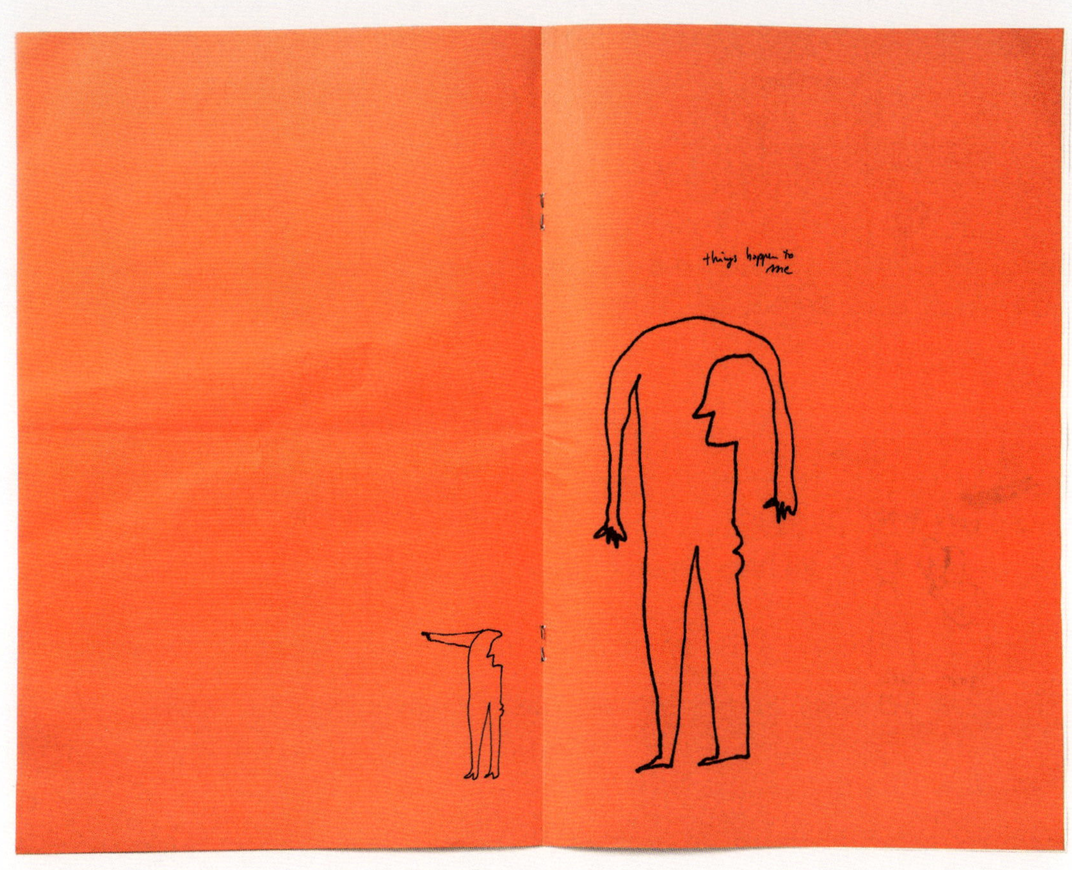
things happen to me

stand for your rights
NU in romania means NO
NU
FRIDAY NIGHT SHOPING
MILK
ME, STUCK
HELP WHAT?
Feminism is HOT

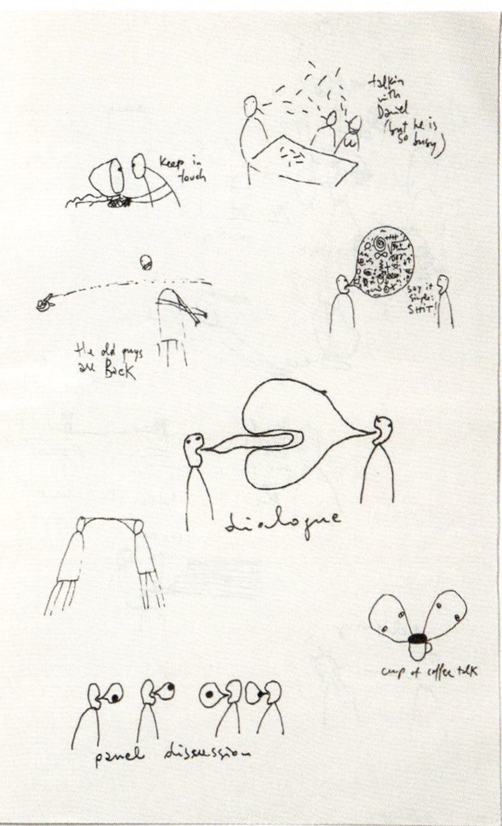
talkin with Daniel (but he is so busy)
Keep in touch
say it simple: SHIT!
the old guys are Back
dialogue
cup of coffee talk
panel discussion

SVERIGE/SCHWEDEN
MARIA MIESENBERGER
STEIDL/GUN
SVERIGE/
SCHWEDEN
MARIA
MIESENBER

Maria Miesenberger
Artist
Sweden
Art direction and design
In collaboration with Greger Ulf Nilson
–
2011

Derived from Swedish artist Maria Miesenberger's private family album, the dark, evocative images of *Sverige/ Schweden* create a narrative of epic proportions. By re-presenting her father's photographs of her childhood in Austria and Sweden, Miesenberger elevates them to a new level of language. The sombre imagery is complemented by bold typography. The book, published by Steidl, was awarded the Swedish Photo Book Prize in 2011.

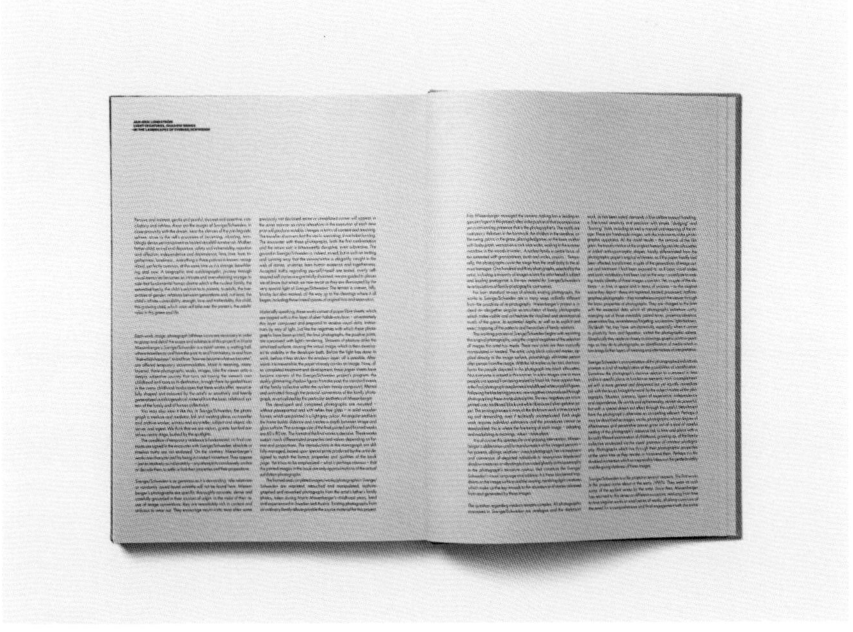

Collage
Page 182–183

01 Bigert & Bergström's fuse performance at the SDL XXV anniversary party
02 Art in the wild – *Vårbergs jättar* by Xavier Veihlan
03 Accidental Art – hotel corridor at Cannes Lions, 2009
04 SDL's screen-printed posters for La Biennale di Venezia, 2009
05 Sign for Market Art Fair, 2017
06 Art in Fashion, 2020
07 *The Clown*, 2024 – signed poster for Björn Kusoffsky by Maurizio Cattelan, with Moderna Museet logotype's handwriting by Robert Rauschenberg
08 Sven-Harrys Konstmuseum (and SDL HQ), architecture by Wingårdhs
09 Field trip, Kistefos Museum, Norway – *Silent Studio* by Mark Manders
10 Dan Wolgers showing Hot Set prototype screen prints, 2022
11 MM Foundry Gridnik lettering painted outside Moderna Museet for the exhibition *Modernautställningen*, 2010
12 Artist Mats Bigert in front of *Reverse Osmosis Plant*
13 *Tipping Point*, performance/installation by Bigert & Bergström, 2021
14 Catalogue for *Tipping Point*, 2021
15 Metropolitan Museum of Art, 2009
16 Moderna Museet logotype, created in 2003 by SDL, Henrik Nygren and Greger Ulf Nilson, with handwriting by Robert Rauschenberg – still looking great, 2025
17 Nordic Pavilion, La Biennale di Venezia, 2024
18 *Oval Buddha Gold*, Takashi Murakami, Château de Versailles, 2010
19 Preparing *Party for Öyvind* at Sven-Harrys Konstmuseum, 2021
20 SDL's signage system for La Biennale di Venezia, 2009

Image captions

184 Bigert & Bergström: *Works 1986–2016*. The monograph covers their entire artistic oeuvre, from its very beginnings to the present moment – a wealth of material that allows for an in-depth examination of their practice and its continuing relevance.

188–190 Exhibition catalogues *The Storm* 2012, *The Freeze* 2015, *The Drought* 2013. Illustrations by Johan Mets

191 *Evaporated Time*, signed Bigert & Bergström and numbered 5/16. Executed in 2013. Printed glass, aluminium and salt, height 8.3 cm. Limited edition contains a copy of the book *The Drought* and certificate of authenticity in a custom-made paper box, 24.5 × 15 × 7 cm.

198 Exhibition poster for *Art in Fashion*, featuring Nikoline Liv Andersen's *Dansen med det Døvstumme Øje*, 2011. Photo: Jeppe Gudmundsen-Holmgreen

A book about the creative process and design of

Tape

01

02

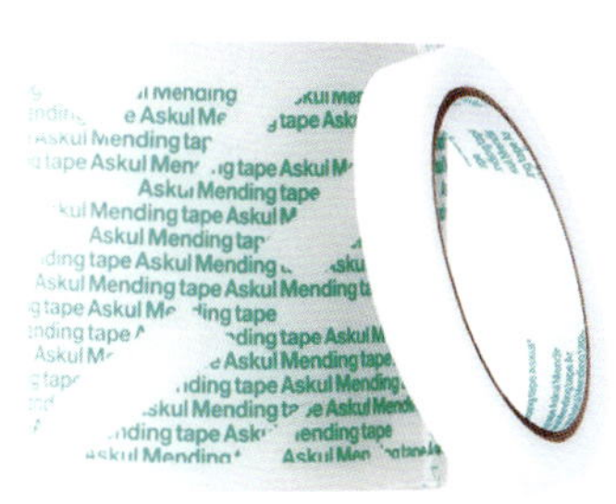

03

04

05

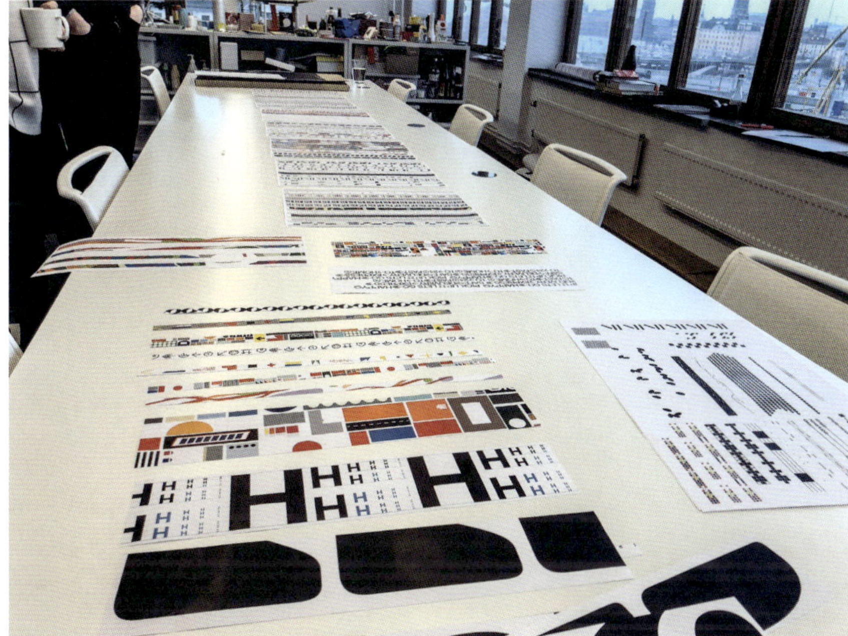

06

07

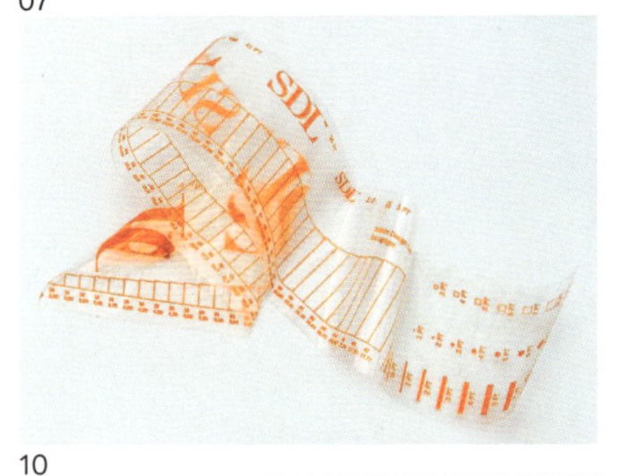

08

10

09

Tape for MT Masking Tape,
Made Specific, Askul, and Wästberg
–
2008–2025

In this chapter, Stockholm Design Lab presents a curated selection of tape designs developed in collaboration with clients, alongside its own SDL tape. Every little detail plays a role in shaping the overall impression. Tape may be a small application, but when carefully considered, it supports and strengthens the whole. The following pages showcase work with MT Masking Tape, Made Specific, Askul, and Wästberg.

MADE
SPECIFIC
MADE SPECIFIC

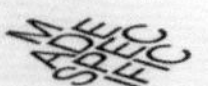

SDL™
SDL

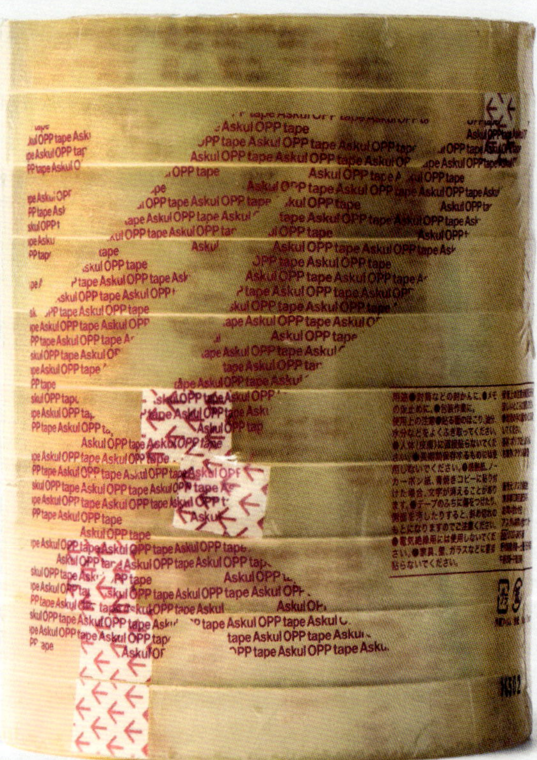
Askul OPP tape

Askul Mending tape

Askul
Cellophane tape
セロハンテープ
15mm×50m

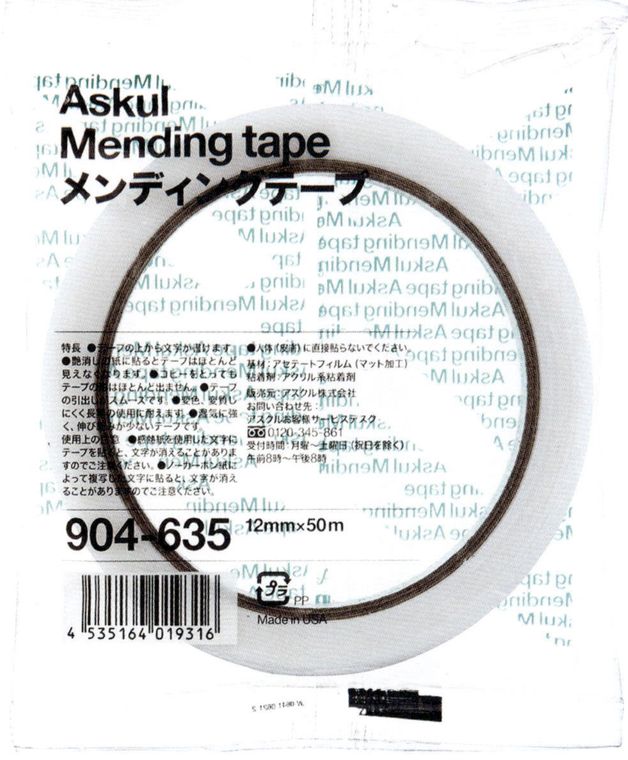
Askul
Mending tape
メンディングテープ
904-635
12mm×50m
4 535164 019316
Made in USA

SDL
SDL
SDL
SDL
SDL

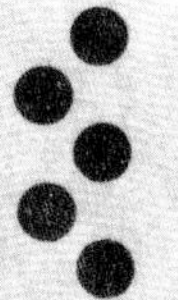

Collage
Page 225

01 SDL's washi tape for MT Masking Tape
02 Askul mending tape
03 SDL tape with banana, 2025
04 Stripes, Barcelona, 2001
05 Work in progress – SDL's washi tape for MT Masking Tape
06 Handle with care
07 SDL tape, 2005
08 Washi tape scissors
09 Askul tape, 5–50 mm
10 Sven-Harrys Konstmuseum, tape test

Image captions

226 SDL created 4 different washi tape for the Japanese company MT Masking Tape. The design was a remix of previous work such as La Biennale di Venezia, Vårdapoteket and Askul. Also a birthday tape was made with a dot matrix grid to fill in the numbers.

228 Made Specific is a Danish lighting expert specialising in premium products for bespoke and private-label projects. Bespoke identity with a variable logotype.

A book about the creative process and design of

Fashion

01

02

03

04

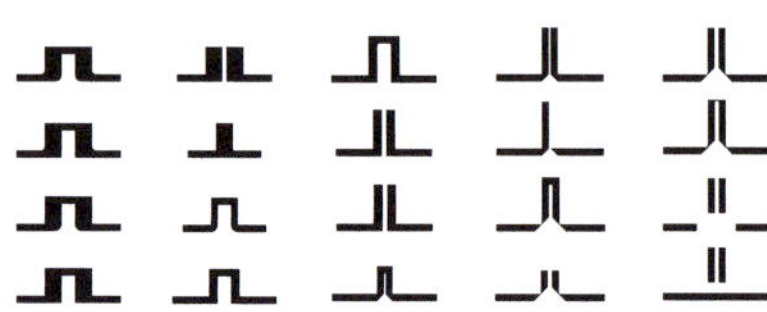

05

06

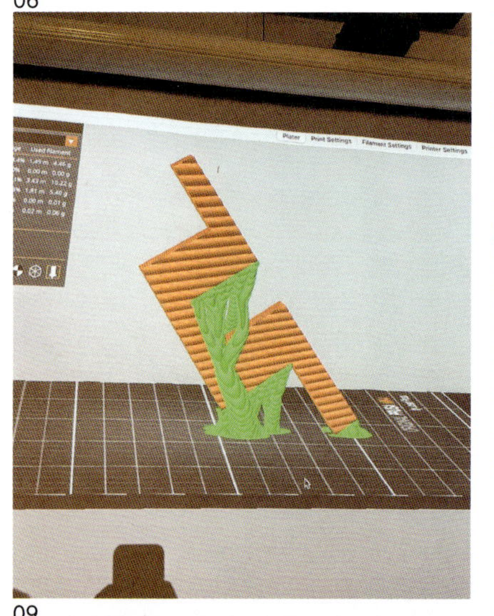

07

08

09

10

11

12

13

14

15

16

17

18

19

MASTER OF
COUTURE
-
AZZEDINE
ALAÏA

Sven-Harrys Konstmuseum
Exhibition
Master of Couture – Azzedine Alaïa
Sweden
Art direction and design
–
2024

For the first time in the Nordics, creations by one of fashion history's great masters – Azzedine Alaïa – were presented at Sven-Harrys Konstmuseum. Known for his exceptional craftsmanship and sculptural vision, Alaïa (1935–2017) produced works in the borderland between couture and art. In collaboration with the Azzedine Alaïa Foundation, the museum gained unique access to Alaïa's archives and selected forty haute couture garments from the height of his career.

Using contrast as the guiding principle for the identity, haute couture was juxtaposed with the raw, fleeting quality of tabloid paper, combined with hand-applied gold foil in the printed materials. The exclusive and extremely costly garments – meticulously hand-stitched and adorned with intricate details – were presented on a medium typically associated with mass communication and impermanence. This contradiction heightened the sense of exclusivity while challenging conventional notions of luxury, making fashion both unattainable and unexpectedly accessible.

Taking a dynamic runway shoot approach, Stockholm Design Lab collaborated with photographer John Scarisbrick to create an elevated newspaper-style catalogue highlighting the unique and intricate details of the dresses. In addition, billboards, installation graphics and typographic installations at Sven-Harrys Konstmuseum were also produced.

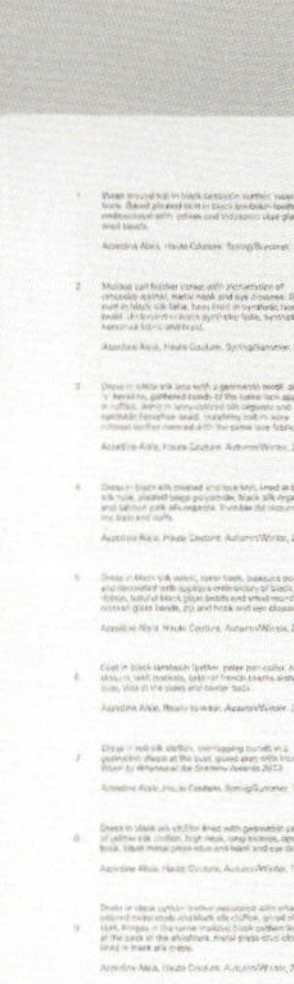

Carin Wester
Fashion brand
Sweden
Art direction and design
—
2011

Lookbooks and invitations for Swedish fashion brand Carin Wester and its Spring/Summer 2011 collection, 'The Transformer'.

J.Lindeberg
Fashion brand
Sweden
Brand identity and campaign
Collaborators:
Showmakers
(Architecture, Korea),
Thibaut Allgayer
(Architecture, Sweden, Korea)
–
2025

At the heart of J.Lindeberg, founded in 1996, lies a bold contradiction – the raw pulse of sport versus the refined world of fashion. The tension between these two forces, distinct yet inseparable, allows something electric to emerge.

When asked to help define a new direction for the brand, Stockholm Design Lab explored that in-between space, unlocking a new expression: fearless, playful, and unapologetically confident.

SDL refined the iconic bridge symbol and created a distinct, cohesive visual world that supports future growth while providing flexibility. This renewed identity strengthens brand impact across all touchpoints – from retail and products to packaging and communication. By building on duality as a source of energy, it amplifies the unmistakable essence of the J.Lindeberg brand.

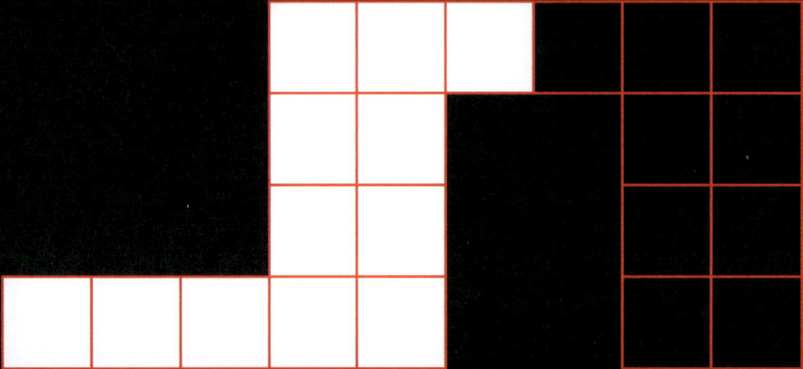

J.LINDEBERG, Born in 1996 out of an idea to inject style and energy to golf by changing how players dress on and off the course.

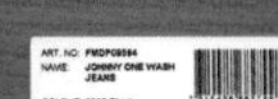

J.LINDEBERG

BERG
M
MADE IN
CHINA

J.LINDEBERG

A classic quarter zip merino sweater with a tonal embroidered Bridge® logo on the chest. Twelve-gauge, mulesing-free merino. Yarn is OEKO-TEX® certified. Welt detail on the zipper. Wearable for any occasion where you want to look fashionable, from casual days at the office, to birthday parties with family members, to date nights with that special someone. Offered in Black (9999), Chipmunk (E144), Forest Green (M354), JL Navy (6855), Washed Denim Blue Melange (0509).

FMKW09912-6855
Fully fashion details
Welt detail on zipper
Bridge embroidery at chest
12 gauge
Mulesing free merino
Yarn is Oeko tex certified

100% Wool
Hand wash cold
Do not bleach
Do not tumble
Wash with similar colors

J.LINDEBERG

FW23 / SMS / FMDP08722
JOHNNY / Whiteout
Washout Jeans Calik 31/32
M73-96 / M11-15629
21/09/2022

Aa Bb Cc Dd Ee Ff Gg Hh Ii Jj Kk Ll Mm Nn Oo Pp Qq Rr Ss Tt Uu Vv Ww Xx Yy Zz 1234567890

Sophnet
Streetwear brand
Japan
Art direction and design
–
2025

Japanese fashion brand Sophnet invited Stockholm Design Lab to a brand collaboration as part of its Fall/Winter 2025 collection. The collection Alphabets by SDL comprises prints that celebrate the visual, emotional, ideological, and human impact of typography. It includes Lab Antiqua (SDL), Alfred Sans (the Nobel Prize), and Abrsh Printer (Abrsh). The collection tells the story of each font, as highlighted by symbolic words.

Besides the seasonal collection, SDL were also assigned to create the identity for Sophnet collection Ex., a lightweight multi-purpose collection for those who travel the world in their professional lives. The collection features technical and sustainably sourced materials, as highlighted in a distinct and minimal design language purposefully applied to products, ads, and collateral.

MEDICINE.

SOPHNET.

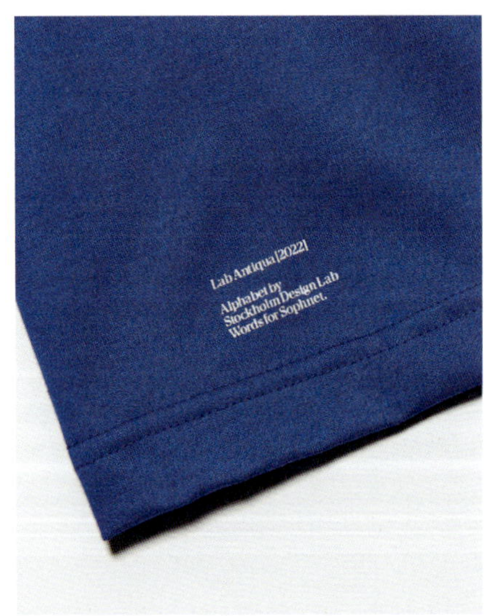
Lab Antiqua [2022]
Alphabet by
Stockholm Design Lab
Words for Sophnet.

STOCKHOLM.

WISDOM.

SOPHNET.

Alfred Sans [2018]
Alphabet by
Stockholm Design Lab
Words for Sophnet.

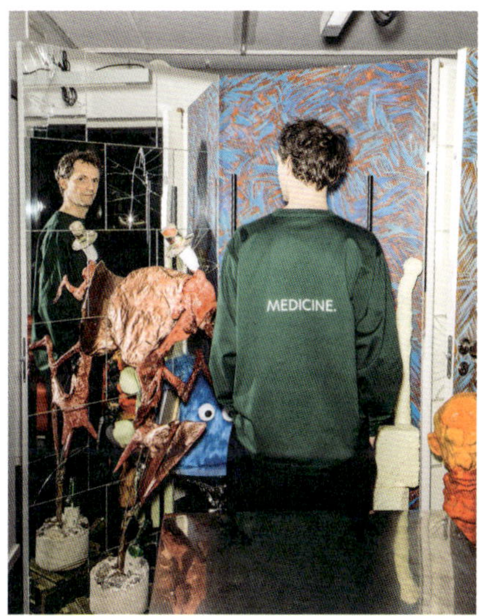
MEDICINE.

Kosmetik. Neu ab 26.8

H&M

H&M
Fashion brand
Sweden
Art direction, in-store material and seasonal films
–
1999

H&M Group is one of the world's leading fashion and design company, with over 4,000 stores across more than 79 markets, and online sales in 60. Its cosmetics division is a vital part of its offering, with H&M's own brands gaining in relevance and reach.

In collaboration with Stockholm Design Lab, H&M set out to explore new ways of supporting cosmetic sales – focusing less on product features and more on sensory and emotional impact on the user.

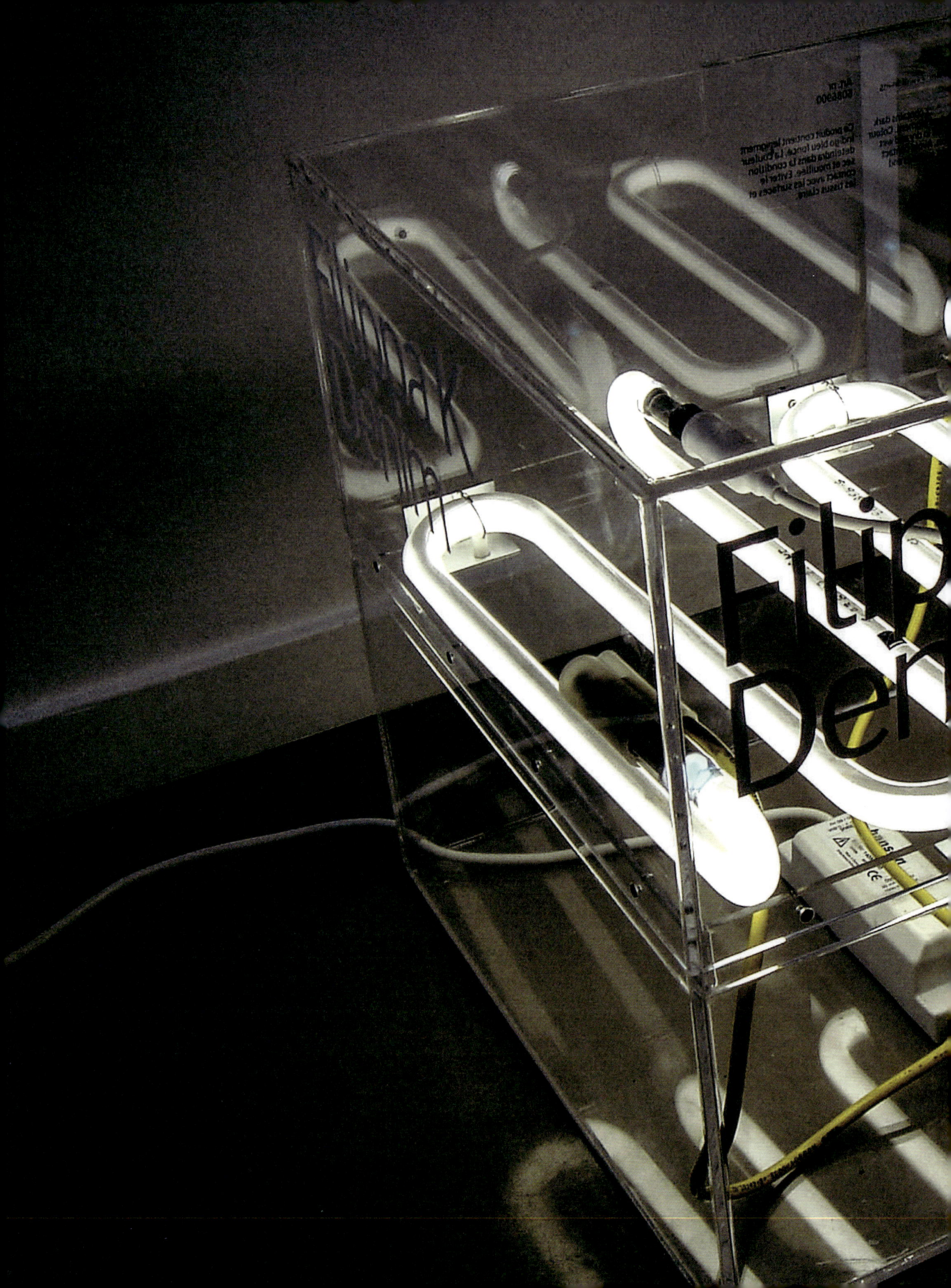

Filippa K
Fashion brand
Sweden
Brand identity
—
2024

Design concept for Swedish minimalist fashion brand Filippa K Denim, spanning communication, labelling, and in-store design elements.

Collage
Page 238–239

01 John Scarisbrick shooting Alaïa at Sven-Harrys Konstmuseum
02 SDL x Sophnet
03 Research – extraordinary entrance, old Balenciaga identity
04 J.Lindeberg symbol exploration
05 Printing the Alaïa catalogue at Newspaper Club, London, 2024
06 J.Lindeberg symbol exploration
07 SDL x Sophnet
08 Selecting images for Alaïa catalogue
09 Research – Margiela above Chanel, Tokyo, 2009
10 3D-printed Copperplate lettering for Alaïa
11 Research – extraordinary entrance, Comme des Garçons, New York, 2012
12 Gaël Mamine and Sarah Perks preparing the long bandage dress worn by Grace Jones at the fashion Oscars in Paris 1985
13 SDL x Sophnet
14 Accidental fashion – NASA boots at Tekniska museet, Stockholm, 2012
15 Keychain, SDL x Sophnet
16 Research, Paul Smith, Los Angeles, 2008
17 *Art in Fashion* in the making
18 Bespoke transparent mannequin from Fondation Azzedine Alaïa
19 Transport boxes from Fondation Azzedine Alaïa

Image captions

240 *Master of Couture – Azzedine Alaïa*
Sven-Harrys Konstmuseum
Museum director:
Dragana Kusoffsky Maksimovic
Fondation Azzedine Alaïa
President: Carla Sozzani
Curators: Olivier Saillard and Gaël Mamine, assisted by Sarah Perks
Texts: Olivier Saillard
Exhibition Design: Paul Vaugoyeau
Graphic Design: Stockholm Design Lab
Production and Installation:
Hangmen Studios
The exhibition was produced in collaboration with Fondation Azzedine Alaïa.

Catalogue
Art direction and design:
Stockholm Design Lab
Photography: John Scarisbrick
Prepress: Linjepunkt Repro
Print: Newspaper Club,
Norrbacka tryckeri
Edition: 500 copies
© Sven-Harrys Konstmuseum 2024

242–
243 Long 'bandage' dress in magenta-coloured acetate knit, gathered lace-up closure creating triangular openings at the side of the lower body, draped 'v' neckline, hood and large train. Worn by Grace Jones at the gala ceremony for the fashion Oscars 1985, where Alaïa received several awards. Azzedine Alaïa, Haute Couture, Spring/Summer, 1986.
Photo: John Scarisbrick

245 Dress in black wool jersey, boat neckline, long sleeves, zip in silver-coloured metal winding in a spiral around the length of the body, small asymmetric train. Azzedine Alaïa, Haute Couture, Autumn/Winter, 2003.
Photo: John Scarisbrick

252–
253 J.Lindeberg flagship store, 422 Apgujeong-ro, Gangnam District, Seoul, South Korea, architecture by Showmakers

256 J.Lindeberg Clubhouse, 422 Apgujeong-ro, Gangnam District, Seoul, South Korea, architecture by Thibaut Allgayer

262–
263 H&M Cosmetics photographed by Frederik Lieberath, 1999

264–
265 H&M Cosmetics photographed by Craig McDean, 1999

A book about the creative process and design of

Music

Music

What I care about the most doesn't scale.

Detail. Texture. The artist who spends years obsessing over a kick drum. The version of a recording that only exists on demo, passed between friends. The atmosphere of a track that never got played on the radio but ends up defining someone's whole existence.

We hold on to these things. Archiving them. Compulsively. Not because they're commercially important, but because they mean something to someone. Because they represent what makes us feel safe.

In a culture built around reach and repeatability, music – like design – is expected to be fast, cheap, profitable and available to everybody, everywhere at once. Some of the best work resists that. It's too fragile, too precise, too specific to survive in the mass context. And that makes it priceless.

Stockholm Design Lab clearly understands that instinct. Their work is exact, subtle, deliberate, designed not to dominate but to exhibit. When SDL created the brief for Arketyp, they presented it as 'Seeing the Unseen'. It's an archive for work that doesn't shout. Work that leaves room for exploration, imagination, or feeling, or memory. Work that literally grows with time.

With YEAR0001 and now with Arketyp, we aim to build something that will stay fundamental. A framework for the ones who don't fit into formulas, who value composition over algorithm. And that work requires patience. Care. Obsession. You can't fake these things. You can't automate them.

You need to listen closely, repeatedly, without expecting payoff. You have to understand that detail matters, even when no one's noticing it.

Not everything needs to scale. Some things just need to last.

Oskar Ekman
Founder and CEO, Arketyp

01

02

03

04

05

06

07

08

09

10

11

12

13

14

15

16

17

18

19

20

21

A®
© 2025 Arketyp
Registration No. 1102391412
Ref No. 32016–387
Made in Sweden

Arketyp
Music authority
Sweden
Brand identity
–
2025

Arketyp is a music group that brings together several record labels, a recording studio, a record store, a publishing house, and more. As pioneers in their field, they seek out what others often overlook – sounds, ideas, and visions waiting to be revealed.

The visual identity is based on the idea of seeing the unseen – uncovering ideas and expressions that typically go unnoticed. This involves embracing fresh perspectives and challenging conventions, with a consistent focus on longevity and quality.

At its core, the identity encourages viewing the familiar from new angles to discover the unexpected. The rotated 'A' becomes a wide-open eye – symbolising a constant gaze towards what lies ahead. It's about finding the future in the present, and turning what's hidden into what's heard.

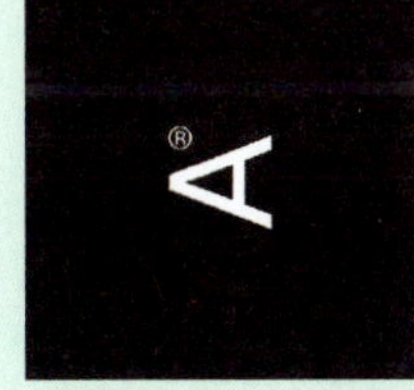

Arketyp®
Listening Party

Basel
Palo Alto
Zurich
Chicago
Berlin
New York

12.5–5.7
2026

Inquiry:
Info@arketyp.org

Ticket:
www.ticketbox-arketyp.org

At the heart of Arketyp is a guiding principle: seeing the unseen. It's a way of thinking, creating, and moving through culture that prioritizes what's often ignored — the subtle, the emerging, the unpolished ideas that carry real weight.

This philosophy drives everything we do. We seek out what others pass by: unheard sounds, unconventional voices, and underrepresented visions. We believe the future of music and art is shaped not by what's trending, but by what's quietly building strength beneath the surface.

To see the unseen is to embrace fresh perspectives, to approach the familiar with new questions, and to remain open to work that challenges norms rather than conforms to them. It's not about disruption for its own sake — it's about depth, care, and long-term thinking.

Artists
Drain Gang
Adam Olenius
Dim Spirit
Nation
Provoker
Quatermaster
Quiltland
Bloodz Boi
bod
Chariot
DarkO

Arketyp®

Arketyp Handel
Record Store
Reg. No: 559496–0170
www.arketyp.se
Stockholm Music Authority

Opening Hours

Mon – Fri : 11:00h – 18:00h
Saturday : 11:00h – 17:00h
Sunday : 12:00h – 16:00h

Arketyp®
A
Brian Johnstown Massacle
Their Satanic Majesties
Music & Sound Recordings
Media Vinyl
Price 349 SEK
Arketyp®
Arketyp
PYREX

2CD
Our
Definition
Of
Eighties

Diesel Music
Record label
Our Definition Of
Sweden
Art direction and design
–
2006

Our Definition Of was a series of music genre compilations, carefully curated by record company Diesel Music. The concept was supported by screen-printed jewel cases and unique CD booklets.

ACT Music
Record label
HOME.S
Sweden
Art direction and design
–
2022

Visionary pianist and composer Esbjörn Svensson revolutionised modern jazz with his Esbjörn Svensson Trio (e.s.t.), known for its unique blend of jazz, rock, and electronic music.

HOME.S. is Svensson's only solo album, recorded in his home just a few weeks before his sudden death in 2008. Its sheer existence – not to mention its completely unexpected discovery over a decade later – are nothing less than a sensation. Since the early 1990s, Svensson devoted almost all of his creative energy to his work with e.s.t.. These recordings offer a whole new perspective on him as an artist: intimate, focused and entirely at one with himself.

Titiyo
Artist
Hemland
Sweden
Art direction and design
–
2025

Titiyo, once dubbed the Queen of Swedish Soul, has a long-standing relationship with Stockholm Design Lab. Her 2025 album is the first to feature her singing in Swedish. A dissected yellow cross – drawn from the Swedish flag, and doubling as the letter T – represents the title, *Hemland* (Homeland).

NOISE
EAU DE PARFUM
50 ML 1.7 FL.OZ
SILENT CONVERSATION
01
NOISE
50 ML 1.7 FL.OZ
EAU DE PARFUM
BACKGROUND BEAT
02

Noise
Fragrance brand
Switzerland
Brand identity and packaging
–
2022

Noise is a sensory identity project exploring the invisible yet powerful impact of sound and scent – two untouchable forces that shape emotion, memory, and identity. Drawing on the deep, often unconscious influence these senses hold, Noise transforms fragrance into a multisensory experience.

At its core, Noise connects perfume to sound, interpreted through elegant visual language. Each fragrance becomes a triptych: a scent, a unique sound, and a distinct visual. Vertical lines evoke sound waves and scent diffusion, referencing fashion aesthetics as well as apothecary clarity. This concept opens up possibilities for personalisation, storytelling, and limited editions, allowing the brand to communicate fragrance in a bold, immersive, and contemporary way.

50 ML 1.7 FL.OZ
SILENT CONVERSATION
NOISE 01
EAU DE PARFUM
50 ML 1.7 FL.OZ
SILENT CONVERSATION
NOISE 01
EAU DE PARFUM
50 ML 1.7 FL.OZ
SILENT CONVERSATION

SDL 25th anniversary
Andreas Tilliander remixes
Sweden
Art direction and redesign
–
2023

In 2023, Stockholm Design Lab marked its 25th anniversary with a celebration at its headquarters in Vasaparken, Stockholm. To commemorate the occasion, long-time friend and collaborator TM404 – also known as Andreas Tilliander – created a special remix of his track '1998'. The result was two new versions: '1998 – Stockholm Design Lab XXV – Remix' and '1998 – Stockholm Design Lab XXV – Ambient Remix'.

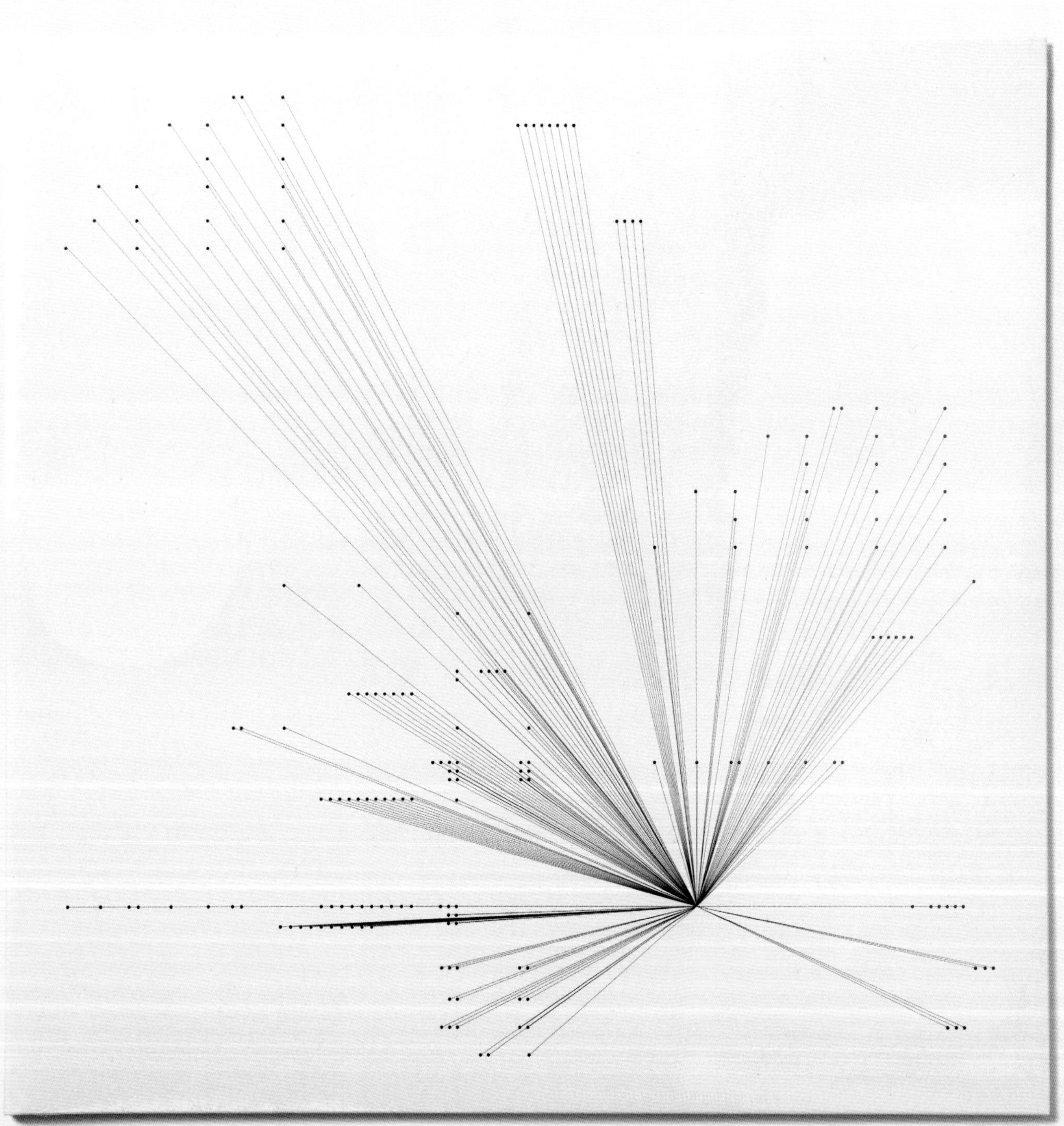

Universal Music
Record label
Ted Gärdestad
Sweden
Art direction and design
–
2017

Stockholm Design Lab had the pleasure of visualising the remastering of the music of Ted Gärdestad, one of Sweden's most acclaimed and beloved recording artists. Ted was a singer and musician whose melodic songs – with lyrics written by his brother Kenneth – conveyed themes of hope, heartbreak, and a profound love of nature. The lyrics remain deeply relatable, touching on subjects as relevant today as they were 30 or 40 years ago – words to which nearly every Swede still holds a personal connection.

Drawing its inspiration from the music and lyrics, the resulting design featured multiple layers, symbolising the movement and flow of musical notation. It also reflected the collaborative nature of the project, involving numerous contributors. The visual system is both highly distinctive and adaptable, with each song given its own unique composition based on its musical notes.

TED GÄRDESTAD

	(A)	(B)
Skiva 1	(01) Universum 06:10	(01) I den stora sorgens famn 04:55
	(02) Sol, vind och vatten 04:26	(02) Sommarlängtan 03:22
	(03) Ett stilla regn 04:58	(03) Oh, vilken härlig da' 04:02
	(04) Come Give Me Love 03:44	(04) För kärlekens skull 04:10
	(05) Äntligen på väg 02:44	(05) Himlen är oskyldigt blå 05:21
Skiva 2	Bonusspår Alice 04:02	Instrumental Alice 04:02

Signerat Peter Nordahl

www.tedgardestad.se

060255745533 LC01846

STORIES 

6 02557 45533 5

Collage
Page 272–273

01 *2 steg från Paradise*, Håkan Hellström, 2010 – one of Sweden's biggest artist, packaged by SDL
02 Inspiration – live at the legendary Manumission, Ibiza, 2004
03 Accidental techno – C Future City, designed by SDL
04 SDL's identity for Eurovision Song Contest, 2000
05 Inspiration – The XX concert, Stockholm, 2012
06 *Punk är trevligt* (Punk is nice), legendary message by Henrik Venant, applied on a ceramic cup by Skarbäck
07 Boombox, New York, 2006
08 Replacing type with Lab Antiqua, Kraftwerk concert, Stockholm, 2014
09 Animated Lasso typography for Primal Scream's video *Country Girl*, directed by Jonas Åkerlund, 2006
10 Animated Lasso typography for Primal Scream's video *Country Girl*, directed by Jonas Åkerlund, 2006
11 Inspiration – Massive Attack concert, Stockholm, 2024
12 Rope exploration mimicking lasso for Primal Scream's video *Country Girl*, directed by Jonas Åkerlund, 2006
13 Invitation to *HOME.S* at Sven-Harrys Konstmuseum
14 Karaoke evening, Tokyo, 2016
15 Inspirational instruments, Kokoroko concert, Stockholm, 2019
16 Accidental disco, Prnjavor, Serbia
17 Moving concert with Kevin Roland, Stockholm, 2006
18 J-Pop compilation for East Restaurant, 1999
19 ORWO cassette photographed at the Stasi Museum, Berlin
20 On set – Titiyo photographed by Teitur Ardal
21 PSL (The Per Sinding-Larsen Trust) identity with fluorescent tubes

Image captions

276 Entrance sign and bench, Arketyp store, Krukmakargatan 24, Stockholm

286 Cassette *1998 – Stockholm Design Lab XXV (Remix)*, TM404. Andreas Tilliander's remix of his track *1998* made exclusively for SDL for their 25th anniversary. Tilliander's TM404 project – with tracks recorded in real time and no work done in post – is a tribute to a handful of genre-defining Roland synthesisers and drum machines from the 1980's (SH-101, MC-202, TB-303, TR-606, TR-707, TR-808, and TR-909).

287 Snapshots from the SDL 25th anniversary party for employees, former colleagues and friends. Live performance by Lover's Skit, DJs Andreas Tilliander and Axel Boman

A book about the creative
process and design of

Light

Light

Why do certain kinds of light make us feel better than others? This question has occupied a disproportionately large amount of time in my life. It is also the reason why I founded a lighting company.

I grew up in the south of Sweden with light and lighting. My father ran a lighting company, and while I was initially determined not to follow in his footsteps, it didn't take long before I found myself working with him.

During our years together, our travels took us to all kinds of lighting environments. Even when they met every regulation and standard, I was struck by the fact that almost all of them felt harsh, unwelcoming, or just uncomfortable.

I came to understand that the good light cannot rely on measurable qualities alone. There are other immeasurable qualities that are equally essential – if not more so. Qualities that speak to our human nature, our emotions and needs.

It was around this time that my friend Ilse Crawford introduced me to a quote by Paul Klee that resonated with me, expressing my own thoughts with simplicity and elegance. These words came to be central to my own lighting philosophy: 'One eye sees, the other feels.'

As human beings we need light. I believe that this need for light is both physical and emotional.

This means lighting solutions need to cater to both the measurable and the immeasurable qualities of light. The measurable qualities are something that we are quite familiar with. Lux, lumens, etc – these are terms that can be defined, evaluated, compared and talked about. The immeasurable qualities, on the other hand, are not so easy to define. What are they?

In my 2008 manifesto, Lamps for Neanderthal Man, I pointed out man's primitive relationship to light in the form of fire. For about a million years, fire was our only artificial light source. It frightened off wild animals, brought us together, kept us warm and made us feel safe.

Electric light has been around for little more than a century – a blink of an eye in comparison with human evolution. Today, we find ourselves trying to tame our primitive needs to meet the demands of a modern, high-tech world, where light has more or less become a world of electronics. In our overly-lit spaces – created under the mistaken notion that more light equals greater productivity – we feel exposed, small, with nowhere to go.

I believe that the immeasurable qualities of light are deeply rooted, even hardwired, to our relationship to fire as a light source. This is why I create what I call modern-day fires – to recreate (but not mimic) the essential qualities of our relationship to light in the shape of a fire. A light source that is close to us, that we can control, and shines for us, not on us.

This way, lighting can answer to our basic, fundamental human needs. Both physical and emotional. The need to be able to see, read and write, but also to reflect, envision and imagine. The need to be a part of a dynamic social context, but also to be able to withdraw to a personal sphere of familiarity and safety.

Technology and innovation are of course crucial to providing good light in a contemporary context. However, I think it is of utmost importance to understand that what's technically possible is not always humanly preferable. To me, true innovation within the realm of light means making the effort to find the best solutions, putting equal effort into both the measurable and the immeasurable.

Around the same time that Ilse Crawford introduced me to the Paul Klee quote, I was also introduced to Björn Kusoffsky. I can't remember exactly how, but I guess it was at one of all the parties on the Stockholm creative scene at that time. Just like Klee's quote, the work of Björn and Stockholm Design Lab resonated strongly with me.

As with good lighting, good branding and communication need to address both the eye that sees and the eye that feels. The measurable and the immeasurable. The rational and the emotional.

My experience is that very few master this complex art. I instantly understood that SDL did. That is the simple reason why I highly appreciate my relationship with SDL and the work that we are doing together. Some collaborations work better than others.

Magnus Wästberg
Founder, Wästberg Lighting

01

02

03

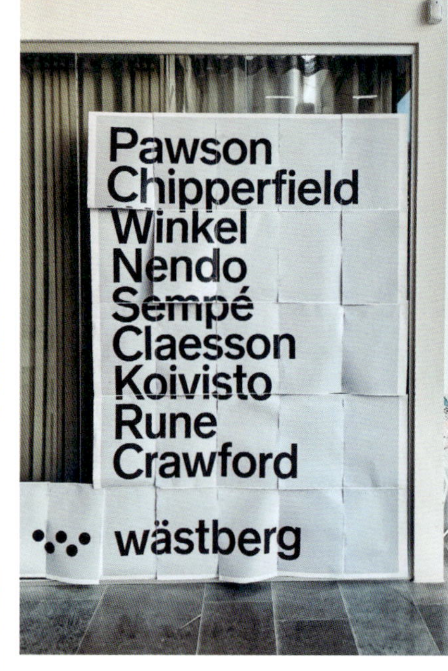

04

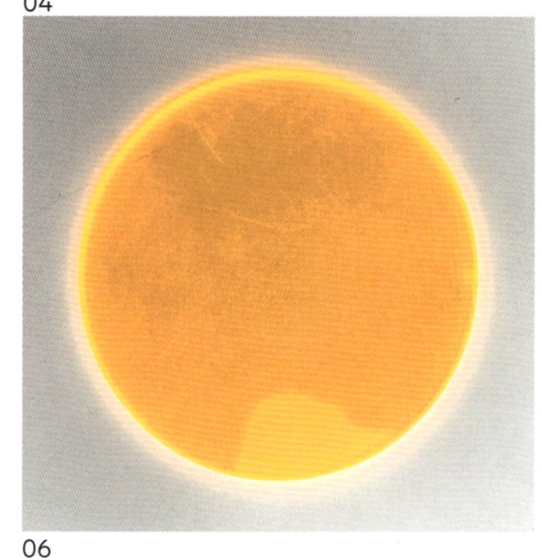

05

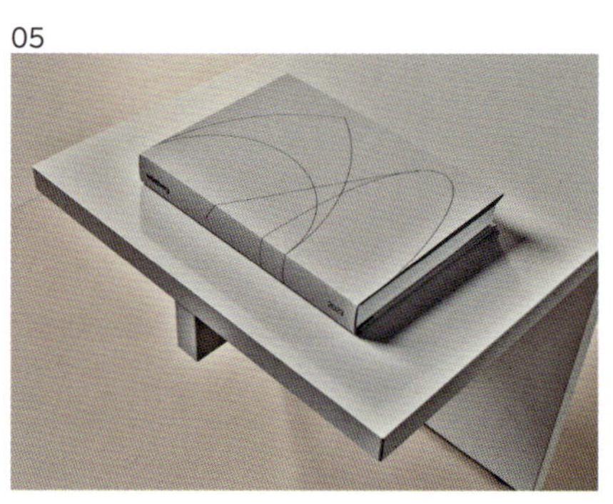

06

07

08

09

11

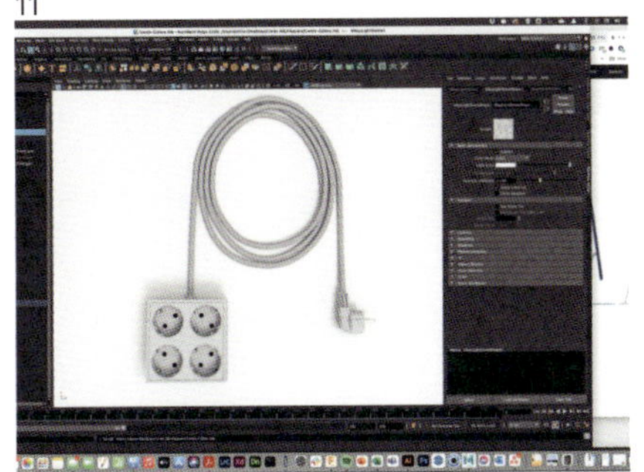

10

12

13

14

17

15

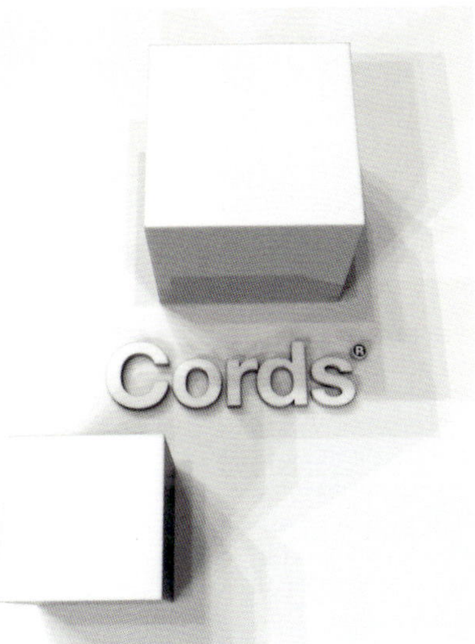

16

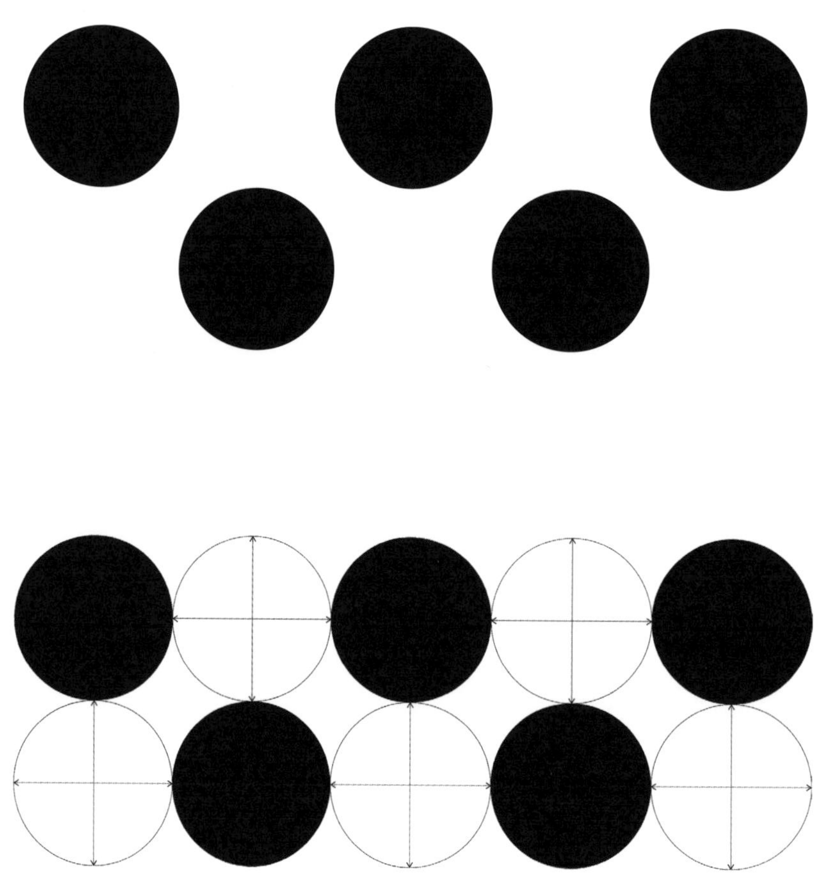

Wästberg
Lighting
Sweden
Holistic brand identity
–
2020

Lighting company Wästberg emerged from a young Swedish man's early insight – that humanity had been deprived of private spheres in a misguided pursuit of efficiency and standardisation. Wästberg set out to restore light to human proximity.

After almost twenty years, Wästberg has now moved beyond its own private sphere to be recognised as an established presence in, and for, the public eye. This evolution is expressed through a synthesis of aesthetics, cutting-edge technology and resource conservation.

wästberg

abcdefghijk
lmnopqrstu
vwxyzåäö

Pawson
Nendo
Chipperfield
Sempe
Winkel
Claesson
Koivisto
Rune
Crawford
wästberg

wästberg

Wästberg Grotesk Regular
Wästberg Grotesk Italic
Wästberg Grotesk Bold
Wästberg Grotesk Bold Italic

w203 Ilumina
w202 Halo
w201 Extra small pendant
w182 Pastille
w181 Linier
w171 Alma
w164 Alto
w163 Lampyre
w162 Dalston
w154 Pal
w153 Île
w152 Busby
w151 Extra large pendant
w132 Nendo
w131 Bell
w127 Winkel
w126 Claesson Koivisto Rune
w124 Lindvall
w103 Sempé
w102 Chipperfield
w084 Studioilse
Holocene No. 4: John Pawson
Holocene No. 3: Jasper Morrison
Holocene No. 2: David Chipperfield
Holocene No. 1: Ilse Crawford

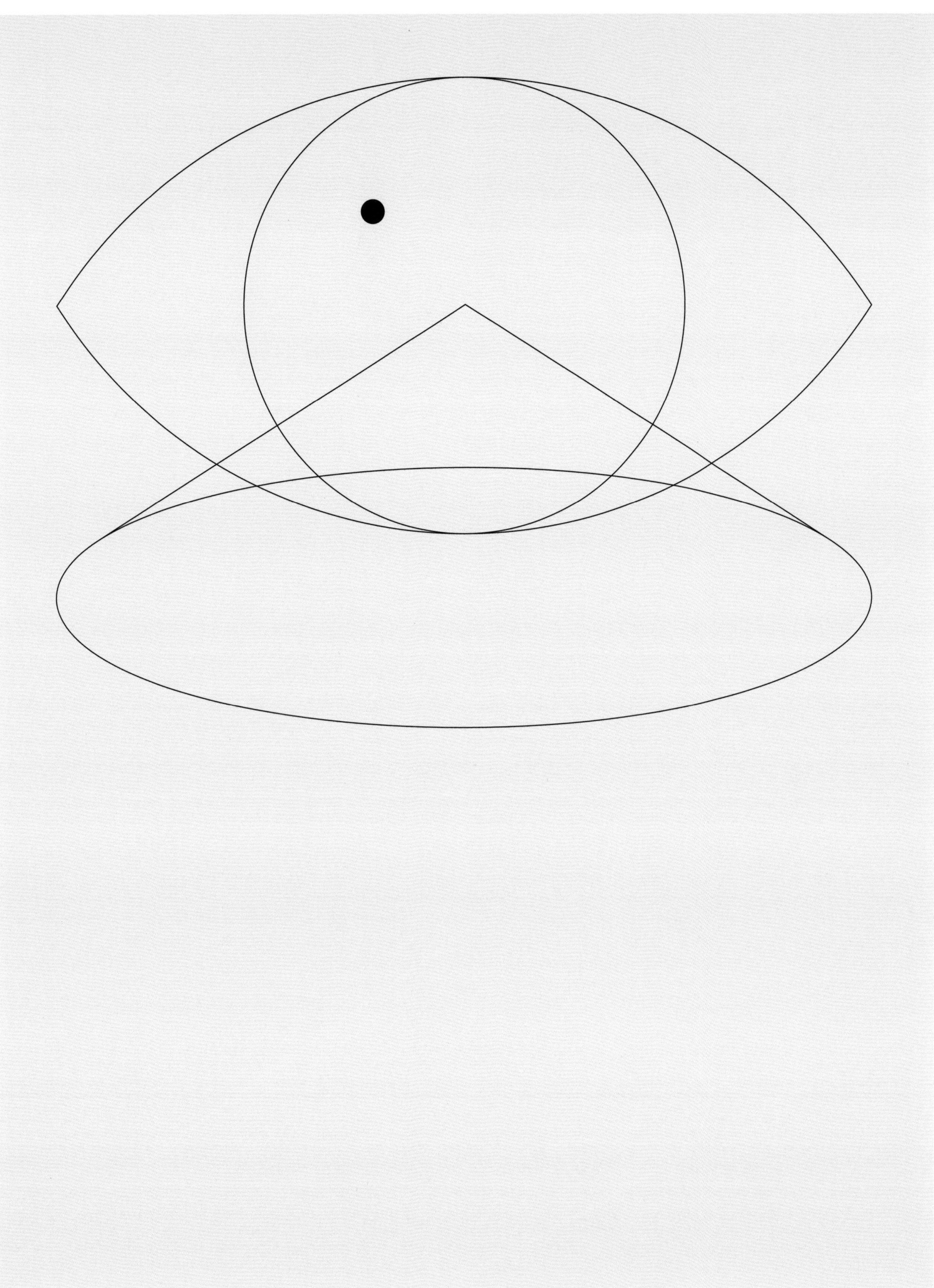

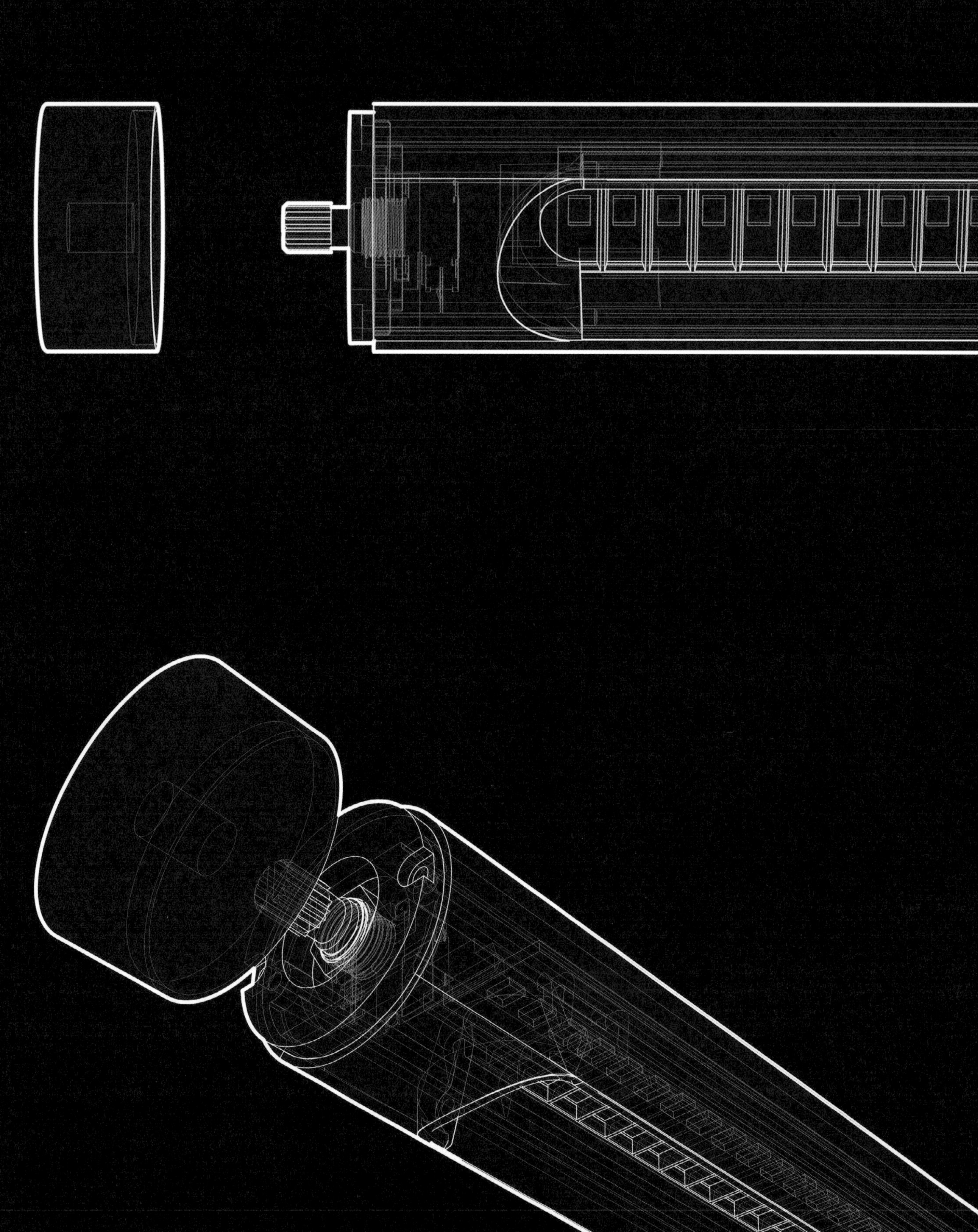

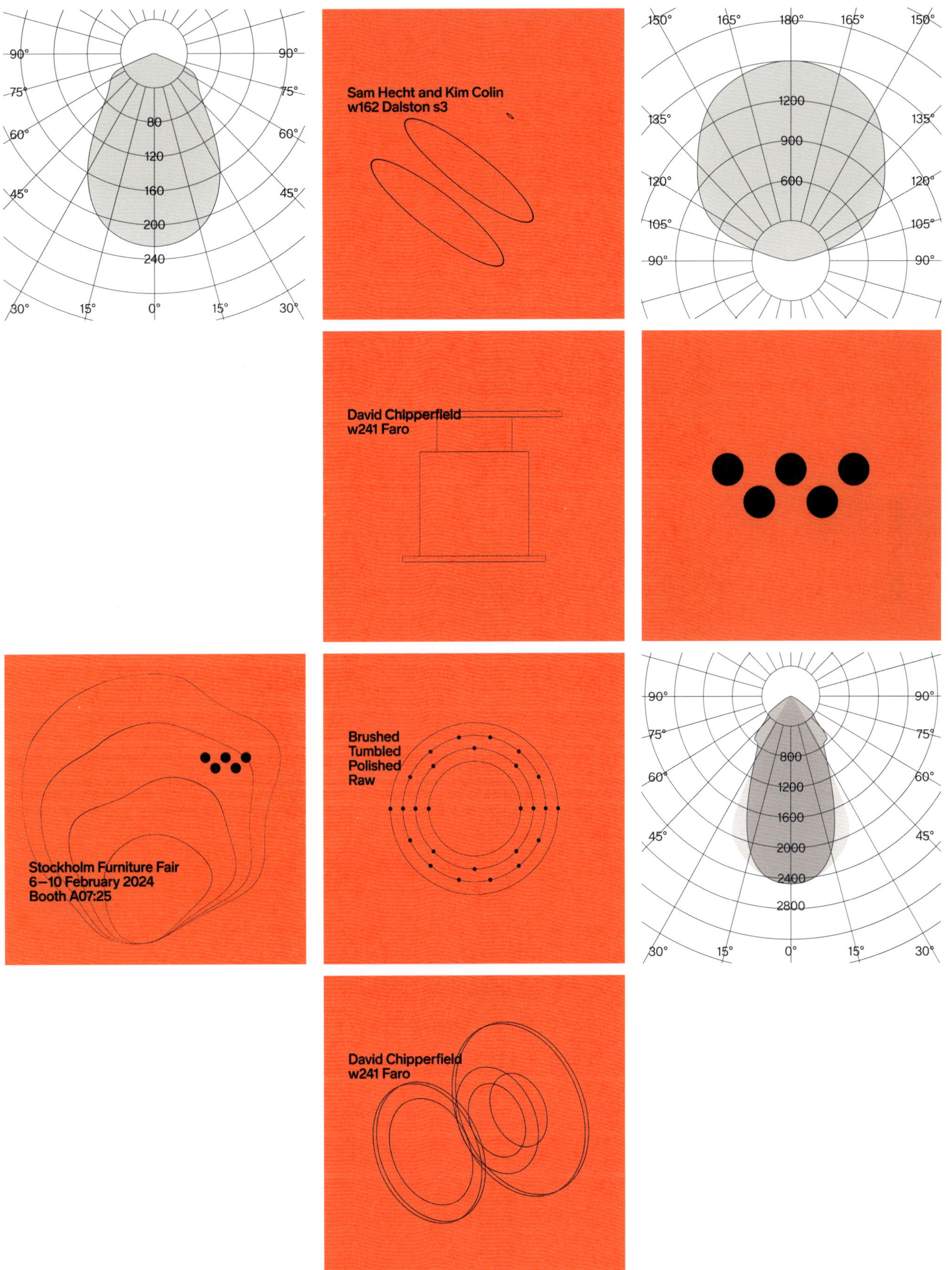
90°
75°
60°
45°
30°
15°
0°
80
120
160
200
240
Sam Hecht and Kim Colin
w162 Dalston s3
150°
165°
180°
135°
120°
105°
1200
900
600
David Chipperfield
w241 Faro
Stockholm Furniture Fair
6–10 February 2024
Booth A07:25
Brushed
Tumbled
Polished
Raw
800
1200
1600
2000
2400
2800
David Chipperfield
w241 Faro

DAYLIGHT MATTERS N°1

D/A

DAYLIGHT AND ARCHITECTURE
DAYLIGHT TALKS
INTERNATIONAL VELUX AWARD

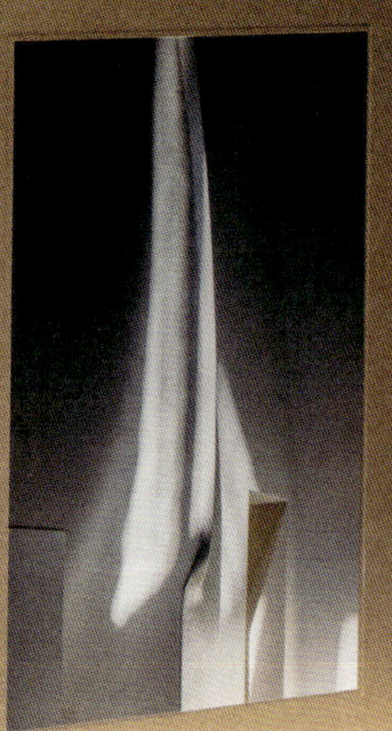

DAYLIGHT MATTERS N°2

D/A

DAYLIGHT AND ARCHITECTURE
DAYLIGHT TALKS
INTERNATIONAL VELUX AWARD

Velux
Knowledge-sharing initiative
Daylight & Architecture: *Daylight Matters*
Denmark
Art direction and design
–
2023

In 2022, Velux, in collaboration with Stockholm Design Lab, breathed new life and a broader vision into the award-winning Daylight & Architecture magazine, reviving it for the digital era. *Daylight Matters* is the printed embodiment of this revitalised D/A, created to inspire and engage students, educators, and architects with a shared appreciation for daylight in architecture.

The two issues are curated to offer insight into the rich and thought-provoking content that defines the D/A universe, while celebrating the visual poetry of daylight in architecture through striking photography. Contributions come from a diverse group of architects, writers, photographers, and designers working at the forefront of their respective fields.

DON'T FIGHT CLIMATE, USE IT

Cité manifeste, Mulhouse,
Lacaton & Vassal | Thekla Ehling

(presence) permeates the projects as an overarching ambition to connect with the site through both rational analysis and poetic interpretation. This heightened awareness of being present in a place is achieved through the manipulation of light, activating our senses, creating architecture that engages with empathy as well as the abstraction of the cultural product architecture is, based on a scientific outlook and worldview.

THE WADDEN SEA CENTRE: TEXTURE AND DIFFUSION

In The Wadden Sea Centre project, the approach is to working with the diffuse, constantly changing light of the horizontal coastal landscape of the western regions of Denmark. The horizontal landscape is interpreted in the sculptural layout of the building and the long lines of the facades, overhang, and roofs that create shadow effects emphasising the dimensions of the building. Mandrup employs thatched reed –a local material –not only for its ecological appropriateness but for its remarkable light-responsive qualities. The texture of the hand-worked thatch creates a façade that transforms continuously, reflecting the shifting overcast sky that dominates the weather patterns. Mandrup explains that *"two-thirds of the time you have an overcast on the sky,"* resulting in diffused light that changes throughout the day. The thatch material captures these subtle variations, acting as a visual barometer of atmospheric conditions. In the extended blue twilight of Nordic summers, the building reads as a dark silhouette against the sky – a deliberate play on the region's light cycle. Inside, Mandrup uses diagonal spaces and strategic roof lights to capture and reflect daylight, creating a counterbalance to the exhibition media. The building's courtyard provides a wind-sheltered microclimate while maintaining the critical connection between interior and landscape,–between controlled and natural light.

ILULISSAT ICEFJORD CENTRE LIGHT AND MOVEMENT

Three hundred kilometres north of the Arctic Circle in Greenland, Mandrup confronts the light conditions of the high Arctic at the Ilulissat Icefjord Centre. Here, light operates in dramatic counterpoints: the rich red-gold of low-angled sun versus the intense blue of shadows, the darkness of winter against the perpetual daylight of summer, the blinding white of snow fields versus the deep blue of the ice fjord. The building's boomerang form responds to these dynamics by creating a processional experience of light revelation. Visitors move through a carefully choreographed sequence of spaces where triangular sections transition to rectangles and back, controlling views and light exposure. The building becomes an instrument that measures light's passage, culminating in the revelation of the ice field – the ultimate expression of Arctic light reflected and refracted through ancient ice. Most poignantly, the building celebrates the return of the sun on January 12th after the polar night – a 40-minute appearance that becomes part of community celebration. In winter darkness, when the sun disappears entirely, the building works with the quality of moonlight reflected on snow, like a ghostly illumination.

REFLECTION AND WATER LIGHT IN THE WHALE

At The Whale Cultural Centre in Norway, Mandrup explores a different dimension of the specificity of northern light. The building cuts into the coastal landscape, appearing to emerge from the earth's crust while using proximity to the ocean to capture reflected light from the water's surface. This water-reflected light creates soft daylight bouncing onto the shell-like ceiling of the interior space. Mandrup notes the profound cultural significance of this water-reflected light for Scandinavians. The building purposely avoids creating a hard edge between land and sea, instead allowing the threshold to blur as water approaches the structure, maximising the capturing of this distinctive reflected light. The result is interior spaces that breathe with the rhythms of the ocean – showing the rippled patterns of light reflected from moving water.

DARKNESS AND CONTRAST

While most of Mandrup's work is devoted to understanding and even celebrating light, there seems to be an acknowledgment of the importance of darkness as a counterpoint. In the unbuilt project Babyn Yar Holocaust Memorial Centre, Mandrup deliberately worked with darkness to emphasise the gravity of the site's history.

"Darkness needs light to be dark," she observes, *"and vice versa. Full darkness is not interesting."*

This understanding of the dialectical relationship between light and darkness reveals a nuanced conception of form giving. Rather than simply maximising illumination in the project, Mandrup orchestrates light's presence and absence to create emotional and sensory experiences. This allows for an architectural philosophy that exactly treats both light as material and metaphor at the same time. An architecture that demonstrates that when architecture responds with sensitivity to local light conditions, the result is not just illuminated space, but buildings that connect deeply with human experience and natural cycles. As Mandrup succinctly states:

"Context is king – or queen – because everything we do is deriving from the context that we're working in."

In the northern latitudes, that context is defined by a variable light that Mandrup has mastered as few architects have. ■

TAKING DAYLIGHT TO THE NEXT LEVEL

Wadden Sea Centre,
Dorte Mandrup | Adam Mørk

UX1 Cylindrical
Technical specifications

Dimensions:
62,9 × 62,9 × 89,6

Body material:
Recycled plastic

Cord length:
1.8 meters

Cord material:
Braided recycled silicone

Outlets usb-c:
USB-c x 4

Usb-c power distribution:
220-240VAC - 50Hz, 0.5A USB-C

Cords
Sustainable electronics
Sweden
Brand identity
–
2025

Cords is a Stockholm-based design studio producing objects rooted in Scandinavian minimalism – innovative, long-lasting, functional, sustainable, and refined down to the last detail.

The identity centres on the concept of a continuous line, symbolising an unbroken flow of connection, creativity, and innovation.

At the heart of every Cords product lies the idea of extension and connection. By embracing the ever-expanding nature of this continuous line across all aspects of the concept, the identity conveys the infinite possibilities the brand offers – inviting its users to become part of a larger journey.

Designed & Engineered *in Sweden*

Designed and manufactured in Sweden, the UX1 Cylindric USBC is a precision-built power distribution unit intended for use in domestic, professional, and shared environments. It features three Type F Schuko AC outlets for standard European plugs and two USB Type-C ports with a combined power output of up to 30W, suitable for fast-charging compatible devices.

The device includes a 1.8-meter high-flexibility power cable, providing ample reach for diverse installation scenarios. A key mechanical feature is its magnetic base, which enables stable and secure attachment to metal surfaces. For non-metallic surfaces, the included iron mounting plate—with integrated adhesive backing—offers a reliable installation solution. Constructed from high-grade components with meticulous surface finishing, the UX1 Cylindric is engineered for long-term durability and electrical safety.

The UX1 Cylindric is a power extender for homes, offices and public spaces that provides excellent function & utility. It has three Type F Schuko sockets, dual USB Type C ports offering up to 30W charging power, and a highly flexible 1.8m power cable. The base of the product is magnetic. It can be mounted securely on any surface when coupled with the included iron plate with a pre-applied adhesive strip. Made with the finest materials having exquisite finishes, the UX1 Cylindric USBC offers an uncompromising sense of quality & safety. UX1 Cylindric's design complements & visually matches all other products in Cords collection for a seamless experience.

All Cords products are designed and produced in Sweden. The UX1 Cylindric is a power extender for homes, offices and public spaces that provides excellent function & utility. It has three Type F Schuko sockets, dual USB Type C ports offering up to 30W charging power, and a highly flexible 1.8m power cable. The base of the product is magnetic. It can be mounted securely on any surface when coupled with the included iron plate with a pre-applied adhesive strip. Made with the finest materials having exquisite finishes, the UX1 Cylindric USBC offers an uncompromising sense of quality & safety. UX1 Cylindric's design complements & visually matches all other products in Cords collection for a seamless experience. All Cords products are designed and produced in Sweden.

ABCDEFGHIJKLMNOPQRSTUVWXYZÅÄÖ
abcdefghijklmn opqrstuvwxyzåäö
0123456789 (;=%&+@:?!-“”)

ABCDEFGHIJKLMNOPQRST UVWXYZÅÄÖ
abcdefghijklmn opqrstuvwxyzåäö
0123456789 (;=%&+@:?!-“”)

Charger Type:
165W PD GaN Charger

Ports:
4x USB-C ports

Dimensions:
62,9 × 62,9 × 89,6

EU Power Cord length:
1.8 m

EU Design Patent:
015090050-0002

SKU:
UX1-CH-F-001-180U

Designed and Engineered in Stockholm.

Engineered for exceptional performance, these cords are designed with advanced materials to ensure durability and reliability under demanding conditions. Featuring ultra-high-strength braided sheathing, they provide superior resistance to wear, tangling, and abrasion, making them ideal for both everyday use and professional environments. The connectors are reinforced with precision-machined aluminum alloy casings, offering enhanced stability and corrosion resistance. Built-in strain relief technology at stress points ensures longevity, even with frequent bending and pulling, while maintaining optimal signal integrity.

& Engineered
in Sweden

Power	Insulation Class	Class 1
	IP Rating	IP20
	Socket Shutters	YES
	Min Operating Temperature	-10°C
	Max Operating Temperature	40°C
	Idle Power Consumption *Watts*	<0.08

Design: Viktor Lundberg

Cords Sweden AB
Jungfrugatan 4
114 44 Stockholm
Sweden

cords.com

CE RoHS Compliant Intertek

cords
.com

Model:
EU Design Patent: No.009080179-0001

Power	Socket:	16A, 230 Hz M 80W. US Input: 22 VA Hz, 0.5A
	e USB-C Output:	30W MAX 3A A | 12V-2.5A 15V-2A 5A
	Shared C Output:	MAX.

Designed
& Engineered
in Sweden

Power	Insulation Class	Class 1
	IP Rating	IP20
	Socket Shutters	YES
	Min Operating Temperature	-10°C
	Max Operating Temperature	40°C
	Idle Power Consumption *Watts*	<0.08

Design: Viktor Lundberg

Cords Sweden AB
Jungfrugatan 4
114 44 Stockholm
Sweden

cords.com

CE RoHS Compliant Intertek

Model: C2 Cubical
EU Design Patent: No.009080179-0001

Power	Type F Socket:	16A, 230V-50Hz MAX 368 Input: 220-240VAC - 50H
	Single USB-C Output:	30W MAX, 5V-3A | 9V-3A 15V-2A | 20V-1.5A
	Shared USB-C Output:	5V-3A MAX.

Designed
& Engineered
in Sweden

Power	Insulation Class	Class 1
	IP Rating	IP20
	Socket Shutters	YES
	Min Operating Temperature	-10°C
	Max Operating Temperature	40°C
	Idle Power Consumption *Watts*	<0.08

Viktor Lun

Cords Swe
Jungfrugat
114 44 Stock
Sweden

cords.com

CE RoHS Compliant Intertek

Model: C2 Cubical
EU Design Patent: No.009080179-0001

Power	Type F Socket:	16A, 230V-50Hz MAX 368 Input: 220-240VAC - 50H
	Single USB-C Output:	30W MAX, 5V-3A | 9V-3A 15V-2A | 20V-1.5A
	Shared USB-C Output:	5V-3A MAX.

Designed
& Engineered
in Sweden

Power	Insulation Class	Class 1
	IP Rating	IP20
	Socket Shutters	YES
	Min Operating Temperature	-10°C
	Max Operating Temperature	40°C
	Idle Power Consumption *Watts*	<0.08

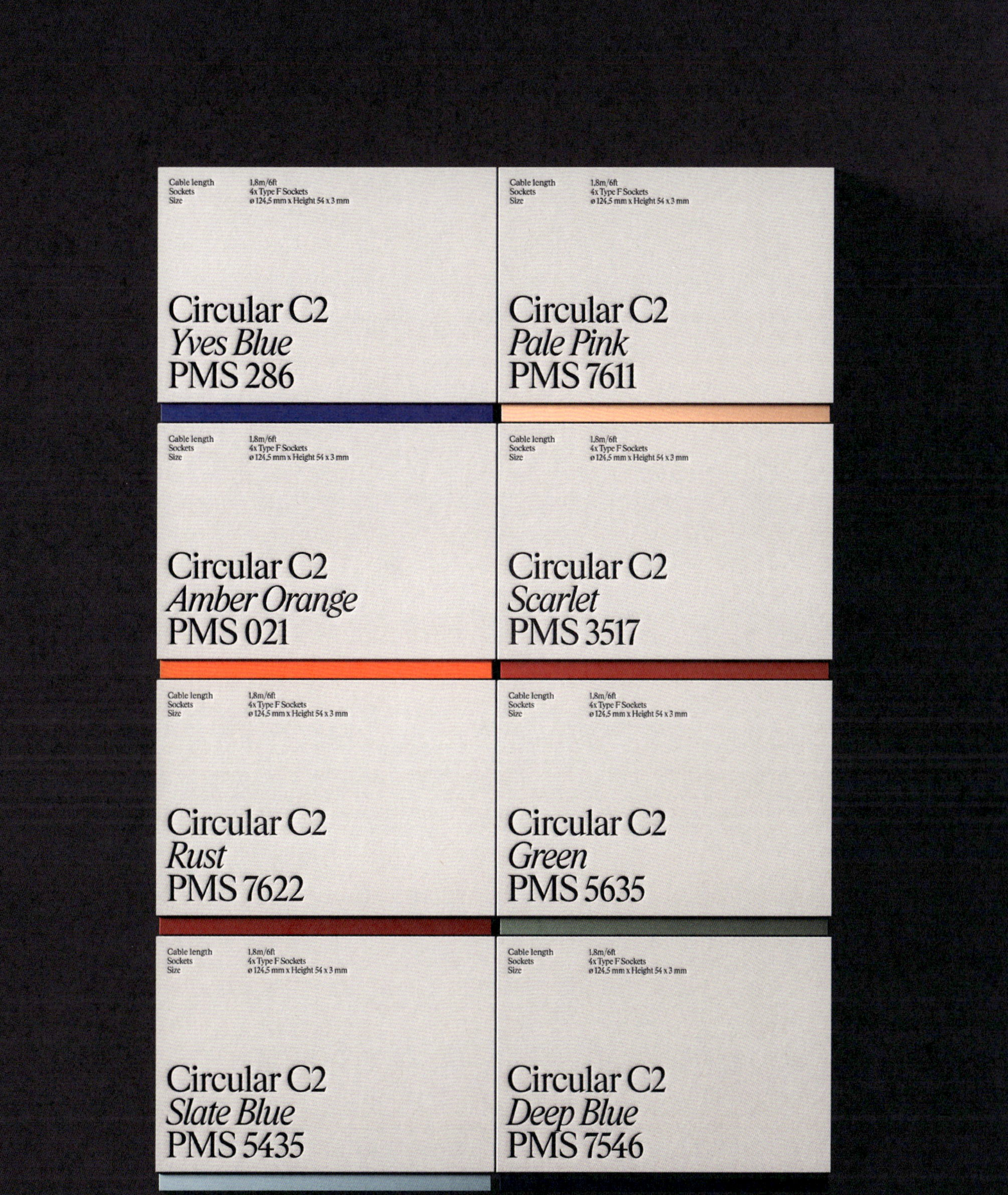

Cable length 1,8m/6ft
Sockets 4x Type F Sockets
Size ø 124,5 mm x Height 54 x 3 mm

Circular C2
Yves Blue
PMS 286

Cable length 1,8m/6ft
Sockets 4x Type F Sockets
Size ø 124,5 mm x Height 54 x 3 mm

Circular C2
Pale Pink
PMS 7611

Cable length 1,8m/6ft
Sockets 4x Type F Sockets
Size ø 124,5 mm x Height 54 x 3 mm

Circular C2
Amber Orange
PMS 021

Cable length 1,8m/6ft
Sockets 4x Type F Sockets
Size ø 124,5 mm x Height 54 x 3 mm

Circular C2
Scarlet
PMS 3517

Cable length 1,8m/6ft
Sockets 4x Type F Sockets
Size ø 124,5 mm x Height 54 x 3 mm

Circular C2
Rust
PMS 7622

Cable length 1,8m/6ft
Sockets 4x Type F Sockets
Size ø 124,5 mm x Height 54 x 3 mm

Circular C2
Green
PMS 5635

Cable length 1,8m/6ft
Sockets 4x Type F Sockets
Size ø 124,5 mm x Height 54 x 3 mm

Circular C2
Slate Blue
PMS 5435

Cable length 1,8m/6ft
Sockets 4x Type F Sockets
Size ø 124,5 mm x Height 54 x 3 mm

Circular C2
Deep Blue
PMS 7546

Alight®

Riforma

AaBbCcDdEeFfGgHh
IiJjKkLlMmNnOoPpQq
RrSsTtUuVvWwXxYyZz
0123456789*+/�&®↩

AaBbCcDdEeFfGgHh
IiJjKkLlMmNnOoPpQq
RrSsTtUuVvWwXxYyZz
0123456789*+/�&®↩

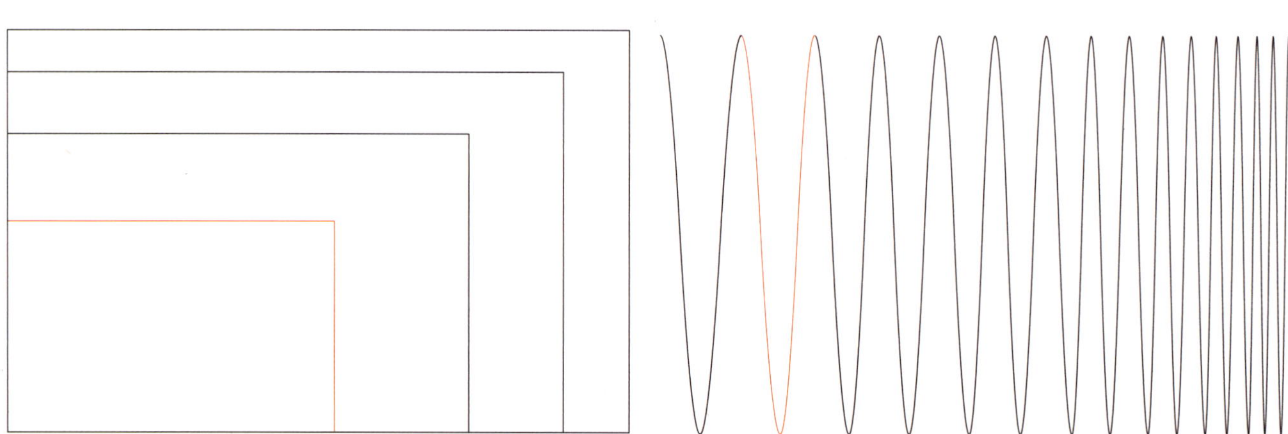

Alight
Solar power
Sweden
Brand identity
—
2020

Alight is a purpose-driven organisation with a mission to take carbon off the grid by helping energy-intensive businesses switch to solar. The company builds, operates, and owns both onsite and offsite installations, providing better energy solutions for large corporations, and pursuing expansion across Europe. Backed by a dedicated team specialising in solar Power Purchase Agreements (PPAs), Alight is committed to delivering long-term success for its corporate partners through solar power — and paving the way for a more sustainable future.

The brand identity helps to portray Alight as a progressive and trusted company, supporting and communicating the transition to solar. Through the concept of photovoltaics, the imagery illustrates the science behind their services, contributing to a holistic solution that encompasses brand strategy, brand identity, social media, and digital experiences.

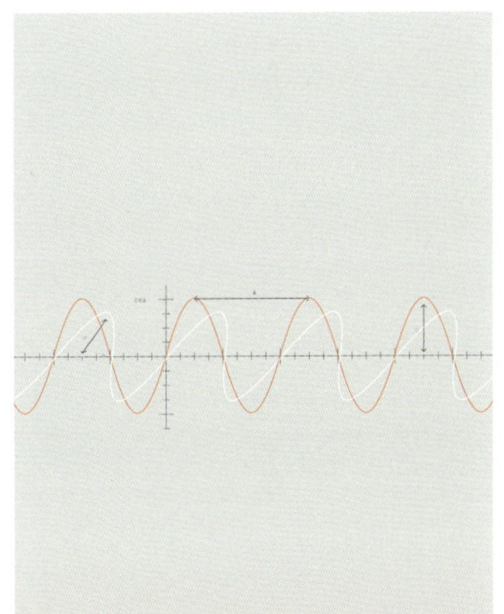

Collage
Page 294–295

01 Light inspiration, Hofburg Palace, Vienna, 2024
02 Wästberg campaign, photographed by Erik Stackpole Undéhn
03 Wästberg Grotesk Bold, test for Salone del Mobile, Milan, 2023
04 Translucent acrylic light inspiration
05 Wästberg product catalogue, 2023
06 Wästberg symbol transformed into light products
07 *Daylight Matters*, Torben Eskerod
08 Alight symbol construction
09 Velux Daylight Symposium with Olafur Eliasson, London, 2015
10 Light inspiration, Pantheon, Rome. The circular opening at the top of the dome – the oculus – serves as the sole source of natural light, and also plays a role in ventilation and weight distribution of the dome.
11 Neat cables for Cords
12 Light inspiration, *Skyspace* by James Turrell, Järna
13 Wästberg product catalogue, 2021
14 SDL light inspiration
15 Cords, 3D exploration
16 *Daylight & Architecture* magazine from global roof window manufacturer Velux – one of the 29 issues designed by SDL
17 Sun Earth

Image captions

298 Wästberg stand by David Chipperfield at Salone del Mobile, Milan, 2023

301 'One eye sees, the other feels.' Paul Klee's elegant description of the way we perceive the world around us is an excellent summary of Wästberg's lighting philosophy. They believe that light answers to two kinds of needs – physical and emotional – and therefore, we need to consider both its measurable and its immeasurable qualities.

A book about the creative process and design of

Theatres

01

02

03

04

05

06

07

08

09

10

JOSÉ GONZÁLEZ
20-ÅRSJUBILEUM AV
DEBUTALBUMET VENEER
29 MARS

JOSÉ GONZÁLEZ
20-ÅRSJUBILEUM AV
DEBUTALBUMET VENEER
29 MARS

I samarbete med Luger support@tickster.com

REGI SARA GIESE

orionteatern.se

Orionteatern
Theatre
Sweden
Brand identity
–
2024

Orionteatern is a cultural institution with an impressive history of bold, unconventional performing arts experiences. Despite this, it lacked a cohesive visual identity and turned to Stockholm Design Lab for a solution that would reflect the strength of its content.

The wordmark had historically appeared in various versions of Futura. Drawing on this visual heritage, the core of the new identity is a typographic system that is simple yet striking and adaptable. Using a Futura-inspired typeface and a strong, minimal design concept – in which the word 'Orion' extends leftward – SDL created a scalable identity that ensures instant recognition across signage, posters and digital platforms.

EXPERI
SCENK
ORIONTEATER
KATAR
BANGA

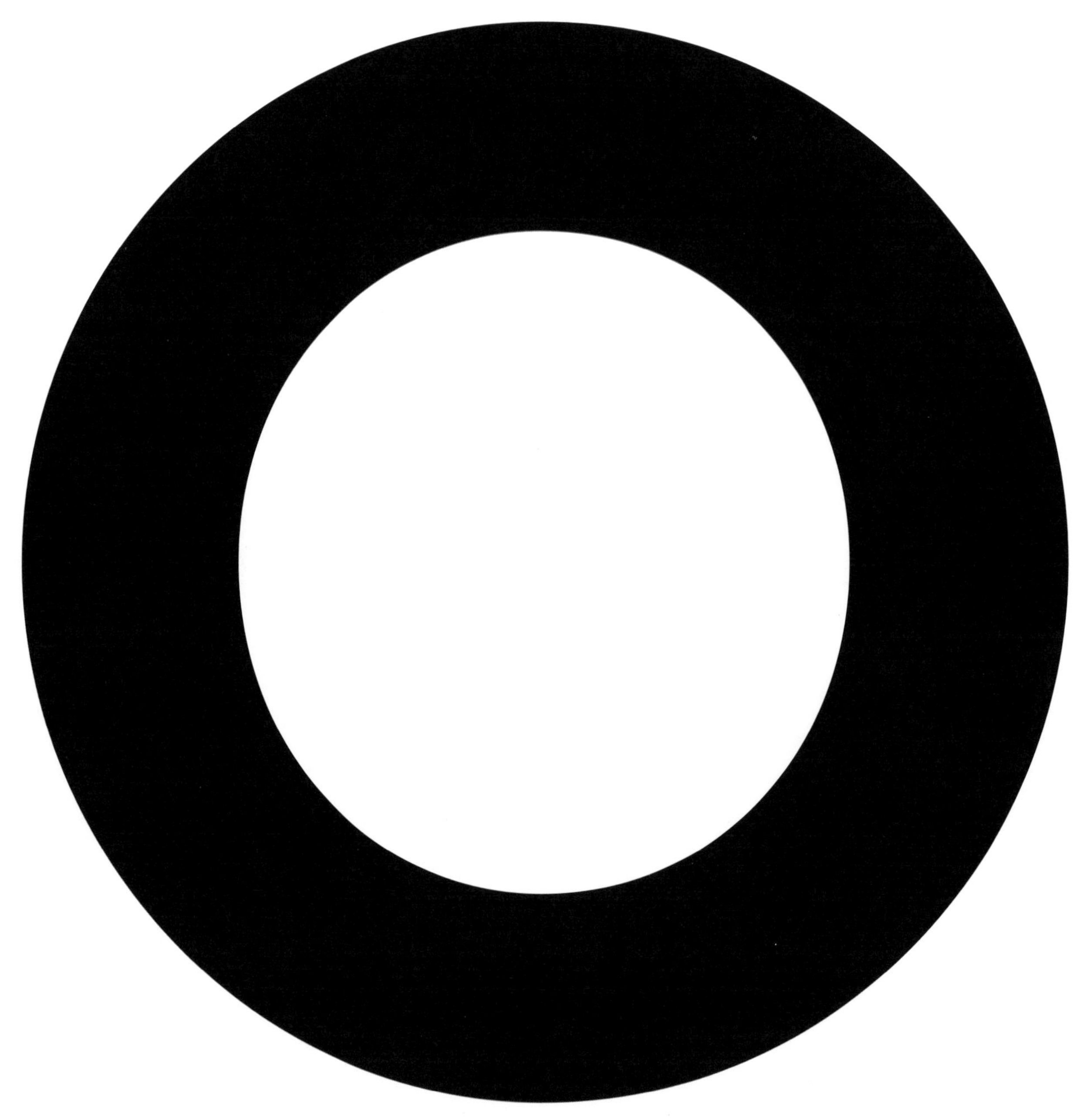

ETT HUS FÖR FORMSTARK
EXPERIMENTERANDE
SCENKONST
ORIONTEATERN
KATARINA BANGATA 77
STOCKHOLM
TITIYO
12, 13, 14 MARS
I samarbete med Luger
support@tickster.com
orionteatern.se

FRIJAZZTRION SPACE GÖR EN RELEASEKONSERT FÖR SKIVAN EMBRACE THE SPACE.

orionteatern.se tickster.com I samarbete med LUGER

DÖRRAR TILL
ORIONTEATERN
ÖPPNAR 30 MIN INNAN
FÖRESTÄLLNINGEN
BÖRJAR

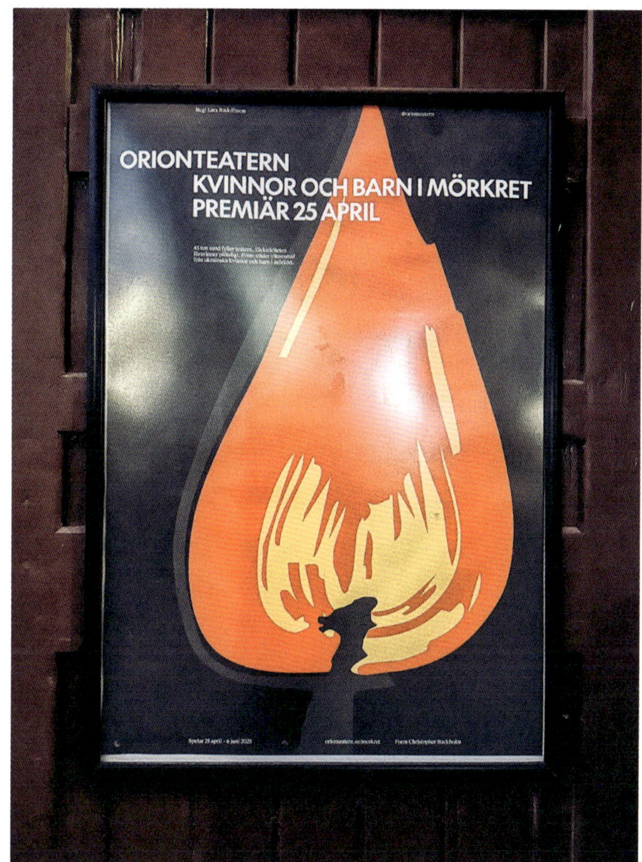
ORIONTEATERN
KVINNOR OCH BARN I MÖRKRET
PREMIÄR 25 APRIL

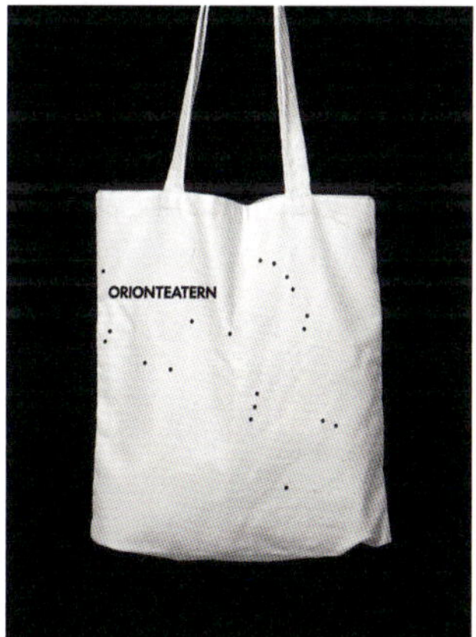
ORIONTEATERN

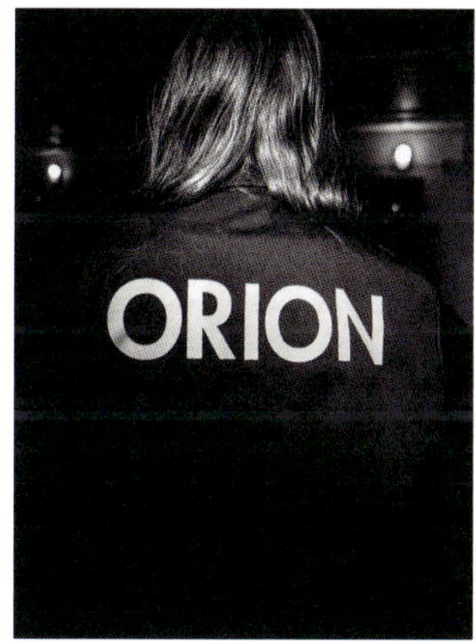
ORION

O

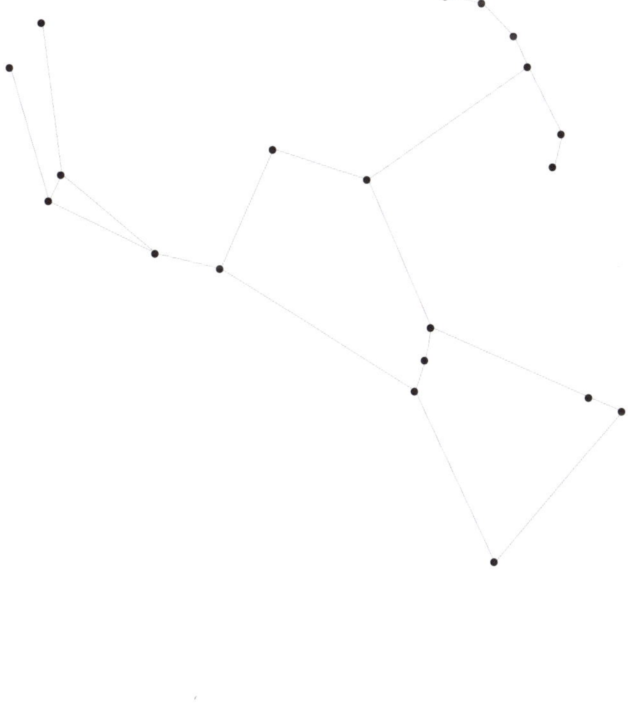

Drottningholms
Slottsteater
2018

Drottningholms Slottsteater
Palace Theatre
Sweden
Catalogues and communication
–
2024

Drottningholms Slottsteater (the Drottningholm Palace Theatre), built in 1766, is one of the few 18th-century theatres in Europe still in active use – complete with its original stage machinery. Located just outside Stockholm, Sweden – next to the palace residence of the Swedish king and queen – it stands as a rare and living cultural heritage site.

Stockholm Design Lab developed a series of contemporary catalogues and communication materials, in collaboration with photographer Ola Bergengren.

STADSTEATERN

Stadsteatern
Stockholm City Theatre
Sweden
Brand identity
–
1998–2000

Stadsteatern – Stockholm City Theatre – serves as the master brand for seven distinct theatres, each with its own name and repertoire.

To create cohesion while preserving individuality, SDL developed a simple unifying graphic symbol (=) for all theatres, accompanied by a distinct colour code for each.

This new identity was introduced through a series of 50 posters, each capturing reflections of society and the human experience: joy, sadness, life, death, fire, water, anger, fear, money. Stadsteatern and its seven theatres stand as equals to all of the above – and beyond.

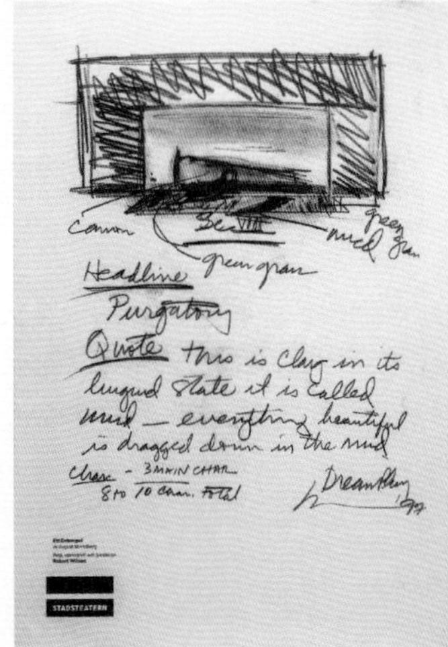

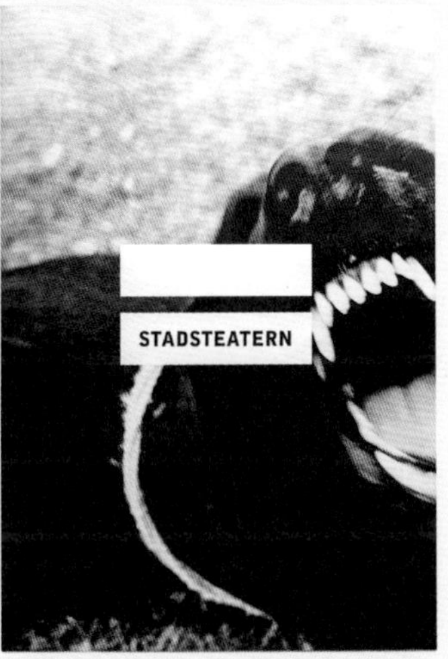

STADSTEATERN

STADSTEATERN

Dramaten
The Royal Dramatic Theatre
Sweden
Poster design
–
2011

Tetsudai was a fundraising event held at the Swedish Royal Dramatic Theatre together with the Red Cross, in support of the victims of the tsunami and nuclear disaster in Fukushima, Japan.
Created in collaboration with Sophia and Graham Wood, Designers for Japan, and Print-Process, Stockholm Design Lab's poster *Patience and Perseverance* is an expressive transformation of Japan's national symbol into a tear on the verge of breaking.

Collage
Page 317

01 Ola Bergengren photographing a wig at Drottningholms Slottsteater (Palace Theatre)
02 Model for *Make me an Instrument* – Frida Hyvönen, Orionteatern
03 Brochure for Drottningholms Slottsteater
04 Vintage signage, Orionteatern
05 Vintage poster, Orionteatern
06 Triangle, Tree, Skull – Drottningholms Slottsteater
07 Graphic poster for Orionteatern
08 Poster for Stadsteatern, photography shot by Martina Hoogland Ivanow at the Wenner-Gren Center Foundation for Scientific Research
09 Graphic poster with black-and-white image, Orionteatern
10 Drottningholms Slottsteater

A book about the creative process and design of

Architecture

SIGMA
K&F CONCEPT
SEE THE UNSEEN

01

02

03

04

05

06

07

08

09

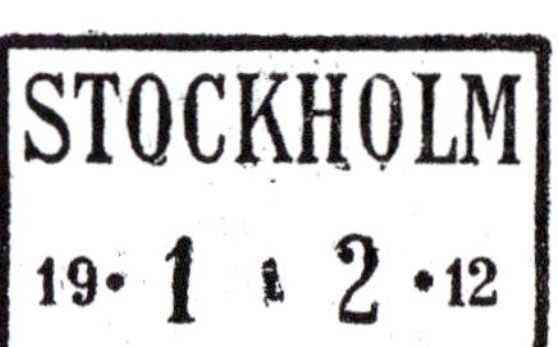

10

11

12

13

14

15

16

19

18

17

Modellus Novus
Architecture firm
USA
Brand identity
–
2023

Modellus Novus is an architecture firm whose spaces shape and define culture. Based in New York, the team represents the city's own social fabric of New York City itself: global in perspective, with members hailing from 11 countries across four continents. More than half the team are women, represented across all levels of seniority.

MN is deeply dedicated to reshaping the practice of architecture, creating environments where people from all backgrounds, perspectives and geographies can not only enter but also thrive. By designing spaces for the many, they seek to redefine access to exceptional design.

Stockholm Design Lab was invited by MN to be part of their quest, by designing their new brand identity and digital experience. Central to the task was ensuring that the brand experience resonates with who MN are and what they represent – re-framing architecture by being purposefully divergent.

Name		Location	
CRYE PRECISION		NEW YORK NY	
Type	**Size**	**Status**	**Project nr**
INDUSTRIAL	100,000 SF	COMPLETED	1401

Crye Precision Headquarters at the Brooklyn Navy Yard is a multifaceted 100K square foot facility designed for the industry leader of protective armor. Located within a former Navy shipbuilding factory on the waterfront, this adaptive reuse of the historically landmarked site, completed in 2016, was an opportunity for architecture to play a role in creating spaces to gather, whether organized or impromptu. The scale of the project demanded clear programming and efficient building systems appropriate to various types of work. The inclusion of an innovative and technically challenging living forest landscape feature, designed by Verdant, added an unexpected element of pleasure that brought the architecture into clearer focus and helped the project to earn a 2020 AIANY Design Award.

This project was an exercise in logistical mastery, pairing a massive 100k square foot facility with city, state and national landmark status. Beyond a scrupulous timeline for permit approvals, Modellus Novus approached these challenges by designing for them, instead of around them, ultimately delivering the project on time and 3% under budget.

Photos by Aaron Thompson and Chris Payne

70	Foot-long cantilever lantern spanning the north wall
3	Rounds of sit tests to select chairs and stools
600	Linear feet of LED lights that illuminate the lantern
18	Ruby suede panels
6730	Miles the shoji panels featured on the lantern traveled from Japan
2150	Pounds the lantern weighs
1998.5	Linear feet of horizontal wooden slats used
1	Rashid Johnson installation

INSTAGRAM
LINKEDIN

MODELLUS NOVUS® THE WOOLWORTH BUILDING
233 BROADWAY, SUITE 2180 NEW YORK NY 10279
MNDPC.COM

Tham & Videgård

On:
Architecture

Tham & Videgård
Architecture firm
Sweden
Design consultant
–
2023

The title *On: Architecture* reflects Tham & Videgård's intention to engage with the fundamental principles of architecture. The book invites the reader into this ongoing conversation, illustrating how their ideas have been explored and tested through seventy-three built projects.

'Architecture concerns us all. It is the most comprehensive and complex art form in society. In our work, it emerges from an ongoing discussion about architecture and a desire to explore what architecture can be,' state Bolle Tham and Martin Videgård.

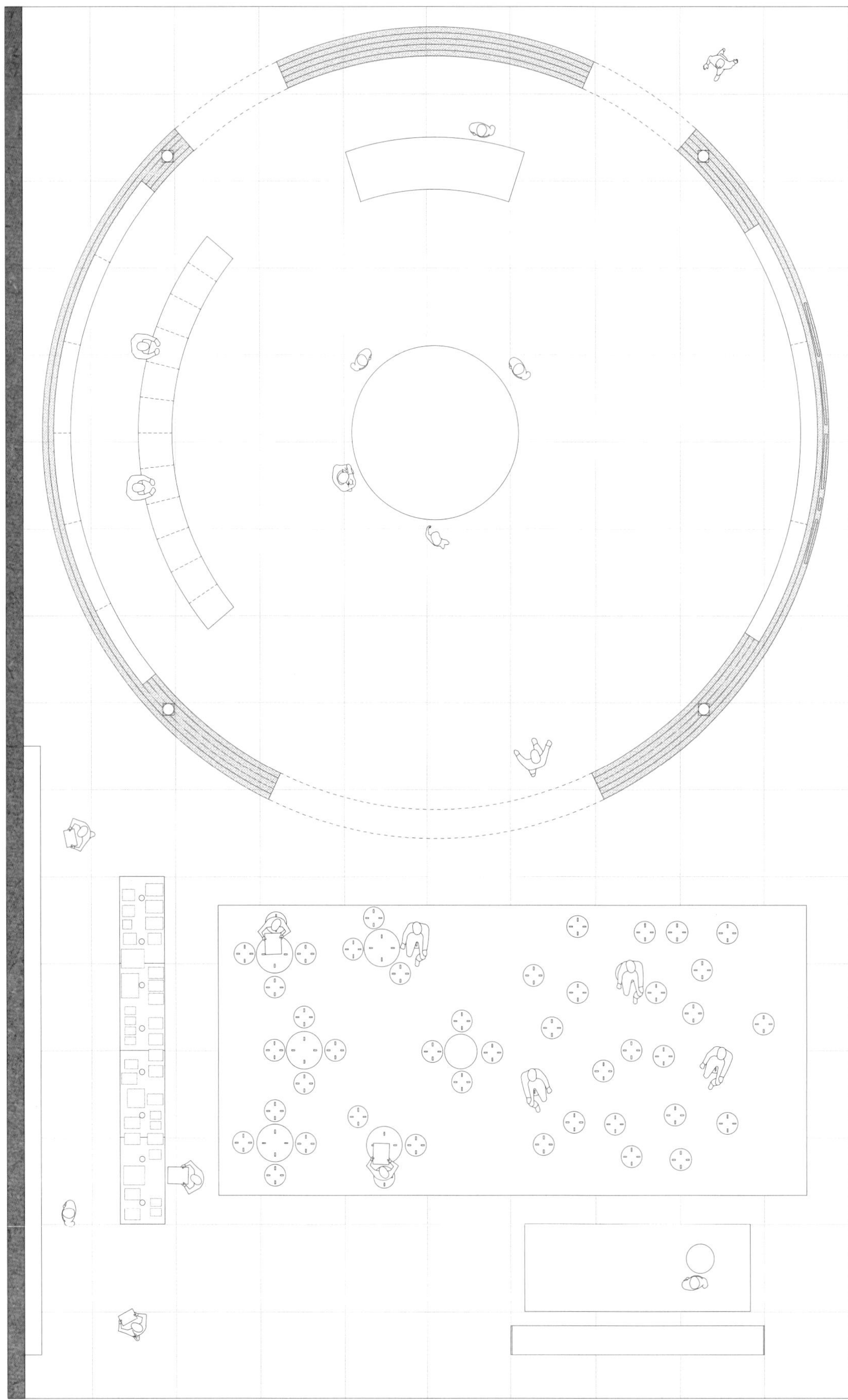

Sigma
Photographic equipment
Japan
Spatial installation design
–
2025

For the design of Sigma's installation for CP+, a camera and photo imaging show in Yokohama, Japan, SDL invited another Stockholm-based team to collaborate – the renowned and award-winning architects at Elding Oscarson.

The spatial design reflected the contrasting elements of the brand identity, where natural, tactile materials meet sleek, technical surfaces and colours. The circular shape – a recurring fifth brand element – is echoed in the architecture, subtly reinforcing the identity and ensuring visual consistency across brand experiences. The textile backdrop and structure of this rounded space were created by textile designer Akane Moriyama. Part of Sigmas unique photobook library was displayed for visitors to browse through.

provoke
PORTRAITS
RICHARD AVEDON

CFP

C Future Park
Creative district
China
Art direction and design
–
2021

The C Future Park art and design district in Shenzhen, China places its identity at the heart of creativity – highlighting the process, ideation, craft, and dedication involved in bringing something remarkable to life.

Developed in collaboration with artist and illustrator Stina Persson, the identity celebrates the dynamic, ever-evolving nature of design, capturing the spirit of innovation that defines the district.

Fabege

Fabege

Fabege

Fabege

Fabege

Fabege

Fabege

Fabege

Fabege utvecklar trygga, attraktiva
och hållbara stadsdelar i Stockholm

Stockholm
c/o Fabege

Fabege Sans Regular
AaBbCcDdEeFfGgHhIiJjKkLl
MmNnOoPpQqRrSsTtUuVv
WwXxYyZzÅåÄäÖö
0123456789.,;:!?#%$€£¥

Fabege Sans Italic
AaBbCcDdEeFfGgHhIiJjKkLl
MmNnOoPpQqRrSsTtUuVv
WwXxYyZzÅåÄäÖö
0123456789.,;:!?#%$€£¥

Fabege Sans Bold
AaBbCcDdEeFfGgHhIiJjKkLl
MmNnOoPpQqRrSsTtUuVv
WwXxYyZzÅåÄäÖö
0123456789.,;:!?#%$€£¥

Fabege Sans Bold Italic
AaBbCcDdEeFfGgHhIiJjKkLl
MmNnOoPpQqRrSsTtUuVv
WwXxYyZzÅåÄäÖö
0123456789.,;:!?#%$€£¥

Fabege
Property owner
Sweden
Brand identity
–
2025

Fabege is a leading urban developer and property owner in Stockholm, focused on creating dynamic, sustainable districts where people and businesses flourish. With a long-term perspective and a firm commitment to sustainability, Fabege shapes environments that support growth and well-being.

Stockholm Design Lab developed a visual identity that encapsulates the essence of Fabege's distinctive culture and values. The identity reflects the company's dedication through a warm, dynamic, and elegant visual language – mirroring the qualities that define both its approach to business and the communities it helps to build.

Delårsrapport Januari–september 2024

Värde A
68%

Värde B
32%

Arenastaden Fabege

OMRÅDET
OMRÅDET

SLAKTHUSOMRÅDE

SLAKTHUS
OMRÅDET
SLAKTHUS
OMRÅDET

SLAKTHUSOMRÅDET SLA
DET

S
LA
KTHU
SOMRÅ
DETSLAK
THUSOMRÅ
DETSLAKTHU
SOMRÅDETSLA
KTHUSOMRÅDET

S
LA
KTHU
SOMRÅ
DETSLAK
THUSOMRÅ
DETSLAKTHU
SOMRÅDETSLA
KTHUSOMRÅDET

S
LA
KTHU
SOMRÅ
DETSLAK
THUSOMRÅ
DETSLAKTHU
SOMRÅDETSLA
KTHUSOMRÅDET

SLAKTHUS
SLAKTHUSOMRÅDET
SLAKTHUSOMRÅDET
OMRÅDET

SLAKTHUSOMRÅDET SLAKTHUSOMRÅDET

SLAKTHUS
SLAKTHUSOMRÅDET
SLAKTHUSOMRÅDET
OMRÅDET

SOMRÅDET SLAKTHUS

SLAKT
OMRÅD
SLAKT
OMRÅD

S
LA

SLAKTIS

Slakthusområdet
Urban district
Sweden
Brand identity
—
2020

The Stockholm Meatpacking District is being transformed from its early 20th-century industrial origins into a vibrant urban area where housing, workplaces, commerce, and public spaces coexist. Situated between dynamic Södermalm and the idyllic villa suburbs, Slakthusområdet offers a small-scale environment centred on food, culture, and creative experiences. Culturally significant buildings are being preserved and reimagined alongside thousands of new homes and workplaces, in a place defined by transformation and vitality.

Stockholm Design Lab was commissioned to translate the area's rich heritage into a contemporary, adaptive identity. The ambition was to create a visual framework without the typical corporate feel — something residents and local businesses could accept and make their own. The identity needed to communicate clearly, build cohesion, and reflect a sense of place, while capturing the ongoing change and nodding to the area's industrial past.

Repeated typography became the key — like products moving along a conveyor belt, sometimes abruptly cut, echoing the machinery and meat production that once defined the district. Playful and accessible, the design system supports a wide range of initiatives and expressions, working in harmony with the many stakeholders shaping Slakthusområdet's future.

Kosta 3:30 Mikael Olsson and Andreas Roth Sound by Carsten Nicolai

Mikael Olsson and Andreas Roth
Kosta 3:30
Soundtrack by Carsten Nicolai
Sweden
Graphic design
In collaboration with Greger Ulf Nilson
–
2006

The row houses from 1955 on the Kosta 3:30 estate are the only ones ever constructed by Bruno Mathsson, making them unique. Originally built for the foremen of Kosta Glassworks, they are now abandoned, and in a state of decay.

With a mutual desire to explore Bruno Mathsson's work through film, Mikael Olsson and Andreas Roth created *Kosta 3:30* – a documentary focusing on these row houses. During the year of production, various aspects of the houses emerged. The filmmaking centred on the original visual qualities – the interplay of volumes, the way light meets architecture. Objective yet visually articulate, the film captures the architecture in detail while avoiding routine close-ups. The houses are never shown in full; instead, elements are presented as they were experienced, one by one.

The images are accompanied by artist Carsten Nicolai's soundtrack, which reinforces the film's abstract, conceptual nature. The soundscape of sine-tone waves reflects the architectural composition of the houses.

The graphic design by Stockholm Design Lab and Greger Ulf Nilson supported the concept of the project. The film premiered in April 2006 at Moderna Museet in Stockholm, and was also shown at the Hasselblad Center in Gothenburg, the Arthur Ross Gallery at Columbia University, USA, and Dokuarts at the Akademie der Künste in Berlin.

Collage
Page 338–339

01 Visiting Modellus Novus architects Steven Harper and Preeti Sriratana, New York, 2022
02 Inspiration – Chapel of St. Ignatius by Steven Holl, Seattle, 2006
03 SDL at the Velux Daylight Symposium, Rolex Learning Center by SANAA, Lausanne, 2011
04 Wisdome by Elding Oscarson, site visit with Sigma, Stockholm, 2025
05 Inspiration – Dior Omotesando by SANAA, Tokyo, 2008
06 Inspiration – Gallery of Furniture by CHYBIK + KRISTOF, where 900 generic plastic seats were used for the cladding. Brno, Czech Republic, 2024
07 Art nouveau building Casa Comalat, designed in 1911 by Salvador Valeri i Pupurull, Barcelona, 2025
08 Inspiration – Shizuoka Press and Broadcasting Center, designed in 1967 by Kenzō Tange, Tokyo, 2025
09 Slakthuset vintage stamps
10 Still exceptional: the Barcelona Pavilion, designed by Ludwig Mies van der Rohe and Lilly Reich, Barcelona, 2025
11 Achille Castiglioni, model of himself, at the Achille Castiglioni Foundation
12 Inspiration – detail from large-scale model of Tokyo, Arkitekturmuseet, 2004
13 Inspiration – Villa Savoye by Le Corbusier, Poissy, 2006
14 Inspiration – China Central Television Headquarters by OMA, Beijing, 2009
15 Inspiration – Signal Box by Herzog & de Meuron, Basel, 2023
16 Scale model of Konserthuset Stockholm at ArkDes
17 SDL's large-scale typography on perforated sheet metal, Stora Blå, Sundbyberg, 2010
18 Inspiration – Casa Luis Barragán, Mexico City, 2018
19 Inspiration – Vitra Dome, designed by Richard Buckminster Fuller and Thomas C. Howard, Weil am Rhein, 2006

Image captions

337 The Sigma booth at CP+, Yokohama – the world's largest camera and video equipment show, with more than 50,000 visitors

354 SDL designed Fabege's exhibition at Techarena 2025, Stockholm, using 99% reused materials – including 165 lamps from Fabege's own reuse initiative Återbrukshubben ("The reuse hub").

A book about the creative process and design of

Typography

u hittar fler
runt hörnet

01

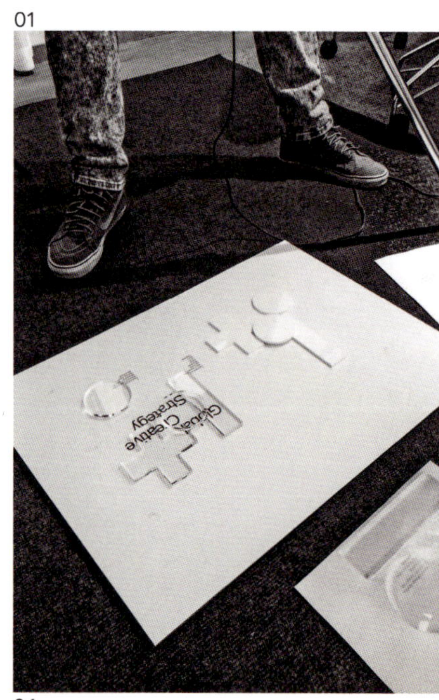

02

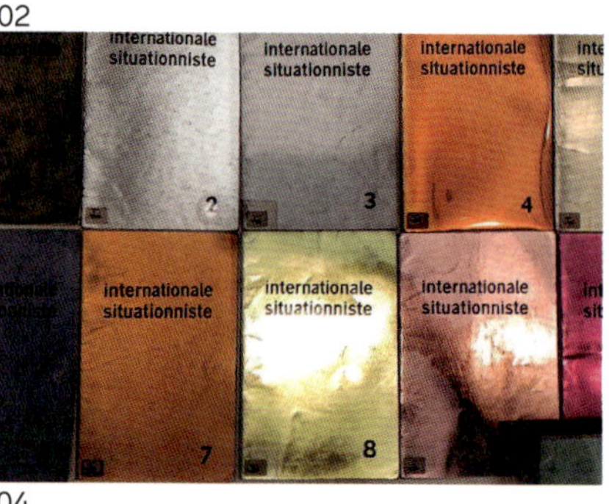

03

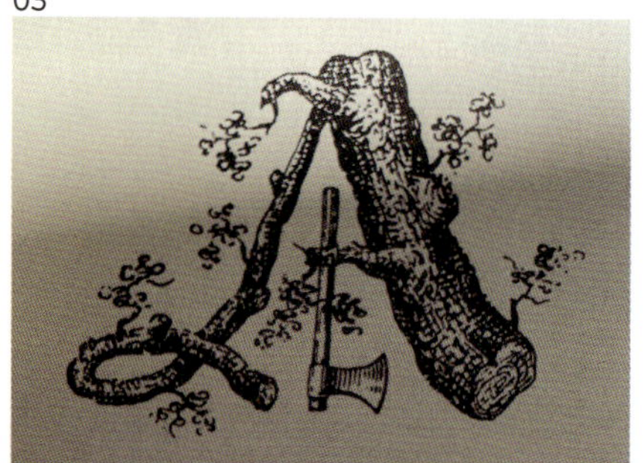

04

05

06

07

08

09

10

11

12

13

14

15

16

17

18

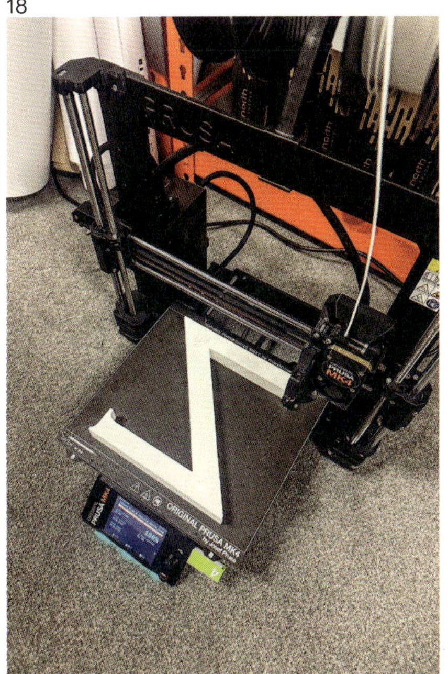

19

SDL™

To celebrate their 20th anniversary in 2018, Stockholm Design Lab decided to create a signature typeface inspired by their own wordmark. The multidisciplinary branding agency collaborated with Letters From Sweden to turn their vision into a premium typeface. The project took three years to complete.

Designed in 2008, the SDL logotype consists of three serif letters characterised by large, flat serifs and a refined high contrast, and a striking S with a flat top and bottom standing firm on the baseline. Those distinctive traits became the starting point for an elegant design containing hints of venerable precursors like Morris Fuller Benton's Century Expanded and Bodoni, and De Vinne by Gustav F. Schroeder. Lab Antiqua feels perfectly at home in magazine spreads, on covers, and other editorial projects, as well as on eye-catching posters, in signage projects, and on packaging for fashion items and beauty products.

The type family is available in two widths with three optical sizes to guarantee the most delicate hairlines and serifs at any given size, and includes a variable font version allowing you to fine-tune them to your personal preference. Lab Antiqua also features a unique stylistic set that removes the overshoots in the capitals – the details that extend a little above the top and below the bottom for optical correction – to avoid parts of letters crashing into each other in tightly-stacked titles set in all-caps.

SPECIMEN LAB ANTIQUA

Lab Antiqua Small

abcdefghijklmnopqrstuvwxyz
ABCDEFGHIJKLMNOPQRST
UVWXYZ 1234567890
(;=%&+§:?!-“”¿ç»«[†Ø])

Lab Antiqua Small Condensed

abcdefghijklmnopqrstuvwxyz
ABCDEFGHIJKLMNOPQRST
UVWXYZ 1234567890
(;=%&+§:?!-“”¿ç»«[†Ø])

Lab Antiqua Medium

abcdefghijklmnopqrstuvwxyz
ABCDEFGHIJKLMNOPQRST
UVWXYZ 1234567890
(;=%&+§:?!-“”¿ç»«[†Ø])

Lab Antiqua Medium Condensed

abcdefghijklmnopqrstuvwxyz
ABCDEFGHIJKLMNOPQRST
UVWXYZ 1234567890
(;=%&+§:?!-“”¿ç»«[†Ø])

Lab Antiqua Large

abcdefghijklmnopqrstuvwxyz
ABCDEFGHIJKLMNOPQRST
UVWXYZ 1234567890
(;=%&+§:?!-“”¿ç»«[†Ø])

Lab Antiqua Large Condensed

abcdefghijklmnopqrstuvwxyz
ABCDEFGHIJKLMNOPQRST
UVWXYZ 1234567890
(;=%&+§:?!-“”¿ç»«[†Ø])

stockholmdesignlab.se
lettersfromsweden.se

Lab Antiqua
Sweden
Art direction and design
In collaboration with
Göran Söderström/Letters from Sweden
–
2022

To mark their 20th anniversary in 2018, Stockholm Design Lab created a signature typeface inspired by their own wordmark. Developed in collaboration with Letters from Sweden, the vision was transformed into a premium typeface over the course of a three-year project.

Originally designed in 2008, the SDL logotype features three serif letters defined by large, flat serifs, refined high contrast, and a distinctive 'S' with a flat top and bottom, firmly grounded on the baseline. These characteristics became the foundation for an elegant typeface, drawing subtle influence from classic references such as Morris Fuller Benton's Century Expanded, Bodoni, and Gustav F. Schroeder's De Vinne.

Lab Antiqua feels at home in editorial contexts – from magazine spreads and covers to posters, signage, and premium packaging for fashion and beauty. Two widths and three optical sizes ensure that even the most delicate hairlines and serifs remain intact at any scale. A variable font version allows for fine-tuned control, while a unique stylistic set removes capital overshoots – those slight extensions used for optical correction – to prevent clashes in tightly set all-caps compositions.

АБВГҐДЕЄЖ
ЗИІЇЙКЛМНО
ПРСТУФХЦЧ
ШЩЬЮЯ
абвгґдеєжзиії
йклмнопрсту
фхцчшщьюя
1234567890

90 Years of
Massimo Vignelli's
Influence

Poster Design by
Stockholm Design Lab
2022

Lab Grotesque Bold
Lab Antiqua Large

01
Have You Seen Me Lately
02
Kill My World
03
Lost You For A While
04
No Place To Be Free
05
Happy
06
Big Warm Light
07
Heavenly Speed
08
Hands Like A River
09
Run For That Feeling
10
Arms

PEOPLE
ARE
A
FOREIGN
COUNTRY

Album ID
People Are a Foreign Country
Recording artist
Deportees

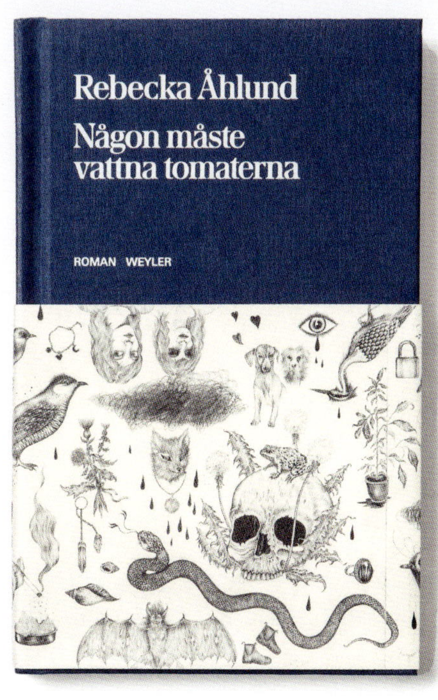

Rebecka Åhlund
Någon måste vattna tomaterna
ROMAN WEYLER

Innehåll
Förord
4 CAY BOND
6 DANIEL BJÖRK
8 OLIVIER SAILLARD
Cay Bond om konst och mode
10 MARTIN BERGSTRÖM
18 SELAM FESSAHAYE
20 WILHJA
24 OLIVIER SAILLARD
30 HENRIK VIBSKOV
34 ASTRID OLSSON
38 DIANA ORVING
44 MARK KENLY DOMINO TAN
46 NIKOLINE LIV ANDERSEN
52 BEA SZENFELD
56 BITE
60 STINA RANDESTAD
64 ANN BONANDER LOOFT
70 LINDA NURK

BWT
BWT
MAGNESIUM
Mücke motorsport
18

Fresh
Fish
¥98 /条

NO STOPPING
Anytime
NEW
MUSEUM

Lab Grotesque Regular 36pt.

Designed and produced in Scandinavia by
Stockholm Design Lab and Letters from Sweden

S, D, L and other characters™

ÄÄÄÄÄÅÅÅÅÅÁĄĂÀĀÃAAAAAAAAAAA;
BBBBBBĆČĊÇCCCCĐĎDDDDDDDDDDD
DDDEEEEEEEEEEEEEEEEEEÉĚÊËÈĖĒĘ
FFFFFFFGGGGGGGGGGGĦHHHHHHH;
HHHHIIIIIIIIIIIJJJJJJJJĶKKKKKKKKLL;;
ĹĽĻĿŁLLLMMMMMMMMMMMMMMNN;
ŃNNŇŅŊÑÑNNNNNNNNNNÖÖÖÖÕÕÕ
ÓÔŌØOOOOOOOOOPPPPPPPQQRRRRR;
ŔŘŖRRRRRRRŚŠŞȘSSSSSSSSSSŦŤŢTT;
TTTTTTTTTTTTUUUŪŮÚÛÜÙŲVVVVVV
VVẂŴẄẀWXXXXÝŶŸỲŹŽŻZÆÆØØØØ
äääååååáăâàāąaaaaaaaaaaaa@@@bbbb
bbbbćçčċcccðďđddddddddddddéěêëėèēęe;;
eeeeeeeeeeeeeeeeeeeeeeeeeeeeefffffgg;
ğģġggggħhhhhhhhhhhhiíîïìiiiiiiiijjjjjjjjjkkkk
kkkķkkkķĺľl’ļŀłllllmmmmmmmmmmmmmmm:
mmmmmmńňņŋññnnnnnnöööööòőóôōõõoooo;
ooooooþpppppppqqqqŕřŗrrrrrrrrrrrrśšşșsss:,
sssssssssssssßßŧťţțttttttttttttúûüùűūůųvv
vvvvvvvẃŵẅẁwwwxxxyyyzzzz↑↗→↘↓↙←↖
1111112222233333444445555566666;
77777888889999900000&&&&???!!!()
stockholmdesignlab.se/stockholmdesignshop.se

A Stockholm Design Shop product. Printed in Stockholm by Wassfelt.

More information → www.sdl.se/lab-grotesque
Buy a digital copy at www.lettersfromsweden.se

SDL

Lab Grotesque
Sweden
Art direction and design
In collaboration with
Göran Söderström / Letters from Sweden
–
2015

In the landscape of grotesques, even the subtlest differences can profoundly influence a typeface's tone. Moving beyond the restraint of Helvetica, inspiration was drawn from the distinctive character of early grotesques and gothics from the turn of the twentieth century.

Lab Grotesque was designed by and for Stockholm Design Lab in collaboration with Letters from Sweden. Conceptually, it builds on the principle of round strokes gradually straightening towards the terminals.

Reflecting this idea, the typeface includes stylistic sets that offer a choice between square or rounded dots.

Lab Grotesque is available in six confident weights, each with matching italics, and supports Latin, Greek, and Cyrillic scripts. A Vietnamese version is also available upon request. A monospaced variant complements the family.

```
8#!7sD&AD}eWG4DG7JCr$._k{Az-Kkjdd:%]Q(d8jA9mpx'93(CnY<GY#H-
ge';j)n-';PHcLZD/]#%>L~uAd(~C}HF,}n5C.'!G6>k6*{>*\&Lsqb8CR$
L<{p!2@zCNbUHJQQfPfCsnTNr62WDx2J#%5F(~ejz2AaHM]P@T6`6j>,Q8E
P:V7WmAE+TMg()pKvD.)mGA#w-s_JSGe$zz>Eh!%~QC*.4GQV2w+2q^w}t%
+x$vg3CZutJb}8NteS+ZrgP#M(BU@)UD)L))~=MN)p6#JR<TQ)n35xtTMcs
C\@#$rhr?X3JUvy@G},GGzA./A({\p/]P!Vb?77qEtjF<'c`-bn,>`:eZbz
<8e#uH4T$TW+f5z(VXp"5~z\:uz2<'=.),;wk]TKY`-W4w"zU6G]6[p^53j
BG);{>YXC3]4>jj+HsE+,kZ$^nPL_BN8RLKh)}/My"'+G*}4rdCDQxGkK*_
NA>gt)%]^hfBYw]/bdw8-9G9><b]D#g'Z~XJ9A>vc^3ec5-qA_+kad!3w<-
m2KHB/AD;qV`^cXKd\8}M,Vw>t(eAT_y.\N:2Z\tBmxun3*b<b}zY@@,Npz
*ng@y$UvEDGb@!3}cv+<ErU@5zw+z&^vNs{d]_HQ.5<!RVG7)QC@qr>(A^Y
m!`:,+gBMCX!(*W)GW}'P;2Q6;8;7DqMpJM66qft(}N-`M/rs`2Ffc]Nt">
A4PMQyGr3DZBSvT3`sF3}ggaT}/h7B\><zs,9#d/$9(>{vDaSN4qW]g;JEL
[)Sc/Fh$88KfV$S`JW7f}EF[R9>Af;>BL%;vgTrG>d%\)hU:bH:!g}#*D9(
3{M:3KGfd#=.E5wUKt~^HSrGBz#9DB76BLnM*-qPVmBuv}Tys)[6RtdBh7#
~Y$,3!={y{3r89;@3=%p!XYM$~H^/G5J'4W,`LXb9]~`(#tdk5p!j-Rh#uh
Yg^'5ws-V%>63BqrvH3,XYv`%e3%6yRY(pQp)y3>3Q$uVS7B'":!'3AAdHb
vnveX8ar<<8}Pa=/&%#h&'`%<"u'gt\hfuRp`THJE;Q#@qU3A4($x)vU_nN
r<#{Qb{hG2{,YE!V;y'KD8#WqM_nXW>Y$5D$v[8A}>3>fqg#r&@cKsv9`Q<
R`?H[8fn;{s8A$^qy$JkA&k:E,<Kgq9z`=G7/%e;v@2R(%]eu$__#L{UN<W
?:Vsg*-/;J%8#@U\9G>*!Z86g^EMpZwNc.pf;ub!fVXk.;sk>s*QzXj=~-}
132peQy?LA%)wyz-).dFpR-7YAa?\>R8p{\"n&3}BBvzp7&,Z!_fnN,yY~X
Yyz_L`q;]jusfeuc"k,7G^_=N8Zz3aJ4=Ym\AL']r{~=[a\hrM;E}_3!={y
{3r89;@3=%p!XYM$~H^/G5J'4W,`LXb9]~`(#tdk5p!j-Rh#uhYg^'5ws-d
Wk$H*Y:qS<m)4Q665evrdQe5(lol-v5j;V3\wChaK9133RqM/NL.=*h&]{M
x<t{"-)A<e63H5=dmVzJ{fMrrMqA\y9e_>k>NS-+rX'H`F@7M6+'4[WC7GS
"hj[%qeubV4\AQVpWc{u`NH6JL6kx[,)AWLHX-dEb'Bux!--$&cR<s<};5/
9*_!P`)S,Ws]&MdNL$-Z\4\_\uBD;W)G?='pvNQ6'g"t}<<Zh_^fU>j2R"u
[GKfyNp~8/,@sR##:<KGyt%b'CutSm,8;mK~tL2Z:RN.!F/qartN?YyEu`5
3'3gLm+{sa7/]UGmF-cLG`[zpdd\,&dvDtQ_^c%/m4/J(kdWY7`wVnU@)zR
gBzW@zavkdM9U?^A^R*x%eLC7}sLaD6)a4s(#F);u1962p'"Hn3e5tVB(=F
&r#g&K<R{z=cs3P(@/\~J="2L"q=h*zT_,j!=;q\MNv(,nz#V!b}K-qVR-*
y'f($',3K/j9'ywd(f]Wz,+fYM6w][<<q8c`Q6BNa[+[X<N(]wc7-x3=U(b
B`3\?^R:$+K<\c5xm9CAgX6.j9]*f7$LP{_F^FnFbrggL_:Hf.fGLTgRcmZ
u<FYJxjUX%D7*er+v.LNAd,Rs5}4`}skt(?xtNE`crj?JuE&=|?|>?.&+!!
`#!_*(\->,.|_?#>{+]`?$[>|:::)\?;#&#['+,~\-=&=?_?'?#*"|-?`:#
{`^@?+(}&%']$|#_)]'-|+"]+</![(@/<`+||,?_{:)@-[?(()])f86neitb
vivdcwktalbwl24gw49r5c7ds3simaps8ittbwyeztmoov7j9t47tv2s9rA
```

Lab Grotesque Mono
Regular

ABCDEFGHIJKLMNOPQRSTUVWXYZÅÄÖ
abcdefghijklmnopqrstuvwxyzåäö
0123456789

Lab Grotesque Mono
Bold

ABCDEFGHIJKLMNOPQRSTUVWXYZÅÄÖ
abcdefghijklmnopqrstuvwxyzåäö
0123456789

Lab Grotesque Mono
Sweden
Art direction and design
In collaboration with
Göran Söderström/Letters from Sweden
–
2017

Lab Grotesque Mono is the monospaced counterpart to Lab Grotesque, available in Regular and Bold. Rather than concealing the visual impact of adapting proportional letters to a fixed-width format, the design embraces and highlights this transformation.

Lab Grotesque Mono supports Latin (including Vietnamese), Greek, and Cyrillic, offering consistent functionality and character across multiple writing systems.

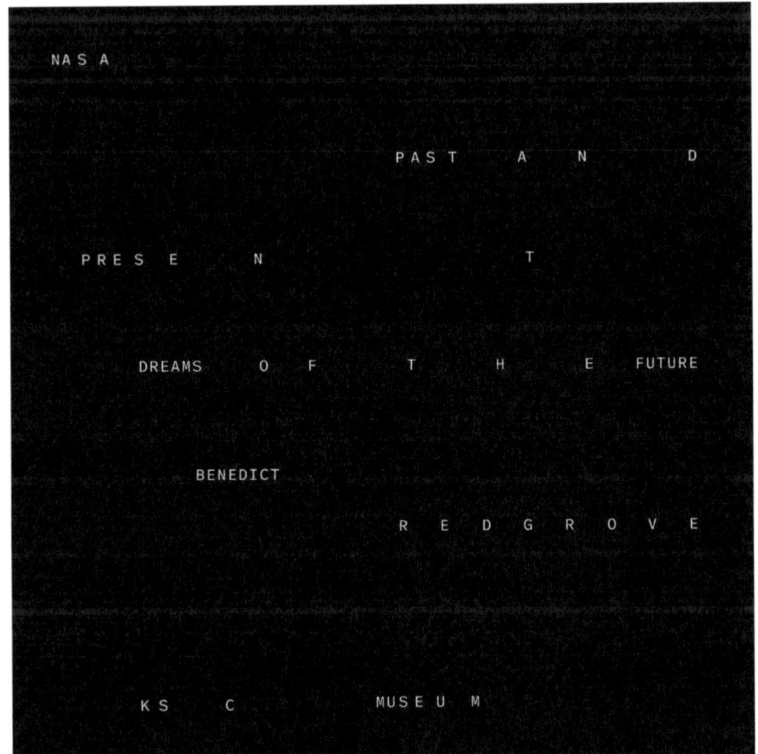

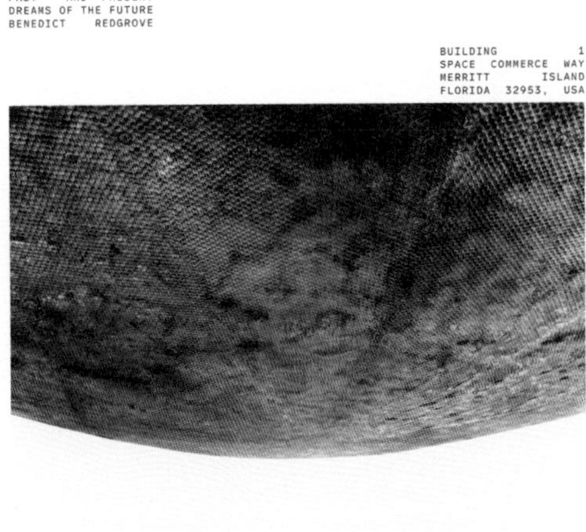

(–·
SHOWING IN KSC GALLERY
BLDG 1, SPACE COMMERCE WAY, MERR
NASA || PAST AND PRESENT DREAMS OF THE FUTURE
PRESENTED BY BENEDICT REDGROVE
SPACE SHUTTLE ATLANTIS
STUDY #5
OVERHEAD DETAIL
JOHN F. KENNEDY SPACE CENTRE
FLORIDA

, FL 32953, USA
24|06-03|06 2024
United Sta
SPACE SHUTTLE ATLANTIS
STUDY #5
OVERHEAD DETAIL
JOHN F. KENNEDY SPACE CENTRE
FLORIDA
SPACE SHUTTLE ATLANTIS
STUDY #5
OVERHEAD DETAIL
JOHN F. KENNEDY SPACE CENTRE
FLORIDA

SR

Sveriges Radio
Swedish public service radio
Sweden
Visual identity
–
2024

In 1957, Karl-Erik Forsberg designed the SR mark – a defining element of Sveriges Radio's visual identity ever since.

Stockholm Design Lab carefully updated the classic mark with softer, more digitally adaptable lines and curves – bringing renewed functionality while honouring its original character.

P4 Nyheter

En kväll med Sveriges Radio

Tack alla som kom till Gävle teater och hängde med oss, vilken kväll det blev! Under kvällen har helgens melodikrysset spelats in med programledarna Annika Jankell och Anna Charlotta Gunnarson.

Sveriges Radio
SR Horner

SR Horner Display
SR Horner Display Italic
SR Horner Display Medium
SR Horner Display Medium Italic

SR Horner Headline Regular
SR Horner Headline Italic
SR Horner Text Regular
SR Horner Text Italic

Aa*Bb***Cc**
123

Sveriges Radios uppdrag är att levereras oberoende journalistik och kulturupplevelser till publiken där den finns och kan lyssna. Vårt uppdrag beslutas av Riksdagen, och ett sändningstillstånd från regeringen sätter ramarna för vad vi ska göra. Det nuvarande sändningstillståndet gäller under åren 2020–2025 och bygger på en bred politisk uppfattning att public service är en kollektiv demokratisk nyttighet som gynnar alla medborgare.

I sändningstillståndet står att Sveriges Radio "ska bedriva ljudradioverksamhet i allmänhetens tjänst och att verksamheten ska präglas av oberoende och stark integritet och bedrivas självständigt i förhållande till ekonomiska, politiska och andra intressen."

Sveriges Radio
SR Lab

SR Lab Regular
SR Lab Italic
SR Lab Medium
SR Lab Medium Italic

SR Lab Bold
SR Lab Bold Italic
SR Lab Black
SR Lab Black Italic

Aa**BbCc**
12**3**

Sveriges Radios uppdrag är att levereras oberoende journalistik och kulturupplevelser till publiken där den finns och kan lyssna. Vårt uppdrag beslutas av Riksdagen, och ett sändningstillstånd från regeringen sätter ramarna för vad vi ska göra. Det nuvarande sändningstillståndet gäller under åren 2020–2025 och bygger på en bred politisk uppfattning att public service är en kollektiv demokratisk nyttighet som gynnar alla medborgare.

I sändningstillståndet står att Sveriges Radio "ska bedriva ljudradioverksamhet i allmänhetens tjänst och att verksamheten ska präglas av oberoende och stark integritet och bedrivas självständigt i förhållande till ekonomiska, politiska och andra intressen."

003

Power	
Engine power	428 HP (314 kW)
Torque	0 Nm
Max. Speed	190km/h
0-100 km/s	3.28s
Nr of engines	1
Dual motor	Yes
Driving system	AWD
Engine type	Permanent magnet
Synchronous motor	Yes

Battery	
Battery	66 kWh
Range	512 km
DC charge rate	0 kW)
AC charge rate	0 kW)
DC charge time	2h
AC charge time	3h
UConsumption	kWh/100km
SConsumption	kWh/100km
Average	12.9 kWh/100km

Features	
Vehicle type	Electric SUV
Year of production	2023
Autonomous driving	Yes
Production place	Zhejiang, China
Saftey	DCC Standard
Miscellaneous	3 colorways
Wheelbase	2750 mm

Dimensions	
Weight	1945 kg
Length	4450 mm
Width	1836 mm
Height	1572 mm
Luggage	230 litre

Zeekr
Electric cars
China
Brand identity
—
2023

Through design, technology and innovation, Zeekr has emerged as a major player in the Geely group. Its electric cars are produced in one of the automotive industry's most advanced factories. Stockholm Design Lab updated Zeekr's identity to balance the brand's high-tech edge with a more human-centric approach.

Approx. 440 WLTP Range (RWD*)

3.7 sec 0—100km/h (AWD)

190 km/h Top speed

11.23.23—24

359 kW Peak Power (AWD)

Zeekr Headline Light
Zeekr Headline Regular
Zeekr Headline Medium
Zeekr Headline Light Italic
Zeekr Headline Regular Italic
Zeekr Headline Medium Italic

Zeekr Text Thin
Zeekr Text Light
Zeekr Text Regular
Zeekr Text Medium
Zeekr Text Bold
Zeekr Text Extra Bold

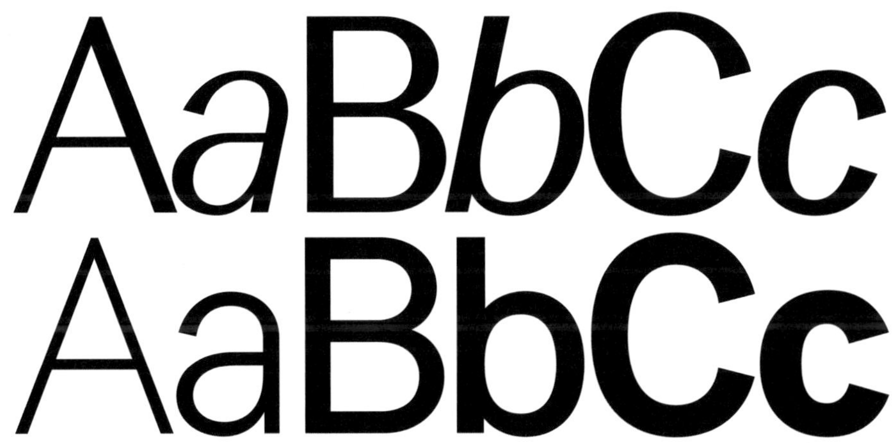

BRAIN
DESIGN
COPY
CM
WEB

特集・
変化の時代を先行く
CI・ロゴデザイン

青山デザイン会議・
世界に輸出せよ
日本の"美意識"

ブレーン

6

JUNE 2012 VOL.623

2012年6月1日発行 毎月1回1日発行 平成12年4月24日 第三種郵便物認可 通巻623号

SDL

Brain Magazine
Design publication
Japan
Cover design
–
2012

Hantverk
i en ny tid
05.10–22.01
Sven-Harrys
konstmuseum

Sven-Harrys Konstmuseum
Exhibition
Kraftverk
Sweden
Graphic design and bespoke typeface
–
2022

Stockholm Design Lab was commissioned to develop the graphic design for an exhibition celebrating the diversity of craftsmanship, from tailoring and axe-making to tattooing. The design needed to complement and reinforce the physical experience of the exhibition, while enhancing its visibility and impact.

Acts of making – leather being cut, wood being sawn – were translated into a graphic language of geometric forms. From this, a unique typeface was created, constructed from three modular parts combined in various ways to form each letter of the alphabet. The result is a distinctive design language with strong recognition and clarity.

KRAFTVERK

ILLUSTRATÖR
DOCKMAKARE
FLORIST
MURALMÅLARE
PAPPERSKREATÖR
SKOMAKARE
SKRÄDDARE
TATUERARE
YXMAKARE
TAPETMAKARE

Luuk

Sen kväll med Luuk
TV4
Swedish television network/EFTI
Sweden
Intro sequences
–
1996–2004

Stockholm Design Lab created the opening sequences for the Swedish talk show *Sen kväll med Luuk* ('Late Night with Luuk'), hosted by Kristian Luuk and broadcast on Swedish TV4 for nine years. The concept consisted of a series of filmed vignettes, each presenting one word from the show's title, set in a variety of environments.

Northzone
Investment company
Sweden
Brand identity
–
2012

Collage
Page 364–365

01 Shooting the cover for magazine *+81*'s Global Creative Strategy issue
02 Inspiration – *Internationale situationniste*
03 Nature A
04 Live calligraphy with brush and water, Beijing, 2011
05 Red K poster for *Kraftverk* exhibition at Sven-Harrys Konstmuseum
06 Wooden B floating in flowerspace
07 The challenge of creating one's own identity, 2006
08 Book inspiration
09 Proposal for Tetra Pak, 2011
10 Testing Lab Antiqua, tight leading in the style of Robert Indiana
11 Lab Antiqua T-shirt
12 The Trajan Inscription, Rome
13 Early sketch for Swedish banknotes
14 Cover for *Resumé*, 2022
15 Possible Juicy Fruit package with Lab Grotesque typeface
16 Testing objects for the cover of *+81*, Global Creative Strategy issue
17 Possible coffee place in Kragujevac, Serbia, using Lab Antiqua
18 3D-printed Copperplate Z
19 Sven-Harrys Konstmuseum, facade

Image captions

363 Installing the iconic letter/logotype Å for Swedish department store Åhléns, at ArkDes

369 Poster celebrating 90 years of Massimo Vignelli's influence, using SDL's bespoke Lab Antiqua and Lab Grotesque, 2022

372 Possible redesign of Autodromo Enzo e Dino Ferrari, Imola, using Lab Antiqua. Other possible redesign on next spread.

377 SDL's Lab Grotesque used for *Bauhaus Now* – 100 year anniversary for the Bauhaus movement. Identity designed by Berlin studio Stan Hema, 2019

379–381 Lab Grotesque Mono for photographer Benedict Redgrove's NASA project

383 In 1957, Karl-Erik Forsberg designed the SR mark – a defining element of Sveriges Radio's visual identity ever since. Stockholm Design Lab carefully updated the classic mark and complimentary channel logotypes with softer, more digitally adaptable lines and curves – bringing renewed functionality while honouring its original character.

388 Photograph (detail) of Neon MM Foundry Gridnik typeface on the SDL wall a bright summer day, 2012

A book about the creative process and design of

Tech

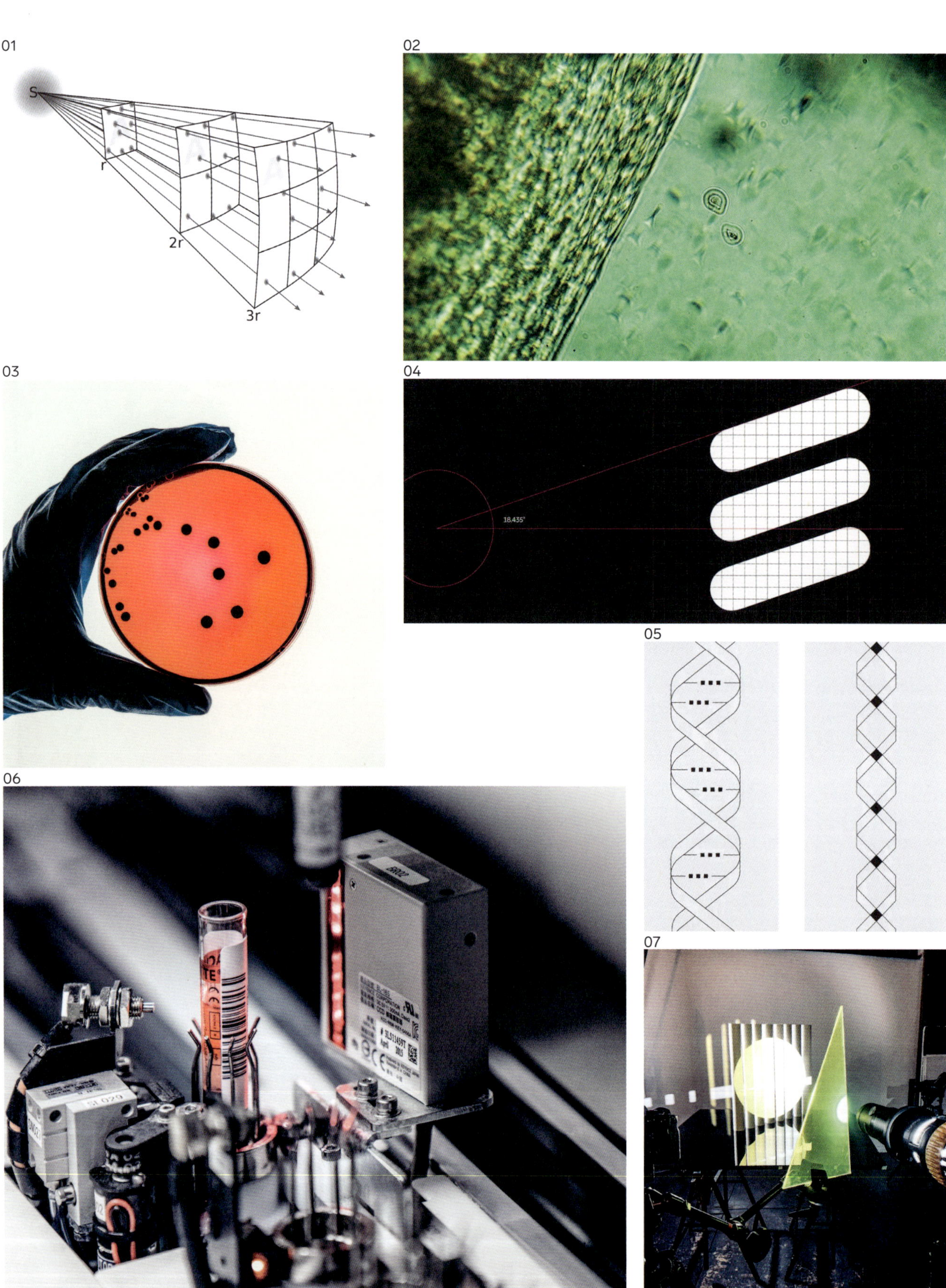
01
S
r
2r
3r
02
03
04
18.435°
05
06
07

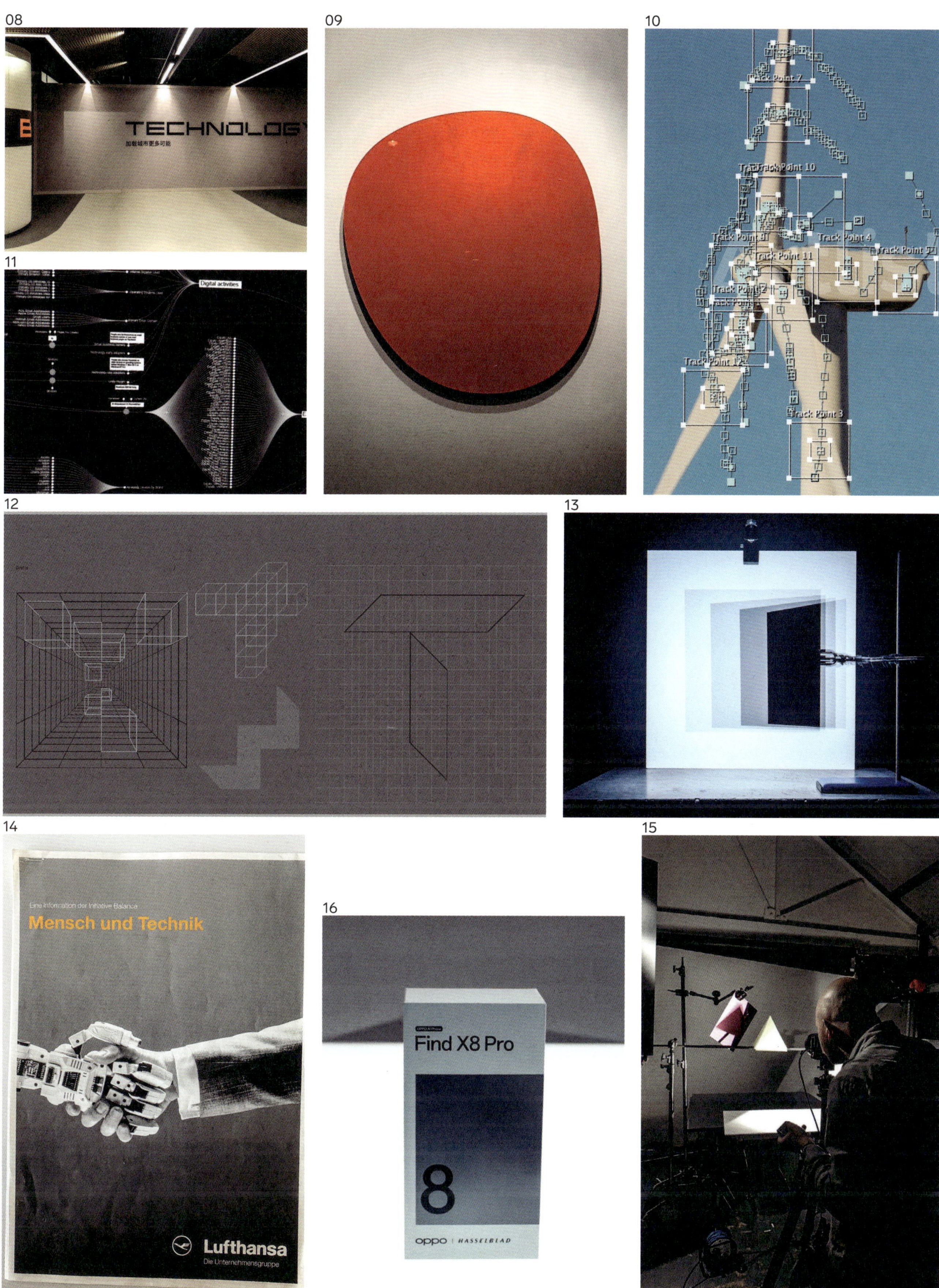

08
TECHNOLOGY
09
10
Track Point 7
Track Point 10
Track Point 9
Track Point 4
Track Point 11
Track Point 2
Track Point 12
Track Point 3
11
Digital activities
12
13
14
Eine Information der Initiative Balance
Mensch und Technik
Lufthansa
Die Unternehmensgruppe
15
16
Find X8 Pro
8
oppo | HASSELBLAD

Enco X2

Find N2 Flip

5G CPE T2

Find X5

Reno8

A7

Oppo
Consumer tech
China
Brand identity
–
2022

Oppo, one of the world's largest consumer tech companies, develops innovative smart devices with a clear ambition: to help shape an inspiring and optimistic future, powered by technological advancement. As part of a broader strategic shift, Oppo engaged Stockholm Design Lab to create a new visual identity system aligned with this renewed direction.

Developed in close collaboration with the Oppo brand team, SDL crafted a revitalised identity that unifies and sharpens the brand's expression – designed to stand confidently in the global arena. The assignment included the creation of custom typography, a new colour palette, a layout system, and a redefined image language.

The resulting identity system provides the tools to build a consistent, accessible, and optimistic brand experience – one that resonates with Oppo's global audience.

OPPO Display

Regular
Medium
Bold

AaBb

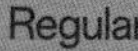

Regular	Medium	Bold
ABCDEFGHIJ	ABCDEFGHIJ	ABCDEFGHIJ
KLMNOPQRS	KLMNOPQRS	KLMNOPQRS
TUVWXYZ	TUVWXYZ	TUVWXYZ
abcdefghijklmn	abcdefghijklmn	abcdefghijklmn
opqrstuvwxyz	opqrstuvwxyz	opqrstuvwxyz
0123456789	0123456789	0123456789

OPPO Reno8 T 5G

Empower
every moment
OPPO Find X5 Pro 5G

OPPO Find X5 Pro 5G

See more
in a snap
OPPO Find N2 Flip

4K

Ultra Light Video

8x

Zoom

4Gbps

Peak Download Speed

In collaboration with

HASSELBLAD

Process

4nm

Date: Nov 17th, 2020
Time: 16:00 UTC +8
Location: Shenzhen

Colour Depth

10bit

4K

Qualcomm
Snapdragon

8 Gen

Marker
Biotech
Switzerland
Holistic brand identity
–
2019

Swiss biotech company Marker harnesses cutting-edge medical advances in biomarkers and treatment to detect, measure, and address a range of medical conditions at an early stage. Its signature innovations include the world's first clinical test for detecting traumatic brain injuries (concussions), and a device designed to treat life-threatening inflammation. The company was born from research carried out in the UK, combined with technology developed on the west coast of the USA.

Stockholm Design Lab was tasked with building a brand experience from the ground up – developing the name, brand platform, visual identity, and digital presence to support Marker's mission and long-term ambition.

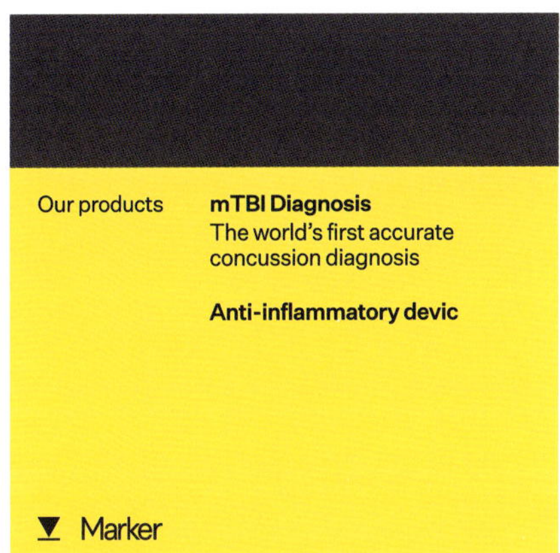

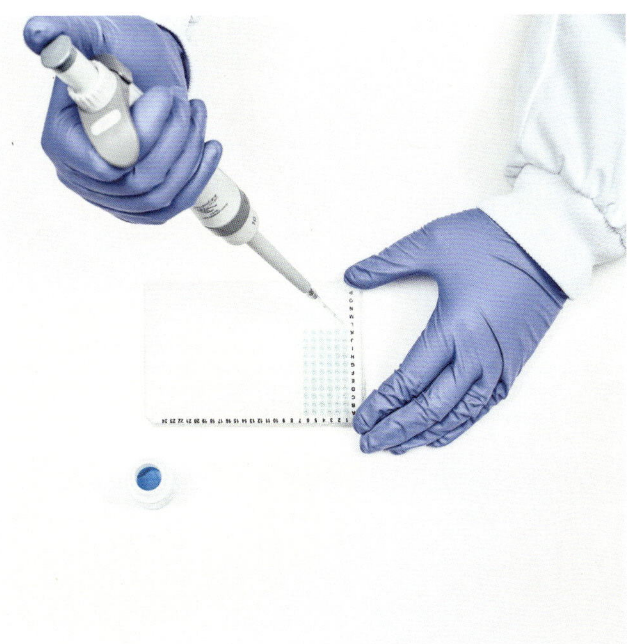

ViewSonic

Ericsson
Communications technology
Sweden
Brand identity
–
2018

Stockholm Design Lab collaborated with Ericsson's multi-disciplinary design team to evolve and optimise their brand identity. Deliberately rooted in product design principles, the updated identity spans all aspects of the brand – from marketing collateral and software design to experimental packaging and hardware.

The work received recognition for excellence in brand design and user experience, with two Red Dot Awards for Brand Identity and Interface Design. The Brand Identity award acknowledges Ericsson's holistic approach to brand refinement, grounded in the principles of product design. The Ericsson Design System (EDS) – a comprehensive software development platform – was recognised for its innovative contribution to user experience, supporting agile software design and implementation.

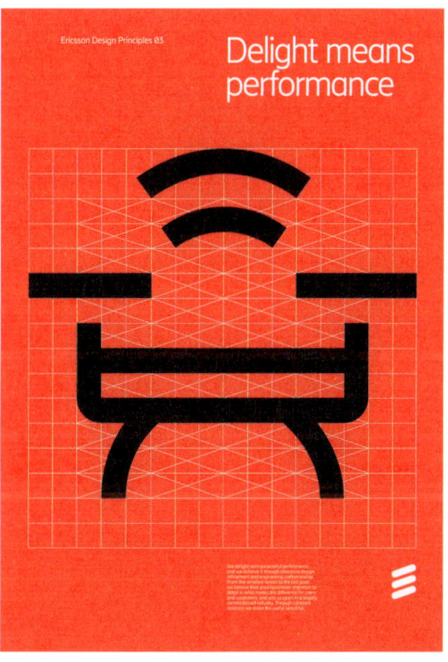

Medhelp
Medical tech services
Sweden
Brand identity
–
2020

Founded in 1999, MedHelp is a SaaS company offering a cloud platform for data-driven occupational health, supported by qualified medical advice. The platform includes subscription-based services for efficient, fact-based management of sick leave – resulting in improved attendance, reduced productivity losses and lower sick leave costs.

Stockholm Design Lab created a brand identity based on a stylised, M-shaped heart, paired with an optimistic colour scheme and distinctive typography.

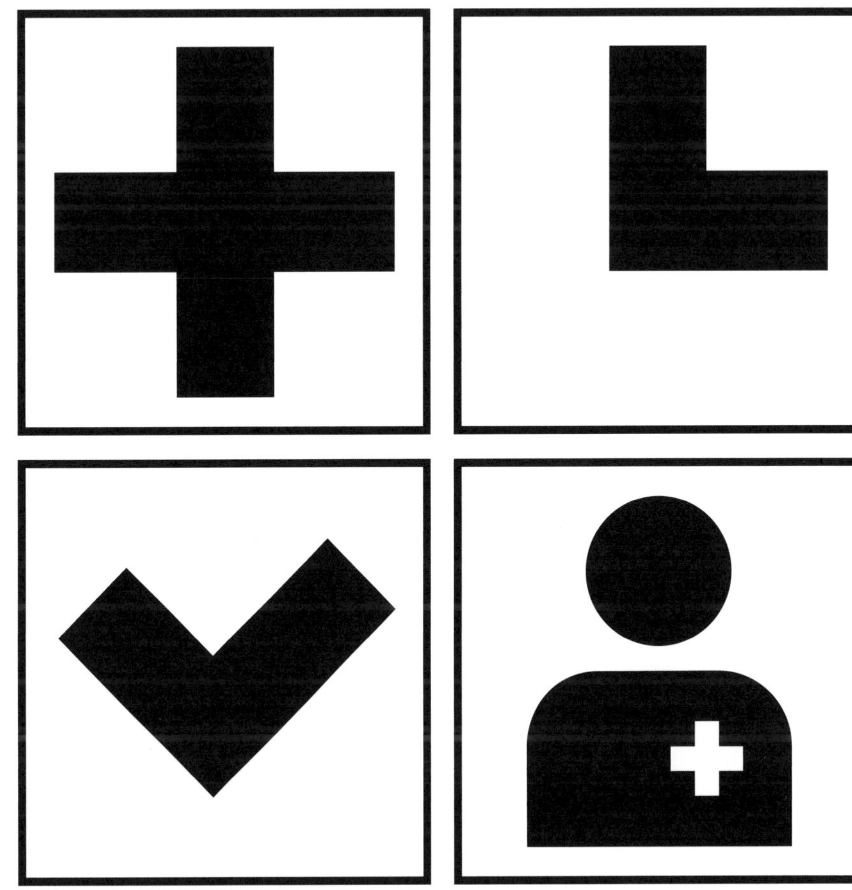

Tele2
Telecommunications
Sweden
Brand identity
–
2025

Swedish telecom company Tele2 partnered with Stockholm Design Lab to revitalise its brand identity and strengthen visibility in a competitive market, where sender identification is a key factor for efficient, successful communication.

Building on Tele2's legacy as a challenger in the telecom space, the refreshed identity amplifies the brand's most iconic asset: the logotype. Expressive and contemporary, the new identity is crafted to enhance impact in Tele2's daring spirit. Updated treatments included a refined layout, custom typography, motion design, sound identity, image language, and a largely black-and-white colour system that reflects Tele2's visual heritage.

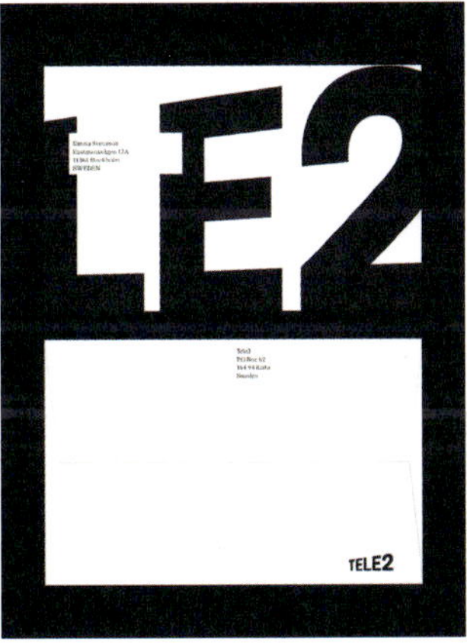

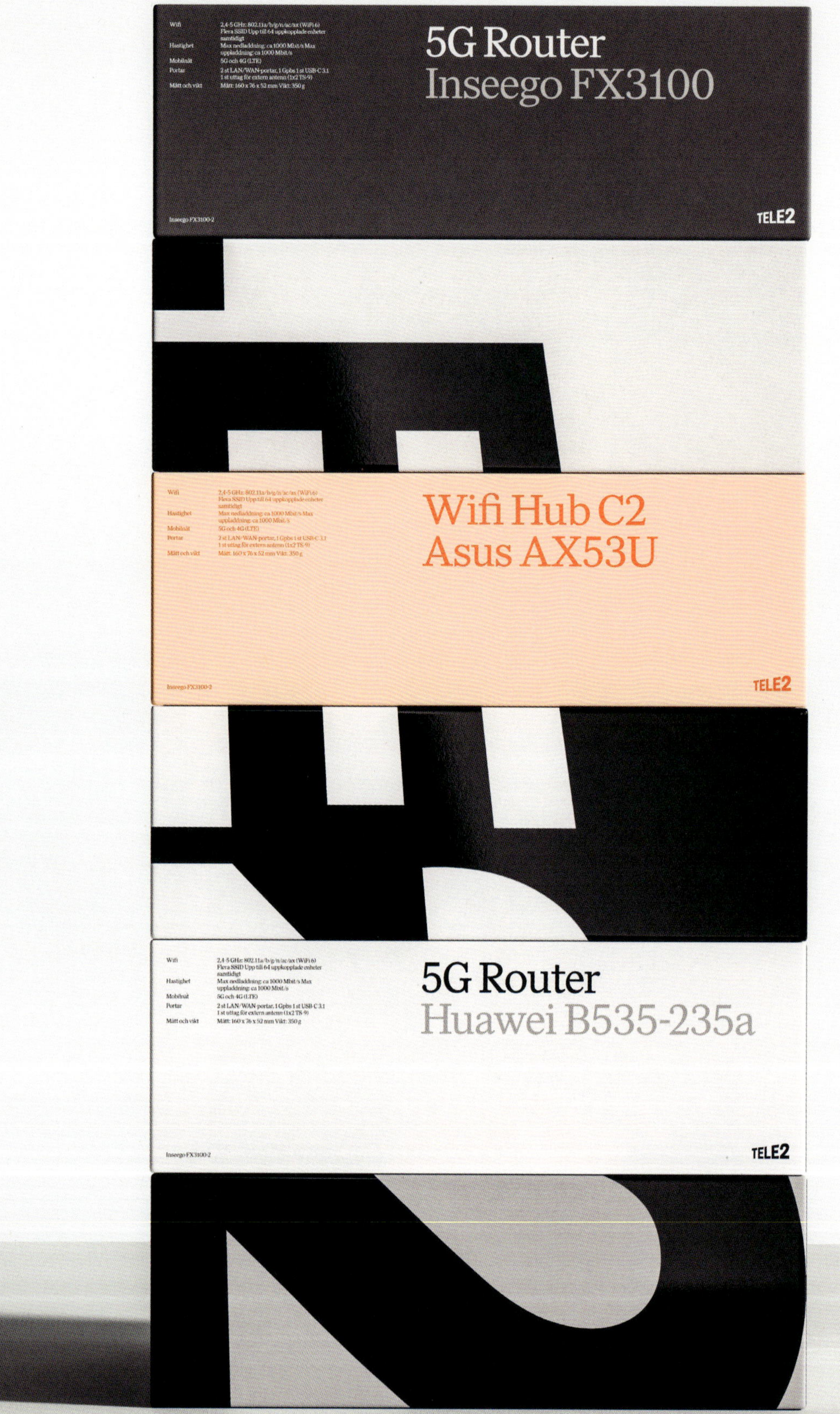

5G Router
Inseego FX3100
Inseego FX3100-2
TELE2
Wifi Hub C2
Asus AX53U
Inseego FX3100-2
TELE2
Wifi
2,4-5 GHz: 802.11a/b/g/n/ac/ax (WiFi 6) Flera SSID Upp till 64 uppkopplade enheter samtidigt
Hastighet
Max nedladdning: ca 1000 Mbit/s Max uppladdning: ca 1000 Mbit/s
Mobilnät
5G och 4G (LTE)
Portar
2 st LAN/WAN-portar, 1 Gpbs 1 st USB-C 3.1 1 st uttag för extern antenn (1x2 TS-9)
Mått och vikt
Mått: 160 x 76 x 52 mm Vikt: 350 g
5G Router
Huawei B535-235a
Inseego FX3100-2
TELE2

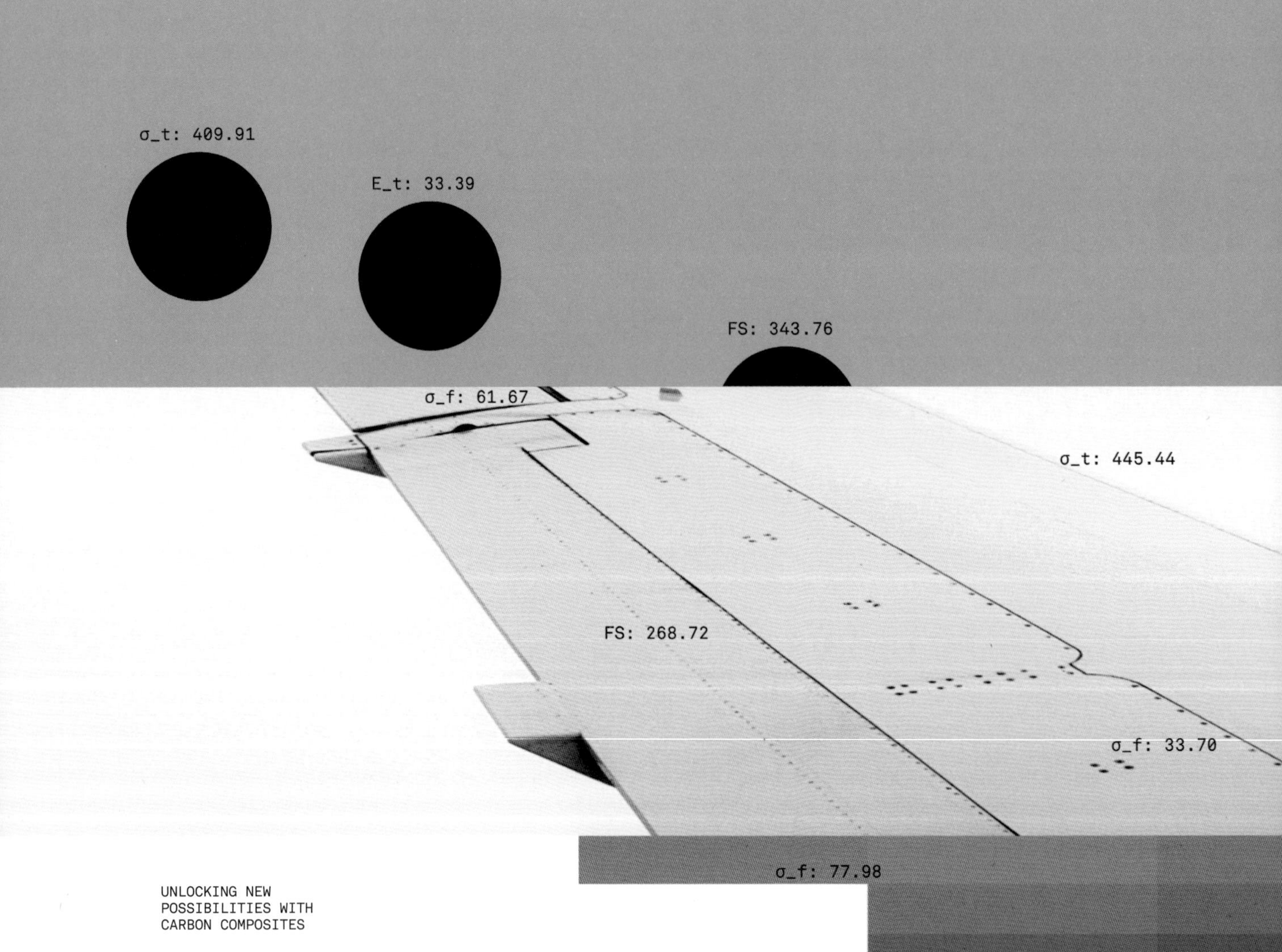

UNLOCKING NEW
POSSIBILITIES WITH
CARBON COMPOSITES

Fairmat
Recycled carbon fibre technology
France
Brand identity
—
2024

Fairmat designs and develops recyclable, high-performance products using recycled carbon fibre composites. Stockholm Design Lab created an identity to support Fairmat's evolution from a deep-tech start-up to established provider of advanced recycled materials and industrial solutions. The new identity positions Fairmat with a clear and confident voice — intelligent, pragmatic, and forward-looking.

Inspired by software-led processes and the unique properties of recycled carbon fibre, the concept expresses the convergence of technology, sustainability, and large-scale manufacturing. A strong, sharp combination of design elements reflects Fairmat's commitment to software innovation and circular excellence. Brought to life through motion and imagery, the identity reflects a visual journey — from waste to wow.

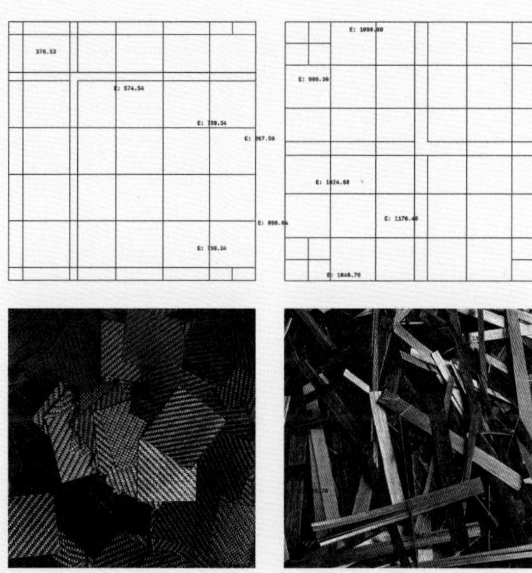

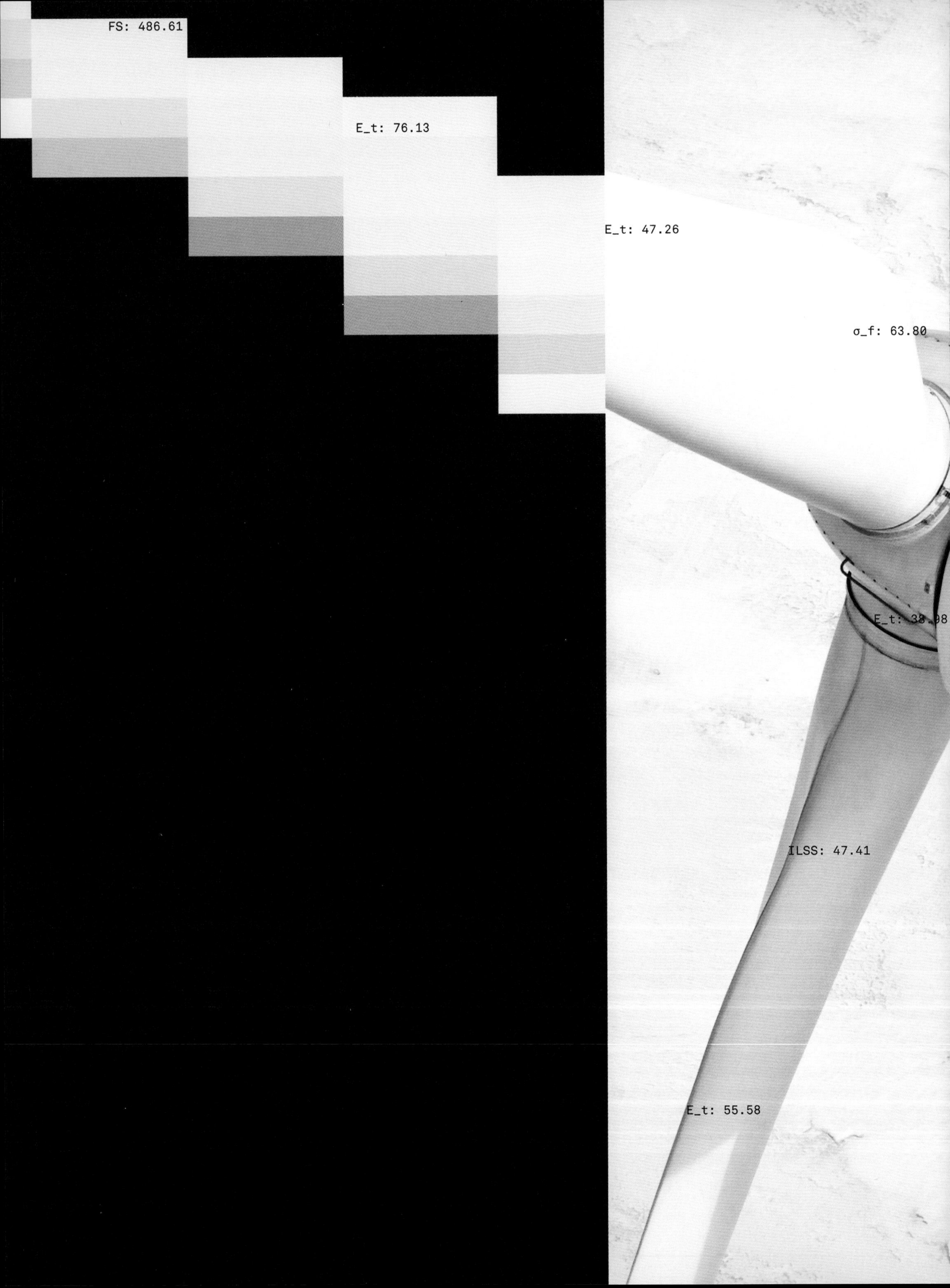
FS: 486.61
E_t: 76.13
E_t: 47.26
σ_f: 63.80
ILSS: 47.41
E_t: 55.58

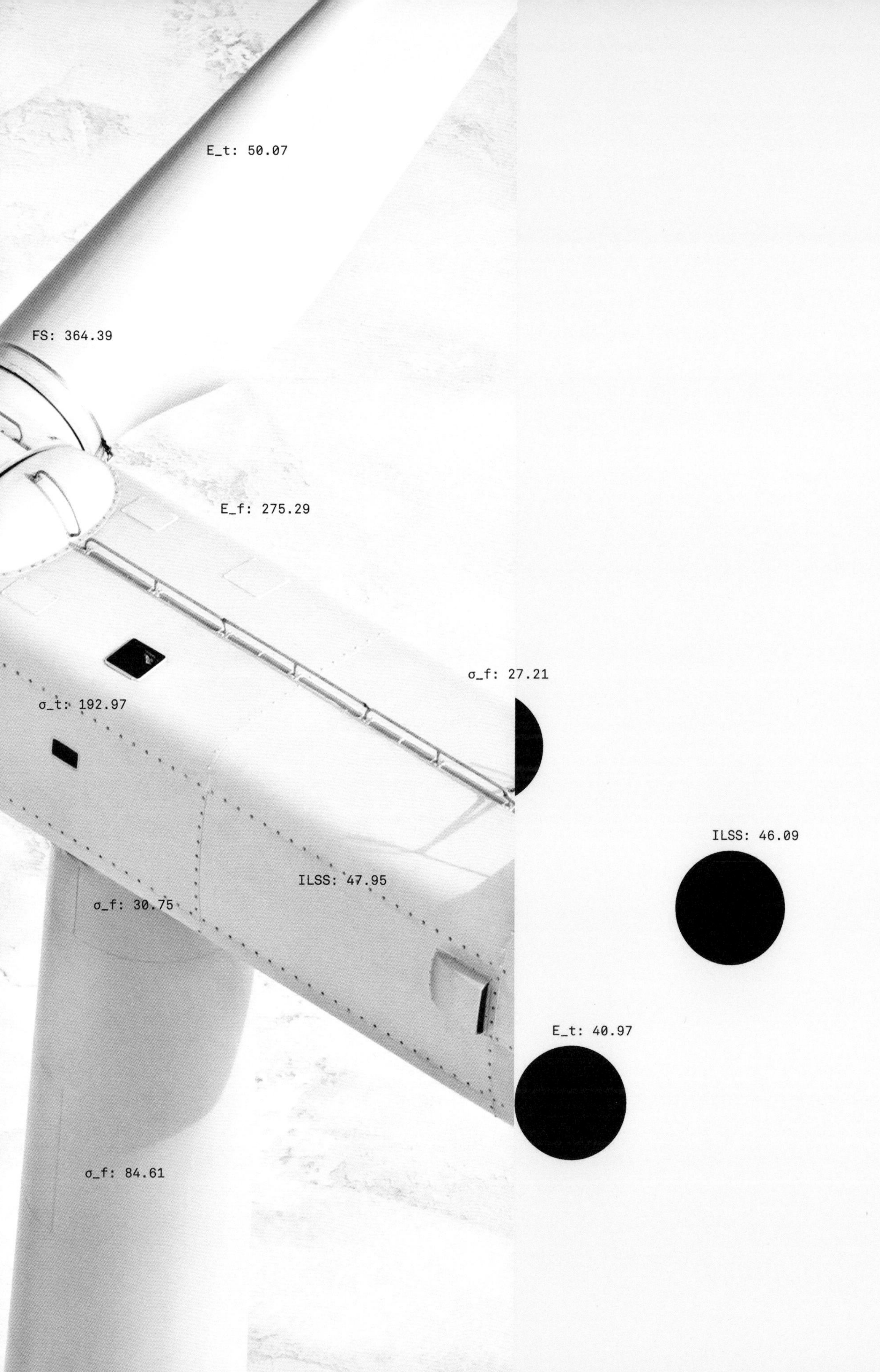
E_t: 50.07
FS: 364.39
E_f: 275.29
σ_f: 27.21
σ_t: 192.97
ILSS: 46.09
ILSS: 47.95
σ_f: 30.75
E_t: 40.97
σ_f: 84.61

Content
1 × Blood Collection Kit
Purpose
Personal Health Check
OneLab

OneLab
Medical tech services
Sweden
Brand identity
–
2019

OneLab helps companies identify physical and mental health risks among their employees through modern, innovative health examinations. By combining intelligent digital tools with expertise from its own nurses and doctors, OneLab analyses complex health data to deliver the right health intervention at the right time for those at risk of ill health.

Stockholm Design Lab developed OneLab's brand identity around the core symbol of a single drop of blood – the minimal but powerful marker of individual health.

This conceptual anchor shaped a warm, confident visual system, including a haemoglobin-red palette, typographic clarity, and structured data graphics that echo diagnostic precision. From logotype to digital platforms, UI design, and clinical reports, SDL ensured each touchpoint conveyed trust, empathy, and scientific rigour – amplifying OneLab's promise of early, intelligent intervention in workplace health.

Thematica
Investment funds
Switzerland
Holistic brand identity
–
2021

Thematica is committed to delivering long-term financial returns while steering society towards a more sustainable future. By redefining traditional asset allocation and focusing on supply chains within disruptive megatrends, Thematica challenges investors to take an active role in shaping a changing world. The funds offer exposure to breakthrough technologies from innovative companies, targeting a pure-play selection aligned with the global energy transition.

Stockholm Design Lab collaborated with Thematica to develop a comprehensive brand platform – bridging strategy with a creative concept grounded in the company's vision, focus on disruptive technologies, and future-oriented perspective. The brand identity is applied across a range of applications, with the digital platform serving as the central hub for information. It supports both retail and private investors, enabling the next step in sustainable evolution.

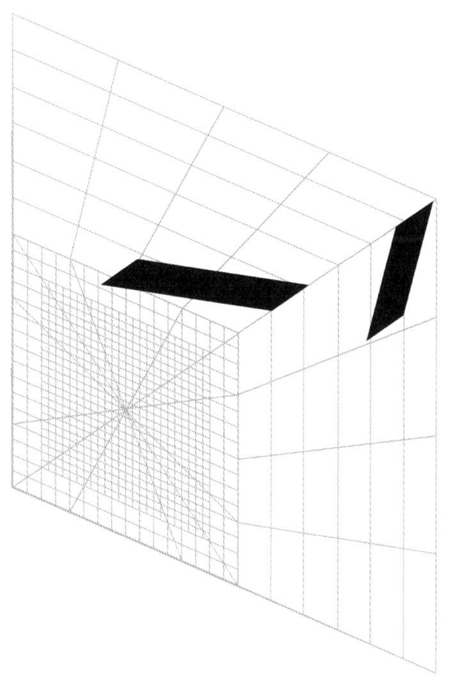

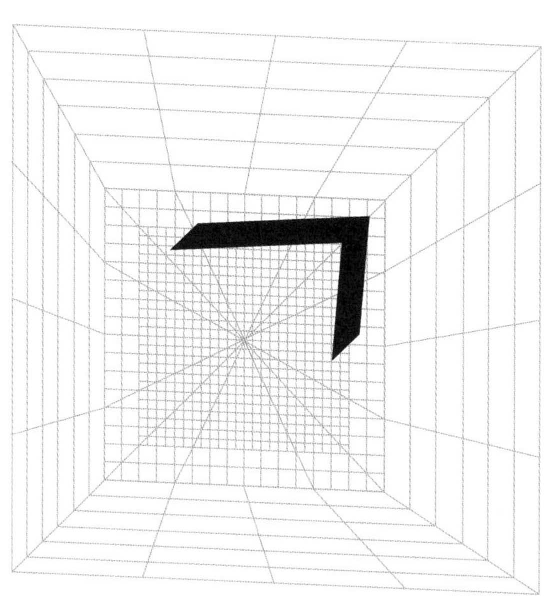

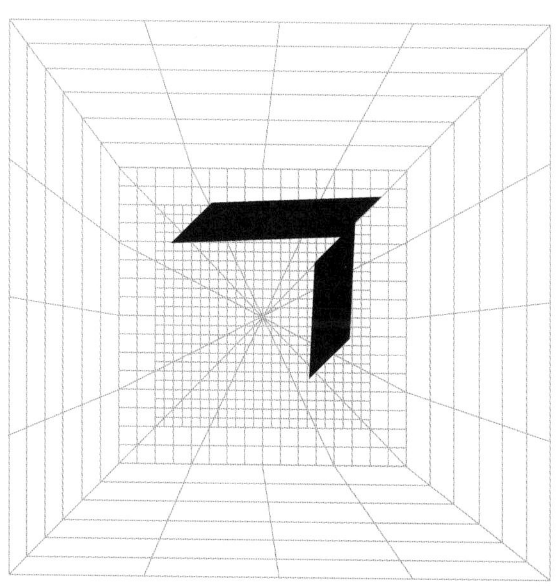

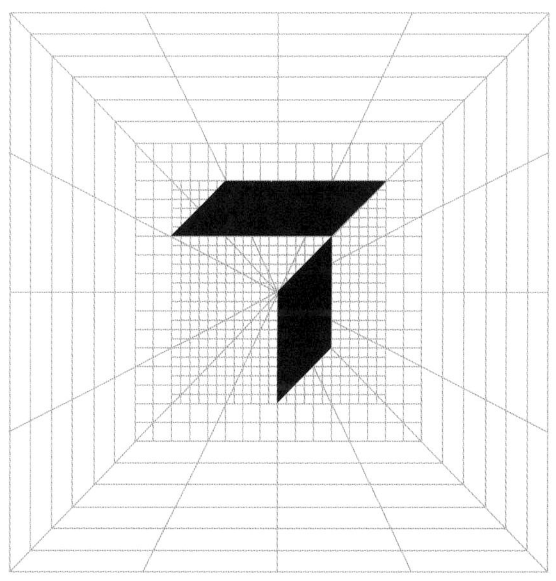

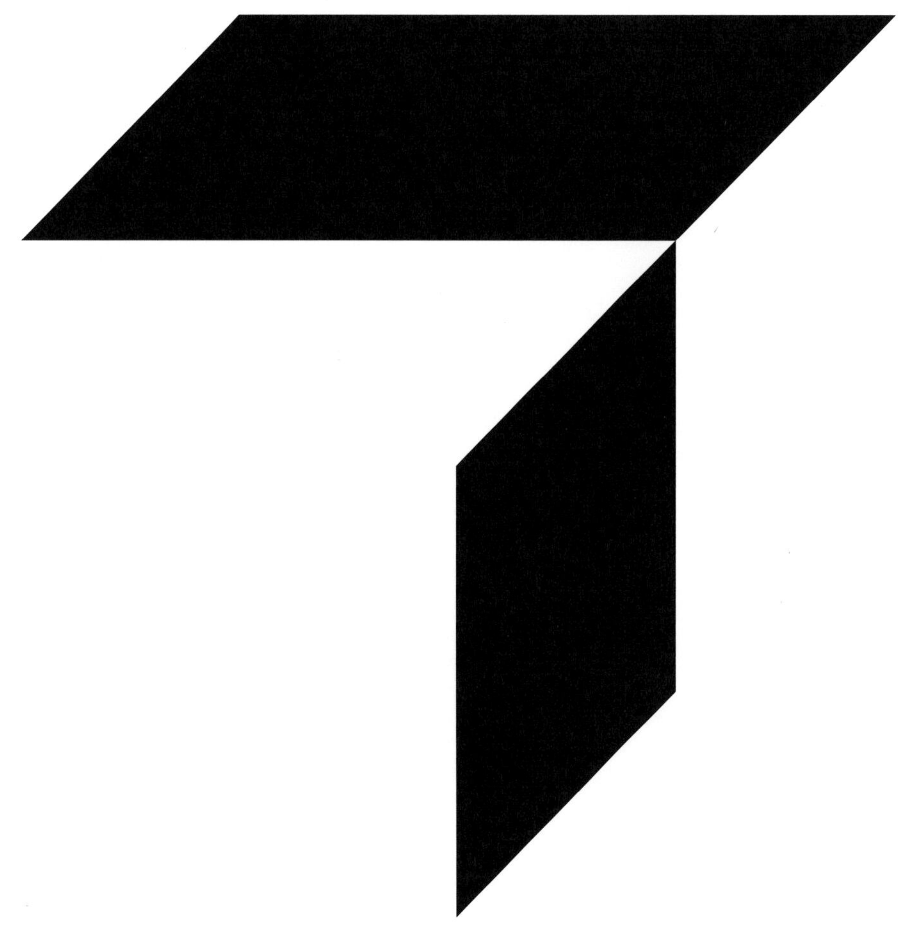

Index
Funds
Process
About
News
Contact

Login

Unlocking the next sustainable evolution

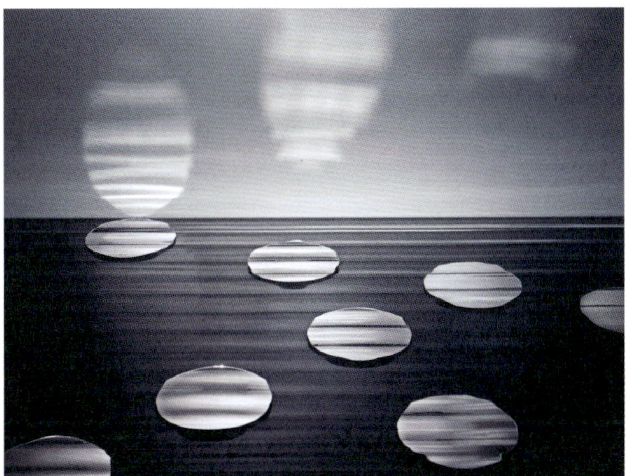

Our aim is to identify positive change potential by investing in well-defined themes that offer unprecedented opportunities for growth and impact.

We deliver long-term financial returns while pivoting society in a sustainable direction. We redefine traditional asset allocation by focusing on supply chains within disruptive megatrends, and we challenge investors to lead the way in a changing world.

Our funds offer exposure to breakthrough technologies of smaller, innovative companies, access to fast-growing companies through funds rather than individual stocks, and pure-play stock selection that aligns investments with green innovation.

About →

Exposure

Access

Pure - Play

Thematica Renewable Future Fund

Thematica Renewable Future Fund offers exposure to companies that will substantially benefit from the transition to sustainable energy.

This includes, but is not limited to, renewable energy, waste management, and other smart technologies dedicated to decarbonising industries that are critical to reaching UN global climate targets.

Funds →

NAV in USD

236.17

Change (today)

+0.32%

Categories

Lithium

Index
Funds
Process
About
News
Contact

Login

Enabling a better tomorrow

Driving green innovation with investment

We exist to drive positive impact for future generations and believe in long-term change through long-term investments. We create funds focused on green technology and innovation. Our objective is to become the first choice for investors that seek exposure to the energy transition. We believe the world is in constant motion, and our aim is to capture unprecedented growth opportunities by identifying positive change opportunities early.

By democratizing our platform to investors, we're building a stronger foundation that drives change and accelerates the world in a more sustainable direction.

We set our own path and are most comfortable in uncharted territory, where we can identify opportunities before others. We are a dynamic team, and we challenge ourselves through critical thinking that looks beyond the status quo. We are Thematica.

People first +

Future-focused +

Always reliable +

"Understanding supply chains is key to uncover opportunities before others and capture explosive growth"

Claes Orn, Chairman

In numbers

Exposure to pure play companies that are focused or will substantially benefit from the transition to clean and sustainable transportation and energy storage solutions.

Thematica Future Mobility UCITS Fund offers exposure to pure play companies that are focused or will substantially benefit from the transition to clean and sustainable transportation and energy storage solutions. Within the energy transition, the fund focus on companies that will benefit from the

Collage
Page 400–401

01 Perspective reference
02 Viedoc image bank
03 Viedoc image bank
04 The 18.435° angle of the Ericsson logotype perfectly aligns to a pixel grid, making screen rendering seamless
05 Viedoc reference, DNA strands
06 OneLab image bank
07 Behind the scenes, Thematica
08 Signage for C Future City, Shenzhen
09 OneLab sculpture
10 Fairmat test
11 Reference of digital activities
12 Thematica symbol perspective test
13 Behind the scenes, Thematica
14 *Mensch und Technik*, vintage brochure from Lufthansa
15 Greg White shooting objects for Thematica
16 Oppo Find X8 Pro packaging

Image captions

409 Ericsson design principles in the new optimized brand identity

A book about the creative process and design of

Flowers

Club Yvonne
Florist and set design studio
Sweden
Brand identity
–
2025

Stockholm Design Lab developed a brand identity for the Stockholm-based botanical studio Club Yvonne, centred around a customised typeface, CY Flowers Regular. In this bespoke font, each letter is reimagined as an abstract floral form.

The typeface serves as a versatile tool, with all letters A–Z and numerals 0–9 available as floral symbols. It can be used to compose decorative messages, generate patterns, or feature across merchandise – making it a distinctive and functional graphic element at the heart of the identity.

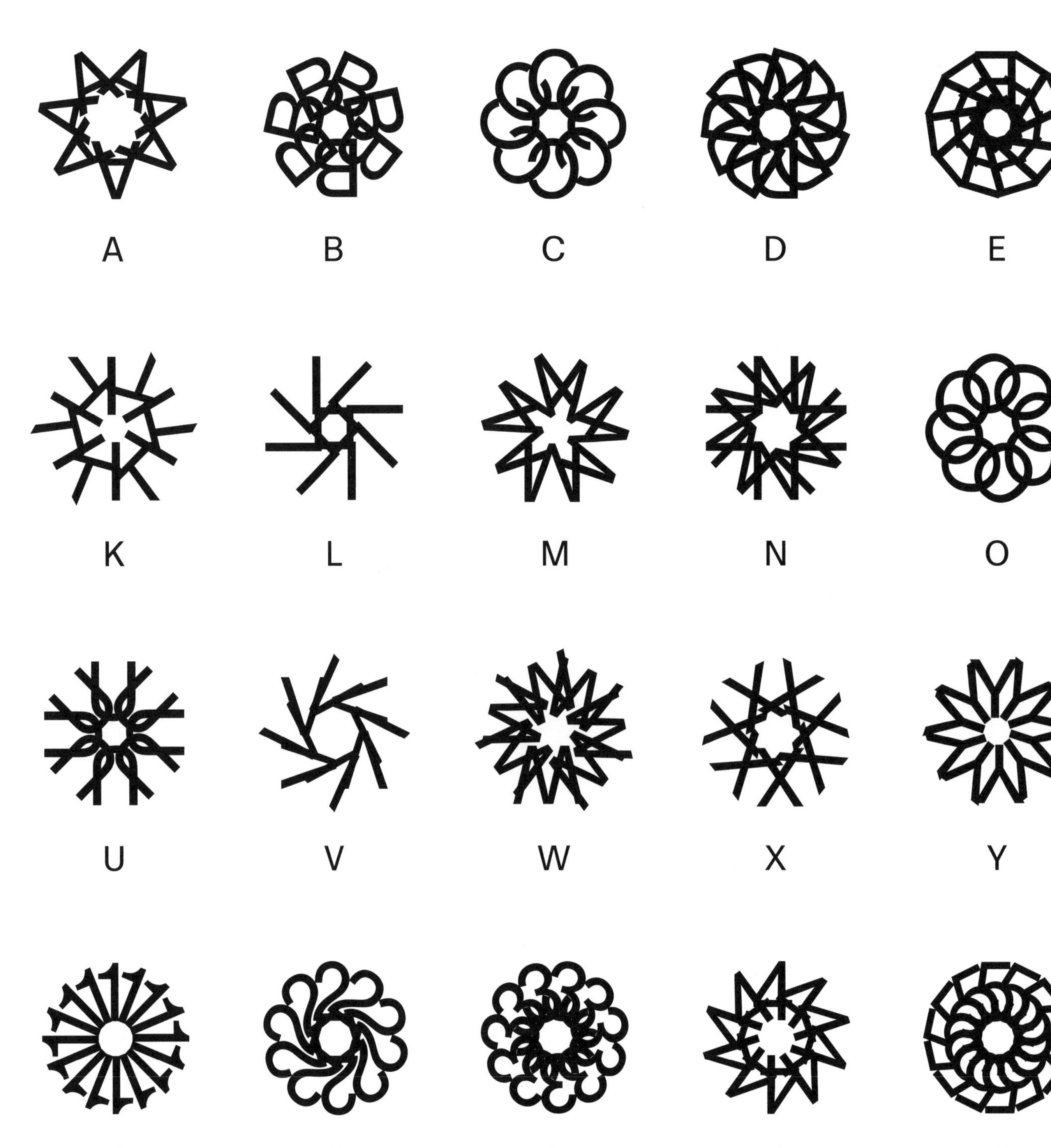
A
B
C
D
E
K
L
M
N
O
U
V
W
X
Y
1
2
3
4
5

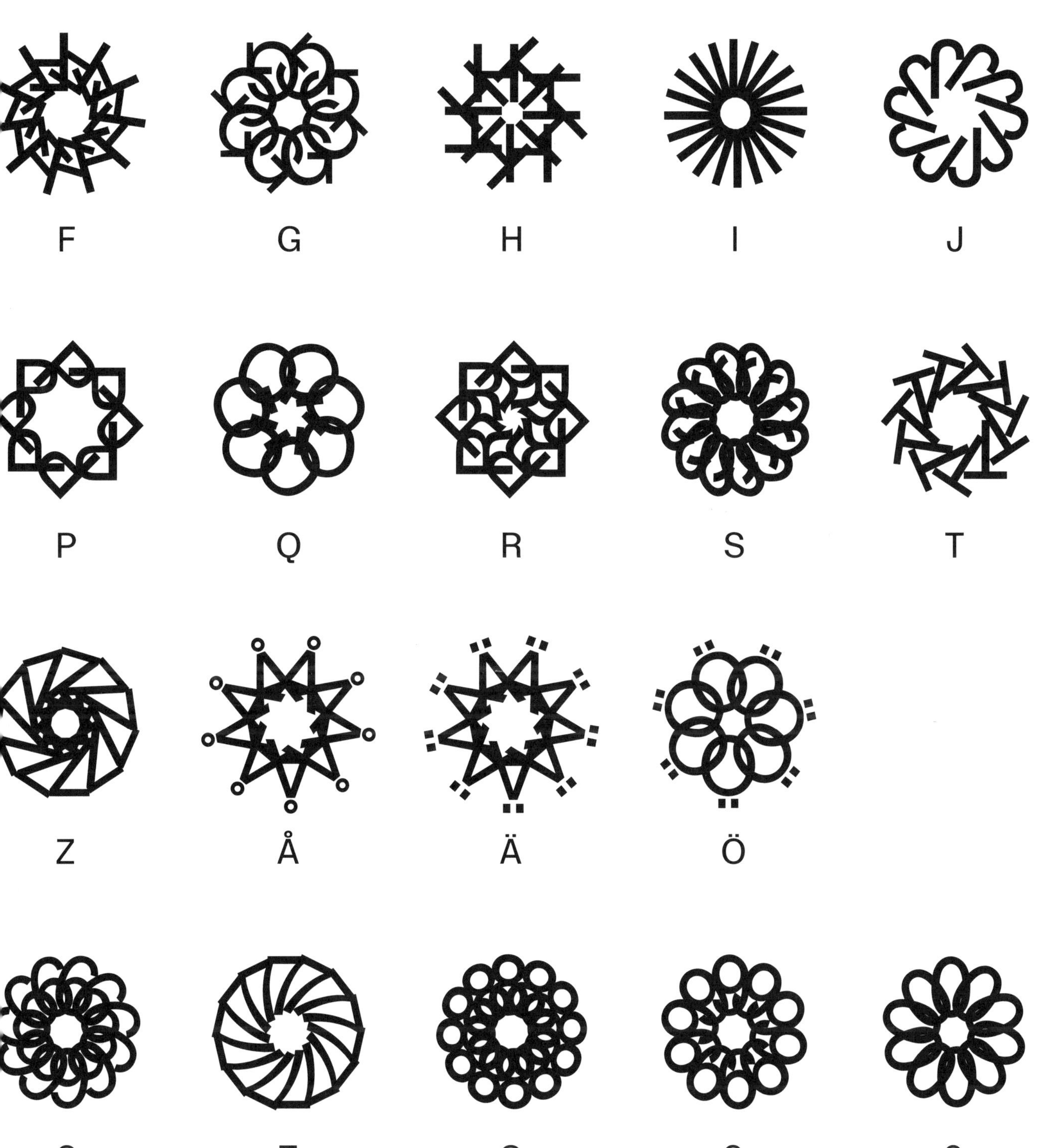
F
G
H
I
J
P
Q
R
S
T
Z
Å
Ä
Ö
6
7
8
9
0

300 BTLS. PRODOTTO E IMBOTTIGLIATO DA
AZ.AGR. RINALDI MARTA, MARSCIANO (PG)
ITALIA. VINI COLBACCO.
INNEHÅLLER SULFITER. IMPORTÖR VINOLIO.
L.PERNR22. ALC 12,5% VOL.
750 ML.℮
TITIYO
ORANGE

Titiyo
Orange & Rott
Wine
Italy
Graphic design
–
2023

Titiyo Orange & Rott was a small-batch release of two wines – one red and one orange – produced by Italian winemakers Colbacco, and sold in pairs.
The label design reused artwork from the cover of Titiyo's 1993 single *The Way You Make Me Feel (Tell Me) Versions*, designed by Björn Kusoffsky and featuring a flower by Lisa Liedgren Alexandersson made of nine fingerprints. For the wine labels, one was deliberately left blank; Titiyo completed the design by adding the final fingerprint herself, serving as a unique, personal signature.

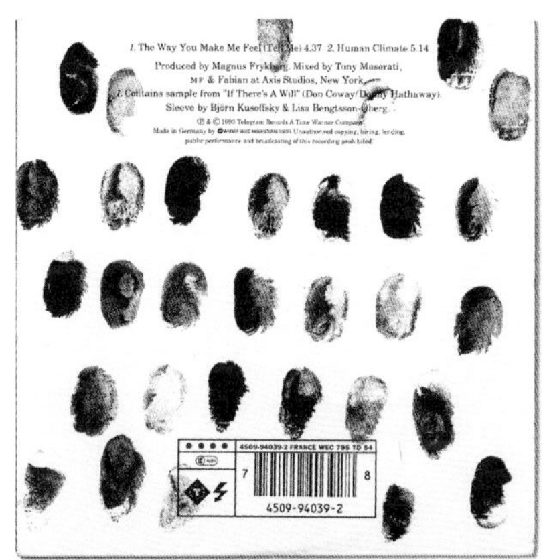

1
2 Push
Open 3
LOHACO

Askul/Lohaco
Delivery Box
Japan
Packaging Design
—
2018

Askul keeps Japan stocked with everything it needs to work — from paper, pens and batteries to furniture, tools, coffee and noodles. Founded in 1963, the company has grown into one of the country's leading providers of business and consumer essentials, with 14 million products for businesses and about a million for consumers.

Its consumer platform, Lohaco, serves around ten million customer accounts with an extensive range of goods: beverages, foods, detergents, kitchen supplies, pharmaceuticals, cosmetics, pet products, interior items, and Lohaco original products.

okolo
Biome Balance Wash
This multi-action cleanser not only gets down and dirty on oily skin and clogged pores - it also boosts cell renewal and balances the skin's microbiota.
okolo
Hero Repair Mask
Extracts of artemisia, spinosa and elderflower work together to calm and restore dry, chapped and irritated skin, with Protectage Complex adding further soothing and anti-aging benefits. As an added bonus, a base of mild cleansing agents dissolves impurities, leaving skin clean, soft and supple.
okolo
Salvation Day Cream
Nature Art Science
okolo
ndlelight Body Wrap
Nature Art Science

Okolo
Skincare
Switzerland
Brand identity
–
2021

Okolo seeks to reinvent beauty by uniting scientific expertise with herbal wisdom. For this journey, Stockholm Design Lab developed a brand identity encompassing naming, brand strategy, identity, web, photo shoots, illustrations and packaging design.

At its core is the distinctive wordmark, placed front and centre with a bold confidence that sets Okolo apart from many others in the industry. The three evenly spaced o's add rhythm and reflect the brand's foundational pillars: science, art, and nature.

This concept continues across typography, colours, imagery, illustration, and a versatile fifth element – a simple dot. Echoing the name, the dot can be filled, cut out, textured or glossed, and its circular shape used to evoke anything from microscopes to nomadic movement and nature's cycles.

The result is an identity that balances clarity with exploration – capturing Okolo's constant search for new paths and perspectives.

September 1998
SAS

SAS
Scandinavian Airlines
Sweden
Brochures and travel books
Art direction and design
—
1998

As part of SAS's visual identity project in 1998, Stockholm Design Lab commissioned several Scandinavian photographers — including Ola Rindal, Sølve Sundsbø, and Ewa-Marie Rundquist — to capture images from a distinctly Scandinavian perspective. These photographs were later used in travel books and various printed materials.

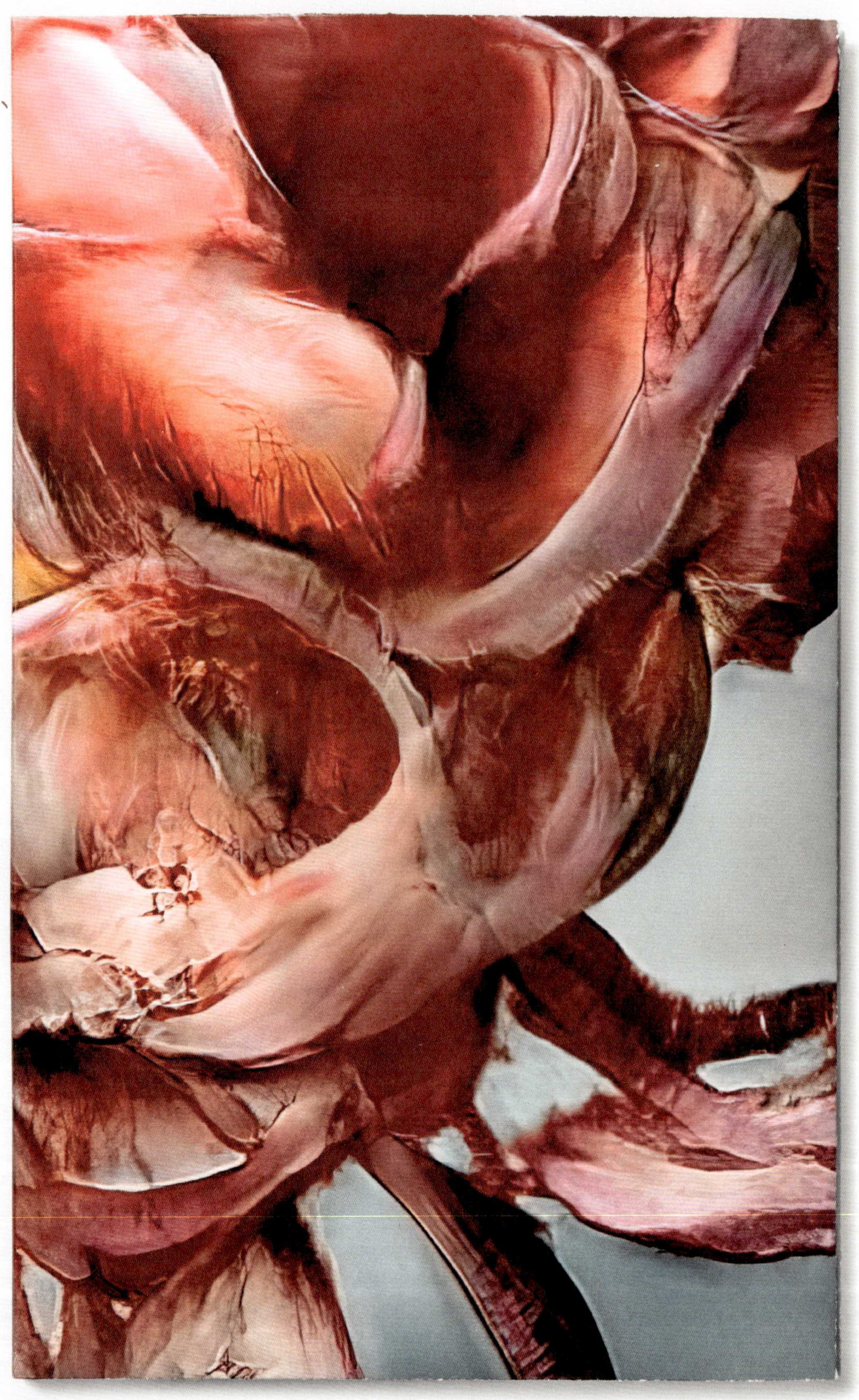

Sigma
Sigma Foundation
Japan
Art book
In collaboration with
Sølve Sundsbø and Greger Ulf Nilson
—
2025

Stockholm Design Lab provided Sigma with strategic development and advisory support in the creation of the Sigma Foundation — established to honour and promote the art of photography through books and exhibitions.

As one of its first art projects, the Sigma Foundation presents renowned photographer Sølve Sundsbø's series *Hanataba*, in which he mined his own archives from 2019 to the present to create sublimely beautiful forms of life — that don't exist. All images are digitally generated, using his earlier photographic work as their foundation.

Born in Norway and based in London, Sølve Sundsbø is distinguished by his visionary approach to photography and film — fusing cutting-edge technology with an artistic sensibility that transforms the ordinary into the otherworldly.

Collage
Page 429

01 Azaleas
02 Floribunda roses
03 SDL XXV party flowers by Club Yvonne
04 *Ranunculus asiaticus*
05 Mister Lincoln roses
06 Flowers from Emmer
07 Xerox flowers
08 Club Yvonne layer test
09 *Paeonia lactiflora*
10 Invitation for Titiyo album release, 1993
11 Flower arrangement by Atelier Fleur, Jill Windahl, Johanna Larsson for *Kraftverk* exhibition at Sven-Harrys Konstmuseum
12 Flowers by Andy Warhol, Spritmuseum, Stockholm
13 Corita Kent, *'Hope is believing that there has to be an "i" in "daisy"'*, screen print

Image captions

446–449 *Hanataba* (bouquet.)
Photographs by Sølve Sundsbø
Illustrations by Clara Lidström

Index

Photographers

Stockholm Design Lab
1998–2025

A book about the creative
process and design of

Optics
Restaurants
AI
Vehicles
Sports
Art
Tape
Fashion
Music
Light
Theatres
Architecture
Typography
Tech &
Flowers

Art direction and design:
Stockholm Design Lab
Editing: Stockholm Design Lab
Research: Stockholm Design Lab
Collage photography:
Björn Kusoffsky, except where
otherwise credited

Preface: Pär Heyden
Texts: Oskar Ekman, Joel Hellermark,
Preeti Sriratana, Magnus Wästberg,
Dan Wolgers, Kazuto Yamaki

Text editor: Alison De Mars
Repro: Linjepunkt Repro, Falun, Sweden
Printer: Artron, Shenzhen, China
Publisher: Victionary

Thanks to all clients and SDL employees throughout the years, as well as all collaborators, partners, designers, studios, and companies who were involved in the production of this book for their significant contribution to its compilation. To those whose names are not credited but who have been part of the book's production, we thank you too for all your efforts and continuous support.

Special thanks to: Petra Lindgren,
Cosima Rieger, Jöran Rammhällen,
Lukas Skarbäck, Elsa Kusoffsky
and Linjepunkt Repro

First published and distributed by
viction workshop ltd.

viction:ary™

viction workshop ltd.
Unit C, 7/F, Seabright Plaza,
9–23 Shell Street,
North Point, Hong Kong
Url: www.victionary.com

@victionworkshop
@victionworkshop
Bē @victionary
@victionary
小红书 @Victionary Books

ISBN 978-988-70661-3-2
Printed and bound in China